PROBLEM SOLVING: A Logical and Creative Approach

Harvey J. Brightman

Department of Quantitative Methods
Georgia State University

Business Publishing Division
College of Business Administration
Georgia State University
Atlanta, Georgia
1980

Library of Congress Cataloging in Publication Data

Brightman, Harvey J.

    Problem solving

    Includes bibliographical references and index.
    1. Problem solving. I. Title.

HD30.29.B74   658.4'03   80-25078

ISBN 0-88406-131-0

Published by:
Business Publishing Division
College of Business Administration
Georgia State University
University Plaza
Atlanta, Georgia 30303

Cover design by Richard Shannon

Printed in the United States of America

Contents

Dedication

Across

1. To a wife who made it possible for me to concentrate on this book

3. To a younger daughter who asked, "Why is Daddy always in his study?"

Down

2. To an eldest daughter who tried to solve all the exercises in this book

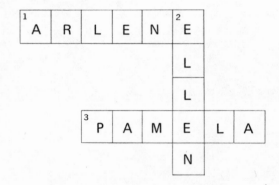

Preface

The problem with problem solving is that no one takes it seriously. By and large, few universities or business organizations offer courses in problem solving, and what training there is, is relegated to second-class citizenship. The purpose of this book is to reverse the trend by training practicing managers to develop systematic and creative approaches to solving the problems they face.

My interest in problem solving resulted from my experience with the Small Business Institute—a Small Business Administration pilot program. The purpose of the program was to allow undergraduate business students to work with firms that were having serious financial problems. In the three years I coordinated the program at Miami University of Ohio, we channeled our best students into the SBI program. However, the students were generally ineffective because of their inability to solve real-world business problems. Interestingly, it was not a lack of technical knowledge that prevented the students from solving the problems; it was their inability to isolate the real problem from all of the symptoms. If someone (including the firms) could have told the students what the real problem was, they could have solved it.

In retrospect, we should not have expected more from the students. While they had received intensive training in the functional fields of business, they had been given no training in the principles of effective problem solving. That's like giving a fine set of tools to a mechanic and then neglecting to provide training in how to use them.

As a result, I began to develop problem-solving courses at both the undergraduate and graduate levels. It occurred to me, however, that practicing managers could also benefit from courses in problem solving. In the past five years I have been offering continuing education courses in problem solving and decision making. As I developed the courses, I noticed the absence of books on problem solving written for managers, and I made a note that when time permitted I would write such a book. Finally, five years later, here is the book.

The presentation of topics basically follows my continuing-education courses on problem solving. Chapter 1 presents an overview of the types of problems managers encounter and the available methods for solving them. Operating problems are characterized as deviations from expected performance. For instance, suppose a firm suddenly loses its share of the market in a particular area. The manager must first identify specific causes for the deviation or drop in market share; then he must generate solutions and verify them. This activity is referred to as *operating problem solving*. Often the goal in problem solving is not to correct a deviation but to make something happen, such as "increase the profits of the XYZ division by 17 percent." The manager must diagnose the opportunities available, generate alternative courses of action, and finally select the *best* alternative. This activity is referred to as *strategic problem solving or decision making*.

Problem solving is more than a series of techniques; it requires the proper frame of mind. Chapter 2 examines the most common blocks that keep us from being successful problem solvers. These include cultural, organizational, managerial, and individual blocks. Once the blocks have been introduced, Chapter 3 suggests general strategies for overcoming them. These blockbusting techniques will be useful in solving both operating and strategic problems. Throughout this chapter, mini-examples and problems are provided to sharpen your critical thinking skills.

Chapters 4 and 5 discuss the Experential Model for solving operating problems. These chapters include several operating problems that will serve as a focal point for the discussion.

The art and science of diagnosing and solving strategic problems is presented in Chapters 6 and 7. Through the use of a merger-acquisition focal problem, various techniques for setting objectives, designing alternatives, choosing the best action, and implementing it are discussed.

Chapter 8 contrasts the strategic problem-solving process presented in the previous chapters with the way it really is in the business world. Suggestions for bridging the "is-should be" chasm are offered.

Finally I would like to thank Jenny Lentz and her staff for typing the manuscript. Given the author's neat but miniscule penmanship, this was no easy task. I would also like to thank Cary Bynum, Peggy Stanley, and Brenda Pace of the GSU Business Publishing Division for their assistance. Their suggestions have greatly improved the readability of the final product. Whatever difficulties remain are, unfortunately, the responsibility of the author.

1

Introduction to Problem Solving

Many years ago I worked with two engineers who were given the job of improving the quality and reducing the number of rejects in a production process. Between them they had over forty years experience in business, or so they said. After a brief study of the problem, they concluded that it could be solved by installing high-precision bearings in the machinery. They defended their solution with assurances that the same solution had once worked in a similar problem. They ordered the bearings and were given a four-month delivery time. When queried on the progress of the project, the engineers told their supervisor that as soon as the new bearings arrived, the problem would be solved.

I remember sitting at the problem-solving meetings and wondering how the engineers had concluded that the major (and only) problem was bearings. It seemed to me they had not yet proven that low-precision bearings were causing the problems. The bearings finally arrived and were installed—and the process failed to improve. At that point someone suggested to the two engineers that rather than having forty years experience between them, they had one year's experience forty times. Those engineers had failed to grow as professional problem solvers.

The moral of this story is that in solving a problem there are more wrong solutions than correct solutions, and when you "solve" a problem, you should be reasonably sure that your solution *will*, in fact, *solve* the problem.

Looking back on that problem, how could the engineers have determined if the installation of high-precision bearings would improve the process without waiting four months? Had they had appropriate training in problem solving, they might have realized that if high-precision bearings would improve the process, then lower quality bearings (than were in use on the production line) should further degrade the process. This line of reasoning would have provided a basis for obtaining objective data on the relationship between bearing quality and the quality of the production process. The engineers could have readily purchased lower quality bearings, installed them on a bank of machines, and recorded the product quality level. If the process degenerated, they could have logically argued that installation of high-precision bearings would improve the process.

Problems in medicine, manufacturing, engineering, and education are similar in nature. Problems are problems, period. In medicine or manufacturing we begin the problem-solving process by first recognizing that something is wrong—the patient has a pain in his chest or absenteeism is on the increase in a department. From the symptoms the doctor or manager must first diagnose the problem and then proceed to solve it. It may turn out that the symptoms are misleading (the patient has appendicitis and the chest pains are sympathetic), so before the doctor prescribes a treatment, he must be reasonably sure that he has diagnosed the *real* problem. Unlike our two engineers, the doctor will attempt to verify his solution (we hope) before he prescribes a treatment.

Until recently, problem solving was not considered a field of study. The first course in problem solving was designed by the late Robert Crawford, Professor of Journalism, in 1931.[1] The General Electric Company developed an in-house course on problem solving six years later; however, it was not until the 1950s that problem solving became a legitimate field of study. During that period advertising executive Alex Osborn developed the brainstorming technique now employed by many companies, the armed services, and the federal government. In the early sixties William J.J. Gordon formed the Synectics Corporation whose main functions are (1) solving design engineering problems, (2) training professional problem-solving groups, and (3) developing inner-city educational materials based on creative thinking. (The term synectics is a derivative of the Greek word *synecticos*, which means the joining together of apparently unrelated elements.) More recently, C. Kepner and B. Tregoe, formerly of the Rand Corporation, developed a systematic approach to problem solving. They now conduct over one hundred problem-solving seminars throughout the world each year. Their clients include banking institutions, governments, service, and manufacturing industries.

In the field of education, the training of problem solvers is still in its infancy. While there have been many programs directed at the elementary and secondary level in education,[2] there has been an appalling lack of work at the university level. A recent encouraging sign is the implementation of problem-solving courses in the curricula of several medical schools; however, more must be done to develop professional problem solvers.

Is Problem Solving Important?

Problem solving *is* important. Indeed Adrian McDonough places problem solving at the very core of the managerial process. He defines managing an organization as a:

1. Collection of problems to be solved, by
2. Assigning problems to the most qualified individuals,
3. Where the most qualified person is the one who will need as little information as possible to make the best decisions.[3]

In an article entitled "The 3-D Process of Management," R. Alec MacKenzie argues that there are two basic management functions: (1) the *sequential* functions of planning, staffing, organizing, and controlling; and (2) the *continuous* functions of solving problems and making decisions.[4] To be successful, the manager must be competent in both functions. Traditional management theorists have directed their efforts toward developing general principles for the sequential functions but have been less concerned with the important continuous functions.

Support for MacKenzie's dual-management functions was provided by a study conducted by Brightman and Urban.[5] In developing a personnel test battery for use in the promotion of workers to first-line management, they analyzed those factors that differentiated effective from ineffective managers. Effective managers were flexible thinkers, were nonrigid, searched for problem opportunities, and were capable of making important decisions; ineffective managers were dogmatic, liked set routines, avoided potential problem situations, and were incapable of making important decisions. (The ineffective managers had no problems with trivial decisions, such as who should be captain of the department's bowling team.)

Problem solving is one of the most essential skills of the effective manager, and yet little attention has been paid to problem solving as a field of study. In fact, organizations and individuals frequently construct roadblocks to effective problem solving.

How to Avoid Problem Solving by Really Trying

According to David Ewing, the attitude that characterizes the professional manager is a willingness to probe, to "look for trouble."[6] An important assumption is that problems provide a springboard for men and women who seek change and improvement. In short, the most dangerous problems facing an organization, from a managerial viewpoint, are the failure to recognize problems and, once having identified them, to correct them. This does not mean that all managers are successful problem solvers, for some managers have ingeniously contrived a variety of techniques for avoiding problems.

Putting Harmony First

Managers who subscribe to this philosophy operate under the following set of premises:
1. Problems rock the boat;
2. A rocky boat is not a happy or harmonious boat; therefore,
3. If you want a harmonious boat, don't search for problems.

Up to a point, harmony is an important ingredient in a successful organization. But if a fetish is made of harmony, decisions that impair harmony will not be made, even if the decisions are important to the long-term survival of the organization.

Substituting Routine Thinking for Critical Problem Solving

Recurring problems tend to generate what Herbert Simon, recent Nobel Laureate, has labeled as programmed problem solving.[7] Programmed problem solving refers to using either standard operational procedures (SOPs) or solutions that worked in the past to solve a current problem. Programmed problem solving is appropriate when problems recur and there is little time for critical thinking. Unfortunately, all problems may tend to be seen as routine, and the lack of critical thinking could be serious. Managers often opt for facts that suggest that a problem is a routine one, even if it is not. Evidence inconsistent with the suggestion of a routine problem is devalued. Some managers who substitute programmed problem solving for critical problem-solving skills are thought to be "fast on their feet" because they immediately generate SOPs to solve a problem. Unfortunately, applying routine SOPs to novel problems is like prescribing cold capsules for the treatment of pneumonia. The critical problem solver may be seen as slow, for this individual critically analyzes the problem situation before making recommendations. The two engineers we met at the beginning of the chapter were truly "fast on their feet." When asked why they believed that high-precision bearings would solve the problem, they replied that such a remedy had worked once before (fifteen years earlier, I believe!).

"Schedulitis"

A manager can become so engrossed in daily routine that he or she fails to see that the primary job is problem solving. As protection against the confusion, doubt, and ambiguity associated with real problems, this type of manager opts to avoid these unpleasantries by pointing to a full calendar. If the calendar is examined closely, one may find that the manager's time is taken up with many nonmanagerial duties.

In the next chapter additional constraints to effective problem solving are presented. If you don't want to be an effective problem solver, there are many techniques you can utilize to remain incompetent. But the fact that you are reading this book suggests that you wish to be effective.

To be a successful manager requires more than hard work, guts, and a pleasing personality. Although these may be necessary requisites, successful managers must also recognize that problem solving is an important professional skill. Just as law and medicine are problem-solving oriented, so too must management be.

Terminology

Problems can be classified along three dimensions: (1) their degree of structure, (2) the level at which they occur in the organization, and (3) how the organization first became aware of the existence of the problem.

Ill-Structured/Well-Structured Problems

Problems may be classified along an *ill-structured/well-structured* continuum. Problems are *well-structured* to the extent that they are repetitive, routine, well-defined and can be solved solely by standardized or automated procedures. In contrast, *ill-structured* problems are novel, elusive, and slightly out-of-focus messes in the sense that a problem is often ambiguous and poorly understood. With ill-structured problems a manager cannot exclusively use SOPs to find solutions but must rely on judgment, intuition, creativity, general problem-solving processes, and heuristics.

Ill-structured problems cannot be solved by cut-and-dried methods either because the problem hasn't arisen before or because it is so important that it deserves a custom-tailored solution. Of course, what is one manager's ill-structured problem is another manager's well-structured problem. Thus a problem is not inherently well- or ill-structured but depends on how often the manager has faced the problem or ones similar. In time, many ill-structured problems become well-structured, and SOPs are developed. Because the environment of senior managers is complex, uncertain, ambiguous, and chaotic, they are more apt to encounter ill-structured problems than their middle-manager counterparts.

Operating Level/Strategic Level Problems

Problems can also be classified along an *operating level/strategic level* continuum. *Operating* problems are encountered by an organization on a day-to-day basis. These problems include when to reorder a particular inventory item or how to select a cover for *Business* magazine. While these decisions do not affect the long-term survival of the firm, they must be solved. *Strategic* problems are problems that are important in terms of actions taken, resources committed, or precedents set. Strategic problems focus on such important issues as "whether to merge with another company" or "whether to install a rapid transit system in a city." The answers to strategic problems will decide the ultimate success or failure of a firm or a city. Whereas senior managers must solve both operating and strategic problems, middle managers generally deal only with operating problems. However, operating problems, if left untended, may become strategic problems.

Crisis/Opportunity Problems

Finally, problems can be classified along a *crisis/opportunity* continuum.[8] *Crisis* problems are akin to forest fires in that they require immediate action. Managers cannot avoid crisis problems even if they wish to. In solving *opportunity* problems managers seek to exploit opportunities and fundamental strengths of the firm. Whereas solving crisis problems is *reactive*, solving opportunity problems is *proactive*. By putting harmony first, substituting routine for critical thinking, and pointing to a full calendar managers avoid proactive problem solving. This is unfortunate, for when next they encounter the missed opportunity, it will probably be a full-blown crisis. At that point, the manager won't be able to hide from the problem. Because of the nature of their jobs, middle managers generally focus on solving crisis problems, whereas senior managers must deal with both crisis and opportunity problems.

The operating/strategic problem classification can be merged with the crisis/opportunity classification to produce a two-dimensional framework shown in Exhibit 1-1. The third dimension—the structure of problems—has been omitted for the time being. Since the focus of this book is on ill-structured problems, this dimension will be discussed in detail in succeeding chapters.

Searching for an acquisition candidate is a strategic/opportunity problem when the motivation is to exploit a strength of the firm or an available opportunity. The same problem becomes a strategic/crisis problem when the motivation is to relieve a current serious problem within the firm.

Exhibit 1-1: A problem classification framework

	Operating	Strategic
Crisis	Unexpected drop in productivity	Unexpected entry of firm into marketplace
Opportunity	Consider adopting a new inventory record system	Search for an acquisition candidate

---

Solving III-Structured Operating Problems

Are there any theories to help managers solve operating problems? Fortunately there are several, some of which are more helpful than others. Before discussing the theories, however, I would like to share with you an ill-structured problem that I solved several years ago. It drove me crazy.

At that time I had a problem with my single-lens, reflex camera. During the winter I shot several rolls of film indoors. After the first roll was developed I noticed that all of the slides were dark. I accused a friend who had taken most of the pictures of ruining the slides of my birthday party. Several months later I shot a roll of film at my daughter's birthday party, and again the slides were underexposed. Unfortunately, I could not blame my friend as I had taken the second set of slides. With my scapegoating premise destroyed, I generated three potential solutions:

1. Bad film.
2. Bad electronic flash unit.
3. Improperly operating camera.

The number of potential solutions will, of course, depend on one's photographic experience. I reviewed the facts of the problem:

Fact 1: I bought the film (two rolls) in two different months from a reputable dealer.

Fact 2: All slides were approximately one f-stop underexposed (I could tell by looking at the slides).

Fact 3: The two rolls of film were fresh (film was shot before the expiration dates).

I compared my potential solutions with the facts. It was hard to believe that two separate rolls of film bought in different months would be defective (Fact 1). Fact 2 was hard to square with Solution 1, for if the film were defective, why were *all* the slides about one f-stop underexposed? Fact 3 established that the film had not expired. The three facts destroyed the bad film solution.

The electronic flash unit solution was then evaluated. I borrowed another flash unit and shot a roll of slides. Again, the slides were one f-stop underexposed. If the flash unit had been the problem, why were all the slides approximately one f-stop underexposed? A defective flash unit would have caused greater variability in the degree of underexposure. And so the flash unit was eliminated. That left the camera. But if the camera were the culprit, why had I not experienced any film problems outdoors? I had, in fact, shot a satisfactory roll of color slides outdoors between the time of the two indoor picture-taking sessions.

Because all my solutions bombed, I reconsidered the situation. The fact that all the slides were underexposed by approximately one f-stop haunted me. What could cause film shot indoors with a flash to be underexposed by one f-stop? Then it hit me. Several months earlier I had purchased a polarizing filter to be used for outdoor color photography. The polarizing filter reduces the amount of light hitting the film by approximately one f-stop. Perhaps I had forgotten to remove the filter when shooting pictures indoors. To verify this, I removed the filter (I could not recall if the filter had been on the camera during the previous indoor picture-taking) and shot a roll of film indoors with my electronic flash. The color slides were all perfectly exposed, and so I had solved the problem.

We will revisit this problem in Chapter 4, at which time the specific analytical technique used in solving the problem will be examined.

Summary

We have now discussed several general problem-solving principles. In problem solving, potential solutions require a consecutive ordering of ideas that can be tested. Since each solution generates different corroborating evidence, the evidence that is most consistent with the facts will indicate the probable solution. From the previous example, it is clear that problem solving requires potential solutions and observations. The interaction of observations (facts or evidence) and solutions continues until one solution squares with all the facts. The function of potential solutions is to guide the search for relevant facts. Without solutions one might become overwhelmed by the sheer number of facts. Yet all facts are not equally relevant. By way of definition, the technical name for facts is *data* and the technical name for potential solutions is *hypotheses*.

Models for Solving Ill-Structured Operating Problems

In this section we will examine four different models for solving ill-structured operating problems. The first three are derived from the psychology of problem solving, while the last model is based on problem solving in actual business situations.

Behaviorist Model

Problem solving is viewed by learning theorists as a trial and error process. If we solve a problem and are rewarded, the probability of solving a similar problem at some future time is increased. The behaviorist school is based on E.L. Thorndike's pioneering studies on the problem-solving behavior of cats.[9] If a cat is presented with a problem (for example, if it is placed in a box from which it must escape to be fed, and escape is only possible by releasing a latch), the cat may fumble around for a time. If the cat should inadvertently solve the problem and be rewarded, Thorndike argued that the problem-solving behavior is more likely to be employed in a similar problem situation.

Likewise with human learning, individuals develop solution hierarchies for solving problems. Solutions in the hierarchy are based on previous problem-solving episodes. If a particular solution solves a problem and behavior is rewarded, that solution approach rises in the solution hierarchy. Faced with a similar problem, an individual selects the first solution in his or her hierarchy and continues down the hierarchy until the problem is solved. If a solution is reinforced, it will move upward in the hierarchy. Behaviorists define a hard problem as one in which the correct solution approach is low in the hierarchy.

The behaviorist model reduces problem solving to the simple principles of *stimulus* (problem)/*response* (solution)/*reward* (behavior). While the model may explain or describe animal behavior and human problem solving in performing simple repetitive tasks, it has three serious shortcomings as a model for solving complex business problems:

1. Real-world problems are not repetitive or well-structured, and therefore the development of solution hierarchies may not occur.

2. The behaviorist model eliminates conscious and deliberate activity; problem solving is reduced to stimulus-response mechanics.

3. The behaviorist model does not lend itself to developing techniques for improving problem solving.

Cognitive Model

Rather than dealing with outward problem-solving behavior,

cognitive psychologists are fascinated by man's mental processes. Cognitive psychologists attempt to explain problem solving as a conscious process. W. Kohler was an early pioneer in developing a cognitive model of problem solving.[10] Kohler demonstrated that apes solved problems in ways that suggested complex thought processes were at work. The basic experiment was to place food outside the ape's cage, well beyond its grasp. A stick was placed in the cage. Kohler reported that the ape would sit looking at the problem situation and then quite suddenly use the stick to bring the food within its reach. Such behavior was deemed insightful. Kohler believed that insightful behavior is based on a restructuring of the problem and that the problem-solving process often takes an indirect path to the solution. Before insight can occur it is necessary to view all the elements of the problem. Unfortunately, the development of insightful behavior was never fully discussed by Kohler.

In human problem solving, cognitive school theorists have examined the positive effects of hints and cues and the negative effects of habit and conformity in problem solving. In numerous laboratory experiments Norman Maier and his associates have probed the mental barriers to effective problem solving.[11] Some of the more common barriers are discussed in Chapter 2.

While the cognitive model has focused on developing strategies and methods for improving problem solving, most of the experimental work has been on carefully defined problem situations. Real-world problems are not so neatly structured.

Information-Processing Model

Recently Allen Newell and Herbert Simon proposed a new model of problem solving.[12] They suggest that human problem solving can be modeled by an information-processing machine— a computer. A computer can be programmed to receive information, store it, erase it, make decisions by executing operational rules, and incorporate new data into its memory banks. Information-processing theorists attempt to reduce complex problem solving to a set of simple, elementary processes that produce, imitate, or duplicate human thinking.

Information theorists not only wish to *describe* problem solving, but to explain it. They believe that problem-solving behavior can be explained as a series of elemental information processes (EIPs). An EIP is an elementary operation that can be duplicated on a computer. For example, the ability to make distinctions as to the size of a variable is an EIP. When we string a series of EIPs together, the integrated behavior we call "problem solving" emerges. In the computer-programming language of FORTRAN IV, a program on dieting with a variable of WTLOSS (weight loss) can be represented as follows:

IF (WTLOSS) 10, 20, 30

10 SUBPROGRAM 1   (Your diet is working.)

.
.
.

20 SUBPROGRAM 2   (Your diet is not yet working.)
.
.
.
.

30 SUBPROGRAM 3   (You're definitely on the wrong
                    diet plan.)

If the WTLOSS variable is negative, proceed to statement 10; if zero, proceed to statement 20; and if positive, proceed to statement 30.

The ability to make tests or comparisons is another EIP and can also be programmed in FORTRAN IV. A program on tax computation might be programmed in this manner:

IF (WITHLD. LT. TAXES) GO TO 20

70 SUBPROGRAM 1   (You are entitled to a refund.)
.
.
.

.

20 SUBPROGRAM 2   (You need to write a check to the IRS.)

If your withholding (WITHLD.) is less than (LT.) your tax bill, proceed to statement 20, otherwise proceed to statement 70. There are additional EIPs, all of which can be represented by a computer code. Thus a program is a sequence of EIPs that duplicates human problem solving.

While out for a Sunday drive several years ago, I noticed that the temperature gauge was lodged in the danger zone. The problem-solving procedure by which I attacked this situation can be modeled by the information-processing program in Exhibit 1-2.

To develop programs that simulate human thinking, information theorists ask problem solvers to think aloud while solving chess and logic problems. A program is then written in a computer code such as FORTRAN, PL/1, or IPL. A successful program must (1) solve the problem at hand, (2) duplicate the elemental processes of a human subject in solving the problem, and (3) *predict* how human subjects will behave when faced with a variant of the original problem. The objective of the information-processing model is to both describe *and* explain human problem-solving behavior.

Like the cognitive school, the information-processing school is concerned with developing strategies for effective problem solving. While this is an exciting development, it has been limited to solving well-structured logic problems and thus has been of little use in solving complex business problems. Perhaps in the future, progress will be made in adapting this model to complex, business problem solving.

Exhibit 1-2: The case of the overheated car

Program	Commentary
1. Stop car.	—
2. Determine temperature.	Doesn't everyone keep a thermometer in their car?
3. If temp GT. 200° go to 8.	If the temperature is greater than (GT.) 200° F, car is overheating; otherwise the temperature gauge is faulty.
4. Drive to nearest gas station.	Replace the faulty gauge.
5. If gauge GT. $7 go to 4.	$7 is the most you will spend on gauge. If gauge costs more than $7, drive to next station. When you find a gauge for less than $7, have it installed.
6. Install gauge.	
7. Resume Sunday drive.	
8. Initiate problem-solving activity to determine why car overheating.	

Experential Model

This model is based on observing successful problem solvers at work. There are several variations of this model but it was first proposed by John Dewey.[13] He suggested that there are three steps (not necessarily sequential) in problem solving:

Diagnosis Phase: Here we are concerned with diagnosing the problem. Unlike structured problems, initial problem formulations are vague. All we know is that something is wrong. When initial suggestions don't solve the problem, the problem must be diagnosed. This is a crucial phase because problem solvers frequently attempt to solve problems before they are understood and thereby solve the wrong problem. We have found the Kepner-Tregoe method invaluable in diagnosing ill-structured operating problems.

Analysis Phase: Once the problem has been diagnosed, potential solutions must be generated. The solutions, in turn, must be transformed into working hypotheses that will direct and guide further observation. A hypothesis is a tentative explanation and must be capable of verification.

Solution Phase: A hypothesis is developed to derive its logical consequences. The ability to reason is, of course, limited by the knowledge and experience of the problem solver. The reasoning may be done by "if-then" hypothetical deductions, or by other reasoning methods. The medical profession makes frequent use of such deductions. A doctor examines a patient and observes certain *facts* that suggest several possible ailments. To determine which hypothesis is correct, the doctor uses the hypotheses to make additional observations and to collect more data. The doctor reasons that *if* the disease is typhoid, *then* certain symptoms will be present *and* other conditions will be absent. The *then* consequences are known to him, based on his experience and knowledge. The experential model will be examined in great depth in subsequent chapters. Each stage of the model will be developed, and clarifying examples will be presented. In contrast to the other models, the experential model is directed at describing the process of solving complex problems.

Solving III-Structured Strategic Problems

In the summer of 1952 President Truman seized the steel mills in what up to that time was one of the strongest assertions of presidential authority ever. Several months later the U.S. Supreme Court invalidated the seizure. While the events have great historic and practical significance for the power of the presidency, we are interested in viewing the steel seizure from a problem-solving viewpoint.

After the North Korean attack in June 1950, President Truman established the Wage Stabilization Board to administer wage hikes. In November 1950 he created the Office of Price Stabilization to administer price ceilings. The Chinese attack on Korea in late November forced President Truman to declare a state of emergency. In response to the national emergency, he established the Office of Defense Mobilization with authority over the wage and price stabilization boards. Meanwhile the Korean War touched off a consumer spending-spree, and in a little over six months the Consumer Price Index jumped 10.3 points. In January 1951 President Truman responded by ordering a general wage-price freeze. Toward the end of 1951 the United Steelworkers began negotiations with the steel industry and demanded a large wage settlement. The steel industry was willing to grant the increase, providing the federal government would permit them to pass the cost along to the ultimate consumer. In March 1952 the Wage Stabilization Board recommended a $0.125 raise and the introduction of a union shop. The union accepted the terms. However, when the industry petitioned the Office of Price Stabilization for permission to raise prices by $7.00 per ton, they were denied. The strike deadline was set for April 8.

We know what President Truman eventually decided. What we are really interested in is the problem-solving process. Let's view the decision from the viewpoint of Graham Allison's three models of strategic problem solving.[14]

Organizational Process Model

According to Allison, leaders may decide, but the information on which they base their decisions is generated by organizational tradition and procedure. To explain an organization's decision at time t, we need only examine their standard operating procedures at time $t - 1$. According to the organization process framework, President Truman's takeover of the steel industry was a consequence of the operating procedures of the Wage Stabilization Board, the Office of Price Stabilization, and the Office of Defense Mobilization. The Wage Stabilization Board had developed guidelines and precedents for evaluating wage-hike requests. These did not depend on the companies' ability to pay. The Office of Price Stabilization also had developed guidelines for deciding on price increases. The two boards did not coordinate their activities for fear that this would invite collusion by industry and labor to simultaneously obtain wage and price increases. Thus, because of the operating policies of the agencies, conflict was inevitable and President Truman had no choice but to seize the mills.

The organizational framework views strategic problems as programmable; the organization's policies are the programming process. Proponents argue that in solving strategic problems the decision maker is not starting *de novo* but is a member of an organization with established patterns of behavior. We may view the organization as the walls of a maze, and by and large, strategic problem solving focuses on solving maze problems and not on reconstructing the maze walls.

Bargaining Model

In this model decisions are the result of struggles between different members of the organization who have different preferences, objectives, competencies, and power bases. The final decision is a makeshift compromise resulting from power struggles between organizational members. The seizure of the steel mills can be viewed as a power struggle between Charles Wilson, Director of the Office of Defense Mobilization, and Ellis Arnall, Director of the Office of Price Stabilization. Wilson wanted to permit the steel industry to pass along some of the increased costs in the form of higher prices. Arnall argued that such a move would make a mockery of the Office of Price Stabilization guidelines and would overturn its announced decision not to grant the industry any relief. Although Wilson was Arnall's superior (at least on paper), Arnall had more political clout, and in a showdown President Truman sided with Arnall. Once the price hike was finally rejected, the President had no choice, for without a price hike, the steel industry would have rejected the wage recommendations of the Wage Stabilization Board. And without the wage hike, the union would surely have struck. Thus, in order to prevent a strike that could endanger national security, President Truman had to seize the mills.

Rational Model

In this model we have a unitary (or group) decision maker who is able to (1) state objectives, (2) state preferences among objectives, (3) generate alternative courses of action, (4) assess the consequences of every alternative action on each objective, and (5) select the best alternative. Unlike the other two models (which are merely descriptive), this model is normative—that is, decision makers should make decisions in accordance with these five principles. Leaving this issue aside for the moment, let's view President Truman's decision from this perspective.

Because of political delays in taking action, President Truman faced a crisis. According to the analysis, Truman's sole objective was to prevent a steel stoppage. There were four alternatives available: (1) invoke Section 18 of the Universal Military Training and Service Act of 1948, which permitted seizure of plants if orders were not filled for the military; (2) seize the mills under the inherent power of the Presidency; (3) send a bill to Congress requesting seizure powers; or (4) invoke the Taft-Hartley Act. According to this model, President Truman reasoned that only option 2 would guarantee continued steel output. Option 4 was rejected because he believed that the unions would disregard the injunction and strike anyway. Furthermore, the President did not want to alienate the union (a secondary objective) because of their strong pro-Democratic Party affiliation. Also, the appointment of a fact-finding board required by the Taft-Hartley Act might discredit the Wage Stabilization Board. Options 1 and 3 were rejected because of potential delays involved in instituting these approaches. President Truman argued that before the necessary machinery could be installed, the union would strike, causing serious problems in the war effort. According to this model then, Truman seized the mills because this was the only rational course of action.

Toward an Enriched Rational Model

While the rational model offers a systematic problem-solving procedure (beginning with setting objectives to selecting the best course of action), the model assumes that the problem has already been diagnosed (conceptualized if you like). Thus the rational model reduces decision making or strategic problem solving to a choice process—choosing the action that maximizes the attainment of one's objectives. This is much too narrow a view of strategic problem solving and ignores what may be the crucial phase—diagnosing a problem. Consider the following problem:

The XYZ corporation is having great difficulty in meeting competition. The company sells a single product, and although it is a quality product, production costs must be trimmed to protect its share of market. Even though many alternative solutions were generated and implemented, the XYZ corporation still could not reduce its costs sufficiently. Then one day the financial manager noted that in designing the cost-reduction program, the company had self-imposed a constraint—namely the corporation had focused its cost-cutting program within the physical walls of the plant. Once the problem was reconceptualized, *new* alternatives (as opposed to more of the same kind) were generated. Finally XYZ corporation bought ABC Industries that made a complementary product. Greater facilities and economies of scale lowered unit costs far below what had been achieved earlier. The moral of the story is that a solution to a strategic problem is limited to how we diagnose the problem. A poorly conceptualized problem will never be solved.

Diagnosis is the name of the game. Although a full discussion is left for Chapter 6, it is appropriate to introduce the diagnostic approach now. In conceptualizing a strategic problem, I have found it useful to think in terms of four elements:

1. *Controllable actions*—These are actions that the manager may take in solving a problem. While there are constraints under which the manager must operate (for example, the advertising level cannot be increased without limit), it is important for a manager to differentiate between real and self-imposed constraints. In the XYZ corporation case, management failed to consider that acquisitions were legitimate controllable actions.

2. *Uncontrollable events*—These are events beyond the control of the decision maker which, however, do affect whether he or she solves the problem. Uncontrollable events can be competitors' actions, governmental policies, union demands, etc. Note that while the manager cannot control these events, someone or something does.

3. *Interrelationships*—These describe how controllable actions and uncontrollable events interact to generate the outcomes.

4. *Outcomes*—These result when a manager takes certain controllable actions and certain uncontrollable events occur. Outcomes measure progress toward obtaining objectives. Dollars are a frequent measure of outcomes in business problems.

In diagnosing a strategic problem, I think you will find it useful to conceptualize the problem using these four elements. For the sake of brevity, let's call this approach the decision-sciences method.

The enriched rational model is shown in Exhibit 1-3. It

Exhibit 1-3: The enriched rational model

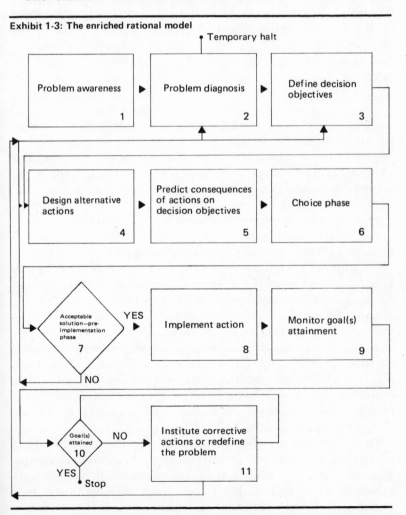

extends the rational model by incorporating a diagnosis phase in solving strategic problems. Although the enriched model is presented in Chapters 6 and 7, let's briefly review it. If a manager is unaware of a problem or an opportunity awaiting exploitation, no problem solving will take place. All too often managers focus on data solely within the four walls of the organization. This is unfortunate because opportunities outside of the organization await those who are informed. Once a strategic problem is detected, it must be diagnosed. Don't worry about the correct conceptualization, for there is no such animal. Rather, as a manager, you should be open to alternative diagnoses of the problem (is the glass of water half-filled or half-empty?). While some diagnoses may ultimately prove more productive, competing diagnoses, at least initially, improve the chances of solving the right problem. At this point the manager may decide that the cost of solving the problem outweighs the potential benefits. If so, we recommend that the manager temporarily shelve the problem and await changing conditions which, like death and taxes, are the only things certain in the world. Once decision objectives have been defined, alternative solutions must be designed. The manager must ascertain to what degree each alternative solution accomplishes the decision objectives. The alternative solutions are then judged to determine the one that best meets all decision objectives.

After a solution has been tentatively selected, we determine if there are any negative consequences in adopting the solution. Sometimes in solving one problem we generate others. Recall that President Truman's decision caused a more serious constitutional crisis that eventually had to be decided by the U.S. Supreme Court. If the adverse consequences of a potential solution are severe, we recommend one of three approaches: (1) design additional alternative actions, (2) redefine the decision objectives, or (3) redefine the problem itself.

From this point, the decision maker should implement the solution and monitor its progress in achieving the decision objectives. If the objectives are not realized, then either corrective action should be taken or it may be that the wrong problem was attacked. Rediagnose the problem and cycle through the process again.

In conclusion, we will be considering two classes of problems in this book—operating and strategic ill-structured problems. Regardless of the problem type, the problem-solving processes exhibit some similarity. Both begin with problem recognition and diagnosis, both require analysis and solution choice phases, and both end with implementation. However, because strategic and operating problems do differ, the specific problem-solving techniques differ. The differences in the problem-solving procedures are suggested by the following analogy: finding a needle in a haystack (operating problems) requires different skills and procedures than designing a house (strategic problems). The differences are summarized in Exhibit 1-4.

Exhibit 1-4: A comparison of problem-solving processes for operating and strategic problems

	Operating problems	Strategic problems
Problem definition	Correcting deviations from standard performance	Moving organization toward its long-term goals
Problem solving process	Dewey model	Enriched rational model
Problem recognition and diagnosis	Kepner-Tregoe method	Decision science method
Design phase	Hypothesis generating method	Alternative generating method
Choice phase	Reasoning and verification method	Weighted product-of-the-consequences method
Implementation phase	Self implementing	Implementation strategies

FOOTNOTES

1. Gary A. Davis, *Psychology of Problem Solving* (New York, Basic Books, Inc., 1973), p. 103.

2. Ibid.

3. Adrian M. McDonough, *Information Economics and Management Systems* (New York, McGraw-Hill, 1963), p. 72.

4. R. Alec MacKenzie, "The Management Process in 3-D," *Harvard Business Review*, November-December 1969, pp. 80-87.

5. Harvey J. Brightman and Thomas F. Urban, "Problem Solving and Managerial Performance," *Atlanta Economic Review*, July-August 1978, pp. 23-26.

6. David W. Ewing, *The Managerial Mind* (Riverside, New Jersey, Free Press, Division of Macmillan Co., 1964).

7. Herbert Simon, *The New Science of Management Decisions* (Englewood Cliffs, New Jersey, Prentice-Hall, 1977).

8. Henry Mintzberg, Duru Raisinghani, and Andre Theoret, "The Structure of Unstructured Decision Processes," *Administrative Science Quarterly*, June 1976, pp. 246-275.

9. Edward L. Thorndike, *Animal Intelligence: Experimental Studies* (New York, Hafner Publishing Company, 1965).

10. Wolfgang Kohler, *The Mentality of Apes* (New York, Humanities Press, 1951).

11. Norman R.F. Maier, *Problem Solving and Creativity in Individuals and Groups* (Belmont, California, Brooks/Cole, 1970).

12. Allen Newell and Herbert Simon, *Human Problem Solving* (Englewood Cliffs, New Jersey, Prentice-Hall, 1972).

13. John Dewey, *How We Think, a Restatement of the Relation of Reflective Thinking to the Educative Process* (New York, D.C. Heath and Company, 1933).

14. Chong-Do Hah and Robert Lindquist, "The 1952 Steel Seizure Revisited: A Systematic Study in Presidential Decision Making," *Administrative Science Quarterly*, December 1975, pp. 587-605.

2
Constraints to Problem Solving

In the previous chapter we introduced the concept of two distinct types of problems a manager faces. While the techniques used in solving operating and strategic problems differ, all problem solvers face constraints—real and self-imposed. In this chapter we will present the more common constraints to effective problem solving. In order of generality, these include cultural, organizational, managerial, and individual constraints.

"There is always an easy solution to every human problem—neat, plausible, and wrong."

—H.L. MENCKEN

In problem solving we are always facing constraints; some are real and some are imagined. The effective problem solver is able to cope with real and self-imposed constraints; the ineffective problem solver cannot. In this chapter we shall examine some of the more common constraints to effective problem solving.

Cultural Constraints

The impact of culture is vividly demonstrated in a short story told by Moshe Rubinstein.[1] He tells of an encounter with an educated, well-to-do Arab named Ahmed. In the course of their discussion, Ahmed asked, "imagine you, your mother, your wife, and your child are in a boat and it capsizes. You can save yourself and one other person. Whom will you save?" Rubinstein thought about it, and although his wife was sitting next to him, he replied that he would save the child. Rubinstein reported that Ahmed was very surprised. As Ahmed saw it, there was only one rational answer. Ahmed reasoned that the mother should be saved since you can have more than one wife or child but you can never have more than one mother.

The broadest constraints problem solvers operate under are those imposed by our culture. Culture is the pattern of all arrangements, materials, and behaviors that have been adopted by a society as traditional ways of solving the problems of its members. Cultural constraints include (1) taboos, (2) differing time perspectives, (3) attitude toward change, (4) beliefs regarding the scientific method, and (5) decision-making style.

In his book *Conceptual Blockbusting*, James Adams demonstrates in a delightful manner how the cultural constraints of taboo operate in problem solving.[2] You, the reader, are given the following task. Assume that a steel pipe is embedded in a concrete floor of a bare room. The inside diameter is .06″ larger than the diameter of a Ping-Pong ball which is resting at the bottom of the pipe. The pipe protrudes 4″ above the concrete. You are in a group of six people and are given the following objects:

100′ of clothesline	a wire coat hanger
a carpenter's hammer	a monkey wrench
a chisel	a light bulb
a box of Wheaties	a file

List as many ways as you can think of (in two minutes) to get the ball out of the pipe without damaging the ball, the pipe, or the concrete floor. Think about it before reading on.

Some common solutions are:

1. Smash the handle of the hammer and use the splinters as chopsticks to pick up the ball.

2. File down the coat hanger and use it as a tweezer to remove the ball.

There is one approach that you probably didn't think of—or thought of but rejected because it is too gross. Why not use Archimedes' principle and float the ball out? But where is the source of water? If you rejected the idea that you are now thinking of, it is because such behavior in public is considered a cultural taboo.

On a more serious vein, cultural constraints distort our time perspective. Suppose you work for a multinational firm as a troubleshooter. You will quickly discover that different cultures have differing time perspectives. These differences impose constraints on effective communication and may lead to conflict rather than problem resolution. Ina Telberg, a journalist attached to the United Nations Educational, Scientific, and Cultural Organization, provides us with the following illustration:

"Gentlemen, it is time for lunch, we must adjourn," announces the Anglo-Saxon chairman in the belief that mankind must have three meals a day. Indeed it is the only proper way to live. "But why? We haven't finished what we were doing," replies the puzzled Eastern European delegate who operates under the belief that people eat when they want to and that people follow their own time table. "Eat by the clock—absurd." "Why, indeed?" asks the Far Eastern delegation where the tempo of life is unrushed, where members of electoral bodies walk in and out of the council rooms quietly, getting a bite to eat when necessary, but where meetings can last hours without formal interruptions.[3]

As each group persists in its own time perspective—the Americans demanding that the length of conferences be fixed in advance and the Asians puzzled at this American need for specificity—mutual friction grows, each side accuses the other of insincerity and unwillingness to come to grips with the problem, and the term sabotage is frequently heard.

Peter Drucker reports that American managers and their Japanese counterparts differ along many dimensions, one of which is time perspective.[4] He notes that Westerners frequently complain that negotiations with Japanese firms are endless. For example, it may take three years before a licensing agreement can be reached. During this time there is no discussion of terms or products. And then within a few weeks, the Japanese are ready to go into production and make demands of the Western partner for information. Generally, Westerners are unprepared to respond so swiftly to these demands. The paradox lies in how each views the term "decision making," which we will address shortly.

One's attitude toward change is very much dictated by culture. Eric Hofer, the longshoreman-philosopher, argues that Americans don't really like change. Even in unimportant things, change can be traumatic. Common reasons for fearing change are:

1. It's against policy.
2. We've never done it that way.
3. It won't work.
4. No one will accept it.
5. It's too radical.

Interestingly, the Japanese show a cheerful willingness to accept change. Their willingness to change is best demonstrated by what the Japanese call "continuous training." This means that managers at all levels train not only for their own jobs but for all jobs at the same job level. Thus a Japanese manager is ready when his job is changed as the result of shake-ups in the organization.

In a different vein, recent research on the brain has demonstrated that the right and left hemispheres operate differently on information. The left hemisphere (right-handed thinking) specializes in symbolic logic, associative reasoning, and analytical processing of data; it is logical. The right hemisphere specializes in visual-spatial representations and processes information in a Gestalt, or holistic, nature (one sees the total picture rather than a series of subparts). Right-handed thinking is equated with the scientific method, reason, and logic. Left-handed thinking includes hunches, feelings, and intuition.

In our Western culture right-handed thinking is considered good, and left-handed thinking is considered bad. When we were young we used hunches and illogic frequently to solve problems. These "bad" habits are eliminated as we learn that scientific method (and lots of money) can solve all of our problems. In addition, right-handed thinking is seen as hard analysis, whereas left-handed thinking is viewed as mushy or even effeminate. Once we recognize that we are male-chauvinistic, right-handed problem solvers, solutions to our societies' problems will improve. And with all of our societies' unsolved problems, there is much room for improvement. Although the models we will be discussing for solving operating and strategic problems are based on the scientific method, they incorporate left-handed thinking in the design phases (see Exhibit 1-4).

There are several ways of measuring the degree of right- or left-handedness in problem solving. The techniques range from analyzing electroencephalograms (EEGs) to paper and pencil tests, such as Street's Picture Completion Test. Some of the figures in that test are shown in Exhibit 2-1. How many can you recognize? The more you see, the greater is the development of

Exhibit 2-1: Street's completion test

1.

2.

3.

4.

Answers: 1. Sailboat, 2. Man on horse, 3. Baby, 4. Rabbit (generally considered most ambiguous diagram).

your right hemisphere (left-handed thinking).

In an article entitled "What We Can Learn from Japanese Management," Peter Drucker noted that to American and to Japanese managers "making a decision" means something different.[5] In the West, the emphasis is on finding the answer to the problem; to the Japanese it is on defining the problem. In defining the problem, much time is spent on diagnosing in an attempt to reach a consensus. To the Western mind this is all a waste of time since the problem is always obvious. While the Japanese do spend incredible amounts of time in defining the problem, there are two advantages to their approach:

- The chance of solving the wrong problem is minimized, and
- When it comes time to implement the solution, those involved in defining the problem have a stake in seeing that the solution is implemented successfully.

In concluding this section of the chapter, I would like to share with you a story told by Russell Ackoff, noted management educator, showing how cultural imperialism can blind a problem solver.[6] In 1957 Ackoff spent time in India at the request of the government to review the family planning program. There he met a group of foreigners who were trying to introduce contraceptive methods. The experiment had utterly failed, and the group blamed their failure on the ignorance, irrationality, and intransigence of the Indians.

Ackoff was not convinced. After several months of study, he reported that the Indians were acting rationally (certainly more rationally than the foreign group). Since India had no social security system, the only way most Indians could survive was by having children who could support them in their old age. However, since only males are generally employable, and the death rate among children is high, large families are necessary insurance for one's old age. Far from being irrational, the Indian peasant was acting in a most rational manner.

Organizational Constraints

The organization is the physical setting within which problem solving occurs and can be a catalyst or a barrier to effective problem solving. While there have been few studies of the impact of organizations on problem-solving effectiveness, there has been systematic research on the impact of the organization on the generation, acceptance, and implementation of innovation. Innovation is defined as the organization's "first-use-ever" of a new product, process, or idea. Before we examine these findings we need to understand the impact of certain organizational variables on individual behavior. These are shown in Exhibit 2-2.

An individual's performance results from three forces: (1) the organizational structure, (2) the managerial climate, and (3) the individual. In turn, the organizational structure is dependent on what organizational theorists label as "contextual" variables. The interrelationships between these forces can be explained by a geological analogy. We can view the organizational structure as

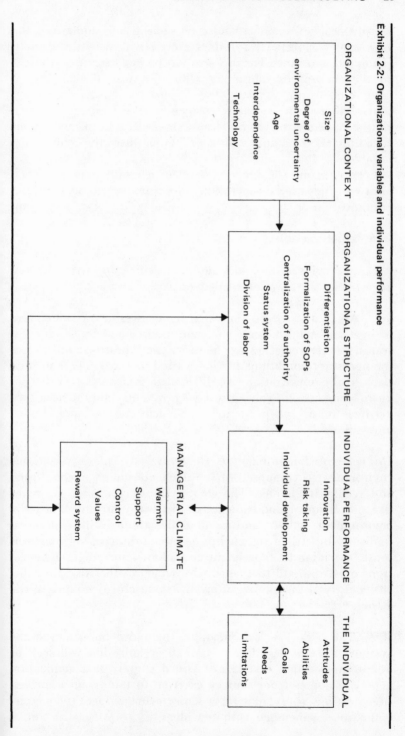

Exhibit 2-2: Organizational variables and individual performance

ORGANIZATIONAL CONTEXT

Size

Degree of
environmental uncertainty

Age

Interdependence

Technology

ORGANIZATIONAL STRUCTURE

Differentiation

Formalization of SOPs

Centralization of authority

Status system

Division of labor

INDIVIDUAL PERFORMANCE

Innovation

Risk taking

Individual development

MANAGERIAL CLIMATE

Warmth

Support

Control

Values

Reward system

THE INDIVIDUAL

Attitudes

Abilities

Goals

Needs

Limitations

the physical terrain of a landscape such as hills and rivers; the individual performance variables are equivalent to the amount of rainfall and wind. The physical terrain has a significant effect on the amount of rainfall or wind. In turn, the amount of rainfall or wind can cause the terrain to change slowly. Of course, there can be sharp changes in the landscape due to natural disasters such as hurricanes or volcanic eruptions. In our diagram, these natural disasters constitute the contextual variables.

Let's examine the impact of selected contextual and structural variables on the generation, adoption, and implementation of innovation or change.

Contextual Variables

Contextual variables include size, degree of environmental uncertainty, age, and interdependence.

Size: Aiken and Alford state that larger organizations are more innovative.[7] While researchers cannot agree on why this is so, it appears that increasing size permits specialization and creates the necessary conditions for innovation to occur. These include slack in the organization (it's difficult to innovate when you are up to your neck in solving today's problems) and the necessary "critical mass" of personnel that facilitate the adoption of innovation.

Degree of Environmental Uncertainty: An organization's environment is composed of suppliers, consumers, competitors, and regulatory bodies. The greater the uncertainty, the more likely that an organization must and will innovate. When the environment is safe and predictable, there is little need to innovate. But when the environment is turbulent, organizations must be willing to experiment and adopt innovation. Organizations must respond to change with change, otherwise, they die. If necessity is the mother of invention, surely uncertainty is the father.

Age: The older an organization, the more bureaucratic the system, and the less likely that an organization will seek or adopt innovation. Aiken and Alford suggest that innovation generally comes from sources external to the organization. As organizations age (read here, as senior managers age) there is less influx of new members with new ideas.[8]

There is a striking parallel in the scientific world. Have you ever noticed that those individuals who led major revolutions were quite young? Einstein and Newton were in their twenties when they revolutionized their respective worlds.

Interdependence: Aiken and Hage report that organizations that develop joint programs with other organizations are more likely to adopt innovation.[9] Joint programs provide an opportunity to import external ideas without the trauma of hiring senior personnel. Organizations locked in joint ventures have the opportunity to question long-standing assumptions and thereby overcome the inertia to stay with a "pat hand." When long-standing assumptions are challenged, organizations are often open to the idea of change.

Structural Variables

Also affecting innovation in organizations are structural variables including organizational differentiation, formalization, centralization of authority, and status systems.

Differentiation: Differentiation refers to the heterogeneity in job descriptions or classifications within an organization. Different classifications require different educational training. Whatever the benefits of education, the debit side of the ledger is that similar educational backgrounds can induce what psychologists call "functional myopia," the tendency to view the organization, its opportunities, and problems from the same set of reference points or world views. For example, two accountants are more likely to view an organizational problem similarly than are an accountant and a liberal arts major. Organizational differentiation stimulates (1) constructive conflict between individuals with different educational backgrounds, and (2) cross-fertilization of ideas. Thus an organizational structure that has occupational diversity is more likely to generate innovation.

However, Aiken and Hage claim that *adoption* of innovation (as opposed to generation of innovation) is less likely in differentiated organizations. What they suggest is that an organizational structure conducive to generating innovation is inappropriate for implementing it.[10]

Formalization: Formalization is defined as the degree to which an organization relies on written standardized rules and procedures. Shepard reports that informal organizations (low formalization) permit an openness that is a necessary precondition for innovative behavior.[11] Unless the standard operating procedures (SOPs) mandate innovative behavior as an organizational standard, innovation is unlikely to occur.

Unfortunately, high formalization is conducive to adopting and implementing innovation. The organizational paradox is eliminated by implementing what Gene Dalton has labeled "venture groups."[12] These are groups within highly formalized organizations whose mission is to venture into the unknown—that is their role. The charter for the venture group is to seek, adopt, and implement change. However, unless these groups are fully supported by senior management, they and their innovation are doomed to failure.

Centralization of Authority: Usually centralization of authority stifles the search for innovation. Clearly, the more time needed for gaining permission from those higher on the organizational ladder, the less time there is to seek innovation. Decentralization results in greater autonomy and individual initiative that in turn generates more innovation.

Once innovation has been identified, the necessary resources to adopt it may be easier to obtain within a centralized organization. Again we have an interesting paradox. Decentralization stimulates the search for innovation; centralization assures its implementation.

Status Systems: Preoccupation with status is to innovation as a nail is to a tire. The inhibitions caused by amplifying status differences within an organization are deadly to the innovation-seeking process. Rollo May believes that preoccupation with status (such as different size desks, different color briefcases, and the ever-present executive washroom keys) and its associated symbols leads to personal insecurity that is incompatible with creative thinking.[13]

The ease of ascending the organizational ladder is positively related to innovation-seeking behavior. Where there is a lack of organizational mobility, you will find incumbents merely doing their jobs and no more.

In summary then:

1. Larger organizations are more likely to innovate.

2. Organizations that operate in uncertain environments are more likely to innovate.

3. Organizations with young senior management are likely to innovate.

4. Joint ventures with other firms are conducive to innovation.

5. Differentiated organizations are likely to generate innovation but have a difficult time adopting it.

6. Organizations that nurture informality are likely to generate innovation but find it difficult to adopt.

7. Decentralized organizations are likely to generate innovation but find it difficult to implement.

8. Preoccupation with status and its associated symbols stifles innovation.

9. Overlaying "venture groups" on formalized or centralized organizations may overcome the organizational paradox discussed in points 5, 6, and 7.

Crisis Decision Making

In the previous section we concluded that the organizational structure does affect the innovation process. We now want to shift our focus and examine how organizations react to crisis decision-making conditions. According to Carolyne Smart and Ilan Vertinsky, organizations, like the people who run them, tend to react poorly.[14]

The term "reacting poorly" when applied to organizational problem solving can mean one of the following: (1) rejecting a correct course of action, (2) accepting an incorrect solution and implementing it (and waiting for the other shoe to fall), (3) solving the wrong problem, and (4) solving the right problem correctly but too late. Under crisis conditions, the likelihood of making the last two errors increases dramatically. According to Smart and Vertinsky, poor problem-solving performance results from the following organizational pathologies:

1. Reaching premature consensus as to what the problem and solution are.

2. Communication distortion resulting from the crisis-like atmosphere.

3. Groupthink.

4. Use of inappropriate SOPs.

Reaching Premature Consensus

During a crisis, decision makers tend to focus on short-range issues at the expense of long-range outcomes. The changing time perspective is accompanied by a drop in problem-solving effectiveness. There is greater concern with reaching consensus even at the expense of finding good solutions. In one sense consensus is made easier because during crises we typically find authority shifting to higher levels in the organization. This, in turn, leads to a reduction in the number of individuals on the problem-solving team, thereby making consensus easier to reach.

Communication Distortion

As the problem-solving group is shifted upward in the organization, the chasm between information collectors and users widens, with an attendant increase in communication distortion, time lags, etc. Because the information collectors are lower in the hierarchy, they tend to have a different world view from the decision makers. The net effect is to further deteriorate the communication process. That is not all. As the problem-solving team shrinks in size, each member must evaluate relatively more information, which can easily lead to information overload and an attendant drop in problem-solving effectiveness.

Groupthink Pathology

As crises deepen we find that the size of the decision-making team shrinks. Small, highly cohesive groups are susceptible to what Irving Janis labels "groupthink."[1 5] Groupthink refers to the deterioration in the decision-making capability of a group irrespective of individual members' capabilities. Group members develop illusions of invulnerability that encourage high-risk solutions. Other groups, including competitors or other divisions within the same organization, are viewed as outsiders and are seen as too weak to take effective counteraction. The groupthink pathology also restrains the group from seriously considering the negative consequences (possible foul-ups) of a solution. Indeed, anyone who expresses doubt over the wisdom of a solution is censored. Janis suggests that groups may go so far as to appoint "mindguards" whose function is to shield the group from those (even within the group) who might challenge its solutions and hidden assumptions.

Janis observed these pathologies at work in the Bay of Pigs fiasco; however, Janis argued that not all small problem-solving groups working under crisis conditions are subject to group-think. In fact, several years later during the Cuban Missile Crisis, the National Security Council (with essentially the same membership as during the Bay of Pigs) did not exhibit any of the groupthink pathologies.

Is groupthink relevant to business decision making? While there have been no empirical studies, it does appear that all decision-making groups are potentially susceptible to the malady. Janis suggests that groupthink results when team members strive for mutual support as a way of coping with the stresses associated with crisis decisions. The greater the stakes, the greater the likelihood that groupthink will be present.

Of course, not all small groups suffer from this pathology. In Chapter 3 we will suggest certain principles of consensus leadership that can reduce the likelihood of groupthink. But when groupthink is at work, poor quality solutions are generated.

Little need be said of using SOPs. Novel problems require novel solutions. SOPs, while useful in dealing with well-structured problems, generally fail to solve ill-structured problems.

Smart and Vertinsky suggest that organizations can be designed to deal effectively with crisis; some of their suggestions are found in Exhibit 2-3. You will note that every prescription has potential negative consequences, and these consequences can outweigh the potential benefits. Beyond those recommendations, decision making under crisis conditions can be improved by hiring executives who are able to deal with stress, by instituting crisis drills to improve reactions (as in war games), and by ultimately creating a dual organizational structure that can be implemented for crisis problem solving. While these suggestions are costly, so too is ineffective problem solving.

Fortunately, some suggestions for improving crisis decision making have an inexpensive price tag. Under crisis conditions, there never seems to be enough time. Thus managers must use what little time they have more efficiently. This leads us to the topic of time management.

Time Management

Asking managers what they do with their time is often nonproductive, since they don't really know. A case in point is the following scenario:[1][6]

Observer: Mr. R—, we have discussed briefly this organization and the way that it operates. Will you now please tell me what you do.

Exhibit 2-3: Design for crisis decision making

Major problem	Symptoms	Prescription	Potential negative consequences
Premature consensus	Size reduction in decision-making team	Discuss alternatives with associates.	Breach of security.
		Obtain fresh viewpoints.	Time consuming process.
	Short-range perspective	Focus on long-term issues by assigning an advocacy role to certain members.	Time consuming process.
	Preferred solution promoted by strong team leader	Encourage critical viewpoints; leader remains neutral and does not express ideas.	Most effective problem solver (leader) may not be used.
Communication distortion	Information overload	Use special formats for flagging critical information, or develop special crisis units for data gathering.	May not be cost/benefit effective.
	Information distortion	Set up channels to cut through hierarchy—allow information collectors to be privy to group decision making.	Breach of security. Time consuming process.
Groupthink	Illusion of invulnerability	Develop worst case scenarios. Set up independent appraisal group.	Time consuming process.
	Group pressure to conform	Require minority opinion by using a dialectic process (develop counter suggestions).	Dialectic process is difficult to carry out.
		Encourage expressions of doubt.	Can lead to damaged feelings if doubters are criticized.
Overutilization of SOPs	Resistance to change (we've always done it this way syndrome)	Allow more individual discretion in decision making.	Loss of organizational economies from standardization; training in problem solving costly.
		Expand SOPs to cover more contingencies.	All problems may be viewed as solvable by SOPs.

Source: Adapted from Carolyne Smart and Ilan Vertinsky, "Designs for Crisis Decision Units," *Administrative Science Quarterly,* December 1977, p. 648.

Executive: What I do?

Observer: Yes.

Executive: That's not easy.

Observer: Go ahead, anyway.

Executive: As president, I am naturally in charge of many things.

Observer: I realize that. But just what do you do?

Executive: Well, I must see that things go all right.

Observer: Can you give me an example?

Executive: I must see that our financial position is sound.

Observer: But just what do you do about it?

Executive: Now, that is hard to say.

Observer: Let's take another tack. What did you do yesterday?

A study by Irvin Choran on chief executive officers (CEOs) of small companies,[17] and one by Henry Mintzburg on CEOs of large companies,[18] tell us a great deal about what these executives do. Their jobs are characterized by: brevity, superficiality, fragmentation, and an unrelenting pace. While that may not surprise you, the actual duration of managerial activities will. See Exhibit 2-4.

If we could save only two to four hours a week through better time management, consider the improvements that could be made in crisis decision making. Four additional hours judiciously applied to diagnosing a complex problem could make the difference between success and failure.

Time management begins with a self-audit. Bonoma and Slevin recommend that you first record all work incidents in a log book for several days.[19] An incident is not a crisis or even an important activity; it is simply a change in what you are doing. Here's how a daily log might look:

    8:00   Start to read mail
    8:15   Plant manager called. Machine breakdown
    8:21   Read mail again
    8:30   Begin scheduled meeting
    9:02   Phone call—interrupt meeting
    9:07   Resume meeting
   10:00   Meet with subordinate re: marketing problem
   10:17   Interrupted—vice-president called regarding budget

Once you have a clear picture of a typical business day, you can improve your management of time in two ways—*do less or work faster*. You can do less by (1) delegating whenever possible and

---

Exhibit 2-4: Duration of managerial activities

	Choran study	Mintzberg study
	3 presidents (6 days' observation)	5 CEOs (25 days' observation)
Number of incidents per day*	77	22
Desk work sessions		
Number of incidents	22	7
Average duration	6 minutes	15 minutes
Telephone calls		
Number per day	29	5
Average duration	2 minutes	6 minutes
Scheduled meetings		
Number per day	3	4
Average duration	27 minutes	68 minutes
Unscheduled meetings		
Number per day	19	4
Average duration	3 minutes	12 minutes
Tours		
Number per day	5	1
Average duration	9 minutes	11 minutes
Proportion of managerial incidents lasting less than 9 minutes	90%	49%
Proportion of managerial incidents lasting longer than 60 minutes	.02	10

*An incident is defined as any change in what the manager is doing (i.e., if the manager is talking to a subordinate and the phone rings, this is a new incident).
Source: Adapted from Henry Mintzburg, *The Nature of Managerial Work* (New York, Harper and Row, 1973), p. 105.

---

(2) learning to say NO. Bonoma and Slevin claim that the use of delegation is the single most important step to time management. There may be some additional positive fall-out from delegation. Subordinates may become more motivated because their job scope is enlarged and better decisions may ultimately be made because of their participation. Saying no is an effective response to activities that have little payoff for improved managerial performance. While some managers fear that saying no will count against them in their drive to succeed, remember that "there ain't no such thing as a free lunch"—put your time where it counts. When an activity is important to improving organizational performance, say yes; otherwise, forget it.

You can gain time by working faster (or smarter). Bonoma and Slevin recommend the following strategies: (1) filter out interruptions, (2) set priorities, (3) develop a paper-flow system, and (4) use dictation equipment.

The worst interrupter is the telephone, followed closely by people. While you can't become a monk, you can take several steps to gain mastery over time. Schedule blocks of time when no telephone calls get through to your office (except from your superiors). Let your secretary run interference for you the rest of the time. Close your office door when you don't want to be disturbed. If your door is open, people will walk into your office even if they have little to say. People walk through open doorways probably for the same reason they climb tall mountains—because they are there. Keep a closed "open-door" policy.

Bonoma and Slevin's remaining suggestions are equally practical and effective. If you can save just four hours a week (assuming a 40-hour workweek), you should be able to gain an additional five weeks a year. Use time wisely.

Managerial Constraints

Managerial or leadership style can be described along a consensus-autocratic continuum. A consensus leader encourages his/her subordinates to participate actively in problem solving and decision making. An autocratic leader makes decisions without any input from subordinates, although they will implement the solutions generated. Is there one leadership style that is best? From a review of studies on leadership style and problem-solving effectiveness, Vroom and Yetton concluded that there was no one best style.[20] The best leadership style depended on the characteristics of the problems facing the group. This led Vroom and Yetton to develop a problem-oriented contingency theory of leadership.

Which Leadership Style?

Their basic premise is that a manager must choose a leadership style to fit the characteristics of a problem. A logical corollary is that a manager's leadership style must be flexible, for not all problems that he or she encounters are the same. Vroom and Yetton believe that a contingency approach does not violate the maxim "consistency in leadership style is desirable," for consistency does not preclude variability if it is known by subordinates in advance.

Problem-solving effectiveness (PSE) can be expressed as a function (f) of the three variables (quality, acceptance, timeliness):

$$PSE = f\ (quality\ (Q),\ acceptance\ (A),\ timeliness\ (T)\ )$$

The Q component refers to the quality or rationality of the solution. Is there a way to demonstrate that one solution is objectively better than others? This is not always possible, for often a "best" solution is one that is merely acceptable to all parties. The A component focuses on the acceptance of a solution by subordinates and their personal commitment to implement it. Commitment is not always important since a manager may be able to implement a solution unilaterally without his or her subordinates feeling that they have been slighted. Good solutions are timely ones. A "best" solution offered too late is worse than an adequate but timely solution.

Recognizing the various components of problem solving, Vroom and Yetton developed a leadership-style selection tree diagram to help a manager determine what style of leadership behavior is appropriate in a given situation. The leadership styles reflect the autocrat-consensus leadership continuum described in Exhibit 2-5.

Exhibit 2-5: Leadership style continuum

Leadership style	Leadership behavior
Autocrat	Manager solves the problem by using whatever information is available.
Consultive autocrat I (CA-I)	Manager obtains information from subordinates. They are not involved in solving the problem.
Consultive autocrat II (CA-II)	Manager shares the problem with subordinates individually and obtains their suggestions. Manager's decision may not reflect subordinates' input.
Consultive autocrat III (CA-III)	Manager shares the problem with subordinates in a group meeting. Manager obtains their suggestions, but final decision may not reflect this input.
Consensus	Manager shares the problem with subordinates. Together they generate and evaluate alternatives. Manager's role is to coordinate and to keep the group on the critical issues. Manager supports the group's solution.

Let's see how a tree diagram can guide a manager in selecting the appropriate leadership style (Exhibit 2-6). The diagram is built on the responses to eight questions and has been pruned to simplify the presentation. The terminal points of the diagram are denoted by the numbers 1 through 6. Associated with each terminal point is a leadership style. First, read the following problem:

> You are the president of a small, but growing, bank with its headquarters in the state's capital and branches in several nearby towns. You follow traditional and conservative banking practices at all levels within the organization.
>
> When you first bought the bank five years ago, it was in poor financial shape. Although the economy has recently gone through a recession, much progress has been made and your prestige in the banking community is high. Your growth has been attributable to good luck and a few timely decisions. However, this has caused your subordinates to look to you for leadership. Although they are capable managers, you wish that they were not quite so willing to accede to your judgment.
>
> You have recently acquired funds to open a new branch. Where should the branch be located? The choice will be made on simple common-sense criteria and "what feels right." As your managers are knowledgeable about real estate in the community, you have asked them to look for suitable sites.
>
> Their support is important to the success of a new branch as they will be asked to supply staff and technical assistance. The success of the project will benefit everyone. Everyone will reap the benefits of an increased base of operations. You have always believed that the crucial key to success is that each member should feel like part of a team.[21]

Before continuing, which leadership style would you choose? Of course, this assumes that you are a flexible manager capable of changing your style when appropriate. Now, let's answer the eight questions:

1. Is there a quality component?

YES. While the manager will use no magic formula in select-

Exhibit 2-6: Leadership-style selection flowchart

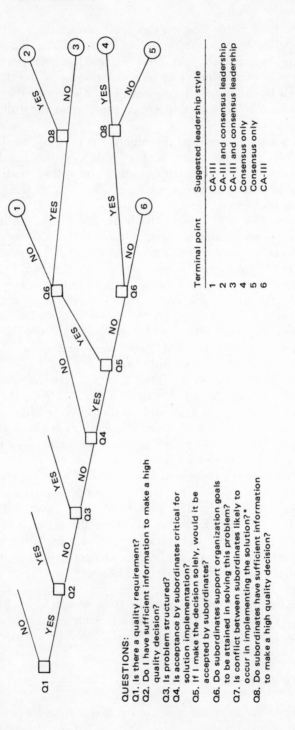

QUESTIONS:
Q1. Is there a quality requirement?
Q2. Do I have sufficient information to make a high quality decision?
Q3. Is problem structured?
Q4. Is acceptance by subordinates critical for solution implementation?
Q5. If I make the decision solely, would it be accepted by subordinates?
Q6. Do subordinates support organization goals to be attained in solving this problem?
Q7. Is conflict between subordinates likely to occur in implementing the solution?*
Q8. Do subordinates have sufficient information to make a high quality decision?

Terminal point	Suggested leadership style
1	CA-III
2	CA-III and consensus leadership
3	CA-III and consensus leadership
4	Consensus only
5	Consensus only
6	CA-III

*A "yes" answer to question 6 in this example precludes the need to answer question 7, therefore question 7 does not appear on the flowchart.
Source: Adapted with permission from Victor H. Vroom and Philip W. Yetton, *Leadership and Decision Making* (Pittsburgh, University of Pittsburgh Press, 1973), p. 748.

ing a site, site selection is a rational process. The "best" site includes more than which site would be acceptable to the subordinates or to the board of directors.

2. Does the leader have sufficient information?

NO. The branch managers know the local real estate market and could be of great help in locating and selecting potential sites.

3. Is the problem structured?

Is the site selection decision so repetitive that SOPs have been developed? While this might be true for some banking institutions, our bank is so small that the problem is unstructured. So the answer is NO.

4. Is acceptance by subordinates crucial?

Does implementing any solution require subordinate initiative, judgment, and creativity, or can implementation be ensured by fiat and the requisite control mechanisms? Stated simply, is compliance by subordinates sufficient or is commitment necessary? This case indicates that the branch managers must be committed to the solution since they will have to furnish staff and technical support. So the answer is YES.

5. Would subordinates accept an imposed solution?

YES. In the past subordinates have been all too willing to let the president "go it alone." In general, the answer to this question focuses on subordinates' needs for independence and the leader's demonstrated problem-solving ability.

6. Is there sharing of organizational goals?

YES. The president believes that the key ingredient in past successes has been a coordinated team effort. As this venture is in keeping with the previous goal of growth, the president assumes that his subordinates' goals remain congruent with organizational goals.

7. Might there be conflict over proposed solutions?

According to Vroom and Yetton, a "yes" answer to the previous question eliminates the need to answer this question. This is not at all clear to me since subordinates could share goals or ends and still disagree on means. Nevertheless, this question is skipped and we go directly to question 8.

8. Do subordinates have sufficient information?

YES. Site selection is dependent on available real estate, and the branch managers are quite knowledgeable in this area.

If we follow the tree diagram to its end, we find ourselves at terminal point 2. Given these problem characteristics, Vroom and Yetton prescribe the CA-III and consensus leadership styles. They suggest that while both styles will be equally effective, the optimal choice depends on which of two additional criteria the manager subscribes to. Criterion A is a short-term criterion that places great weight on minimizing the man-hours required to solve the problem. Criterion B is a long-term criterion and is primarily concerned with maximizing the subordinates' participation. Thus Vroom and Yetton's recommendations for acceptable leadership styles are:

CA-III and Consensus Leadership Style

Criterion A: Consultive Autocrat - Type III Style
Criterion B: Consensus Style

Any other leadership style would be ineffective because it would fail to match the leader's style to the eight problem characteristics.

Vroom and Yetton then worked with over 500 managers in an extensive training program to teach them how to implement the leadership-style selection tree diagram. After several months they concluded that

1. There was an increase in the extent to which managers varied their leadership styles.

2. Training is necessary to increase a manager's ability to describe problem characteristics accurately.

3. Training is necessary for managers to "role play" the five different leadership styles.

4. How a problem is perceived determines how a problem is characterized along the eight dimensions.

The appropriate leadership style is dependent on a manager's perception of the problem characteristics. But managers are not cameras; they do not always capture reality. Each one of us has his or her own peculiarities, and it is to individual factors that we now turn.

Individual Constraints

What stops us from being the effective problem solvers we want to be? In this section we will discuss eight handicaps that problem solvers must overcome. Some deal with who and what we are and therefore are difficult to overcome; others can be successfully dealt with by the left-handed creativity techniques discussed in the next chapter.

Stereotyped Thinking

How do facts affect us especially when they contradict our widely held beliefs? Social psychologists tell us that there are two ways of incorporating controversial beliefs into our belief systems. First, we may disregard the facts and stick to our preconceived beliefs. For example, suppose you believe that union (or management) representatives are basically untrustworthy. This belief is based on many years of experience. If a union representative should do something for the good of the company, how is this fact incorporated into your beliefs? Will this fact change your beliefs about union representatives? Maybe not. You may ascribe some ulterior motive to the union representative's behavior. The result is that, instead of changing your beliefs about the union, you change the data. We will call this behavior stereotypical or dogmatic thinking. A second, and more constructive, pattern of incorporating data into our belief systems is to tolerate the inconsistency between our past beliefs and the present data.

Let's examine how information shapes beliefs (or vice versa). I want you to read the first short description and write a paragraph describing what kind of person the worker is.

DESCRIPTION 1: Works in factory, reads a newspaper, goes to the movies, average height, cracks jokes, strong, active.

Now ask a co-worker to read the following description (and don't let him see description 1) and write a paragraph.

DESCRIPTION 2: Works in factory, reads a newspaper, goes to the movies, average height, intelligent, cracks jokes, strong, active.

Now, compare your paragraph and your co-worker's paragraph. Are there any major differences between the two?

Haire and Grunes conducted this experiment on two groups of college students.[22] They reported that a typical paragraph for the first description reads as follows:

> Likeable and well-liked, mildly sociable, healthy, happy, well-adjusted, not very intelligent but trying to keep abreast of current trends, interested in sports, and finding his pleasures in simple, undistinguished activities.

The inclusion of the adjective "intelligent" in description 2 caused all sorts of difficulties. For many students the terms "works in factory" and "intelligent" were inconsistent. In order to maintain consistent beliefs, the "intelligent" adjective had to be reinterpreted. In some cases the worker was promoted to a foreman (a manager is obviously more intelligent than a worker, right?). In other instances the students argued that the worker, while intelligent, obviously possessed no initiative; otherwise, why would he still be a worker? It is amazing what some people will do to data to maintain consistent sets of beliefs.

Russ Ackoff relates an interesting case of stereotyped thinking.[23] Ackoff was asked to design an educational program to increase upward mobility for a company's black employees. The problem was that although 40 percent of the workers were black, the percentage of blacks in the supervisory and managerial ranks was only 1 percent.

In order to design the program, Ackoff requested access to the personnel records of 500 randomly selected black employees and of 500 white employees who had similar jobs. The personnel director refused permission, arguing that it was difficult because of the personnel system. The director told Ackoff he could safely assume that blacks were deficient across the board. The conflict was finally resolved when the parent company gave Ackoff permission to collect the data.

Ackoff found that blacks were not more deficient than whites in years of schooling (forgetting for the moment the qualitative educational differences). Indeed, on the average, blacks had about one more year of schooling than did the white employees. Ackoff told the company to junk the proposed training program and to educate white supervisors so that they would permit blacks to move up. Ackoff's suggestions were rejected. A year later a federal court found the company guilty of discriminatory practices.

Stereotyping is the antithesis of critical thinking. Why is it that some of us are able to maintain sets of inconsistent beliefs while others, like the personnel director, are not?

Intellectual factors play an important role. We are not all equal. Intellectual factors determine how we restructure our beliefs as we obtain additional information. Do we incorporate inconsistent data into our beliefs, or do we reinterpret the data? More intelligent people are able to incorporate controversial data into their belief systems and to tolerate inconsistency when it is present.

Of *greater* importance is the personality dimension of intolerance of ambiguity. Regardless of the level of intelligence, some individuals find it difficult to tolerate uncertainty or ambiguity. A study by Guilford and associates found that intolerance of ambiguity consisted of two components: (1) a black and white or dichotomous thinking style, and (2) the need for definiteness or closure.[24] Individuals who solve problems along a black-white thinking pattern believe that there are only two ways to attack a problem—a right way and a wrong way. Such thinking is counterproductive because problems frequently are solved by employing two or more problem-solving strategies simultaneously. To some people, need for definiteness is a compulsion. These people are *overly* concerned with need to maintain order and cannot cope with the ambiguity associated with a complex problem. Frequently, in the rush to restore order the problem solver either disregards the problem situation or "solves" the problem before it is well defined. These people are "solution-minded" rather than "problem-minded."

In a recent study, Brightman and Urban examined the relationship between intolerance of ambiguity, problem-solving ability, and managerial performance.[25] We were asked to develop a battery of psychological measures for promoting workers to the foreman level within a company. Since we believed that effective foremen and managers are effective problem solvers, we selected measures that tapped a supervisor's problem-solving skills and attitudes. Problem-solving attitude was assessed by the personality variables of intolerance of ambiguity and dogmatism. These two dimensions were important because effective problem solvers must be capable of solving novel problems. In contrast, recurring problems can be handled by standard policies and procedures. A dogmatic supervisor is closed to new information, cannot tolerate the ambiguous situation, and thus might be incapable of dealing with ill-structured problems. The foremen's problem-solving abilities were measured by the Watson Glaser Critical Thinking Appraisal. This standardized instrument measures the ability to draw inferences, recognize assumptions, deduce logical consequences, and evaluate arguments. The supervisors' performance levels were obtained from the firm.

We found that foremen who were dogmatic and could not tolerate ambiguity tended to be ineffective problem solvers and ineffective managers. Foremen who were flexible and could tolerate moderate amounts of chaos were effective problem solvers and effective managers.

Lack of a Questioning Attitude or How To Be a "Whys-Guy"

Frequently we hesitate to ask questions; perhaps we do not wish to appear ignorant. Given a choice of being ignorant or appearing to be ignorant, many individuals will select the former. Such individuals may never suffer loss of face, but they pay a price, for the difference between success and failure in problem solving often is the amount and quality of the questions generated.

We were all born with a questioning attitude. To a youngster the world is a mysterious and unexplainable place. Children want to know the "why" and "how" of everything; why is the sky blue or how does a bird fly? As children grow up they are taught by the parents ("Don't bother me with those questions!"), friends ("Don't you know anything?"), and by their teachers ("We just covered that material.") that asking questions is a sign of stupidity. The result is that youngsters begin to value ego over knowledge and will go to great lengths to camouflage their ignorance. This strategy is best demonstrated in the classroom by students who continually nod their heads in agreement with your lecture, but who haven't the faintest idea of what you are talking about.

By the time a child reaches adulthood, the lack of a questioning attitude has become his or her *modus operandi* in problem solving. Several years ago I directed a senior-level independent study course run in conjunction with the Small Business Administration in which teams of students were assigned to work with small firms that were in need of management assistance. In concert with their clients, the student teams defined the problems and generated and implemented solutions. We had our share of successes, but when we failed, a prime reason was the lack of a questioning attitude on the part of our student teams. I recall one team that was working with an owner of a retail book store located in an older shopping plaza. After several interviews with the owner, the team concluded that the major problem was a lack of marketing research. They thought that the client was carrying the wrong inventory for the clientele he was serving. In their third meeting the team asked the client why he had not conducted a market research study. The team was crushed when the owner replied that he had indeed conducted a market study. At our next class session you could see the disappointment on the students' faces—the problem just had to be lack of marketing research.

When they asked what they should do now that their solution had already been tried, I asked them, "What does your client mean by marketing research?" and "Is his definition the same as yours?". At that point the team recognized that they had failed to question their client properly and had *assumed* that marketing research is marketing research is marketing research. In subsequent meetings the team discovered that what the client meant by marketing research was asking his friends if they would buy books at his store. Marketing research indeed! After conducting a complete market study, the team recommended a different line of books and the sales skyrocketed.

Should you believe that only students lack a proper questioning attitude, I would like to relate a story (not so amusing) about the academic community. During a series of meetings on developing an innovative educational Ph.D. program, the group was using jargon instead of English. One of the participants, who was upset over the meetings' lack of progress, wished to test his colleagues' lack of a questioning attitude. At one meeting he fabricated a new jargonese term that sounded meaningful. During the meeting he dropped the term into the conversation. Not one of his colleagues blinked an eye, and, in fact, several nodded their heads knowingly (a holdover from their student days?). There wasn't one individual who would bare his ignorance and ask what the term meant.

How do you develop a questioning attitude? First, remember how you were as a child. The trait of wanting to know why things are as they are is an important skill. Don't be intimidated by your parents, your peers, or your teachers. You will quickly find out by repeatedly asking "why" that people really don't understand the world about them. I used to think I understood why the sky is blue (after all, I took two years of physics in college) until my five-year-old asked "Why? . . . Why?" No one can withstand an incessant barrage of "whys" and "hows."

Risk of Failure

Some individuals possess a paranoic fear of failure. Rather than fail, they would rather not try to solve the problem (not trying is in fact failure). Some individuals are willing to assume the risks involved in problem solving, others are not. Why we are the way we are is not clear. Perhaps unwillingness to assume risk is based on objective evidence that we are really ineffective problem solvers. Often we fear failure even when our problem-solving track record is excellent. When the nature of our fears is not understood, they become anxieties. The first step in dealing with anxiety is to locate its sources. Once anxiety has been resolved into *specific* fears, we may be able to deal with each effectively.

One fear that is quite realistic is best expressed as "every solution breeds new problems." You can learn to cope with this specific fear by trying to estimate the future possible negative effects (foul-ups) of taking a course of action before actually doing it. By systematically considering "worst-case" scenarios, you may decide that what you thought was the best course of action has too great a risk factor associated with it.

How can you do this? Before implementing a potential solution, you should assume that Murphy was correct and that the solution will cause more problems than it solves. Your analysis should include the likelihood that foul-ups will occur, together with their seriousness. Potential trouble areas include people, the organization, external factors, and facilities. You want to ensure that the solution is not worse than the problem.

A simple example will be helpful. Suppose you generate two solutions to a problem and conclude that solution A is the better one. Before you implement your solution, you should consider the potential adverse consequences of *both* solutions. It may be that the better solution has greater negative risks associated with it, and you may wish to reconsider. You should then prepare a worst-case scenario worksheet (see Exhibit 2-7). For each solution list all the foul-ups that can occur during implementation, assign values that reflect their seriousness, and assign probabilities that reflect the likelihood of the foul-ups occurring. Next, weight the seriousness components by their

Exhibit 2-7: Worst case worksheet

Consequence	(1) Seriousness*	(2) Probability	(1) x (2)
Potential coordination problem with division Y.	80	.3	24
Critical equipment could break down.	30	.7	21
			45
May reduce organization's reaction time to external changes during solution implementation.	90	.15	13.5
Could hurt morale in division.	70	.20	14
			27.5

*The degree of seriousness is measured on a scale of 0 to 100.

respective probabilities of occurrence and sum. The higher the score, the greater are the negative risks associated with that solution.

Although solution A had been your preferred solution, you might not want to implement it because it possesses greater downside risks. As long as the risks are now out in the open, you can assess the trade-offs between solution effectiveness and new problem creation.

Memory Constraints

Sometimes the difficulty in problem solving is not the lack of information but the failure to utilize the information that we have. In Chapter 1 we presented an information-processing model of the brain. Like a computer, our memory acts as a processing unit, operating on the available data to solve problems. Unfortunately, we have limited capacity of recall. Beyond seven bits or pieces of information, our memory fails us.[26] While it is true that we rarely need to memorize long digit-strings in solving complex problems, the problems are illustrative of the memory constraint.

Consider the following number:

91852719521

If you were given 10 seconds to memorize this number, could you? Most people can memorize up to 9 digits. Try it before reading on. You could remember the number if you had a system.

Memory systems date back to Simonides of Greece (circa 500 B.C.). Many of these systems are based on association (mnemonics). Students in a geography class picture *homes* on the Great Lakes to help themselves remember that the five Great Lakes are *H*uron, *O*ntario, *M*ichigan, *E*rie, and *S*uperior. They may utilize the Indian-sounding phrase *seaana* (SEA-ANA) to recall the major inhabitable continents of *S*outh America, *E*urope, *A*sia, *A*frica, *N*orth America, and *A*ustralia. Engineering students have used mnemonics to learn the electrical wiring code, and medical students have used association to learn the cranial nerves.

In the book (I almost forgot the title) *The Memory Book*, Harry Lorayne and Jerry Lucas present over a dozen memory systems.[27] Harry Lorayne has used these systems to memorize the names of an entire audience. While a member of the National Basketball Association, Jerry Lucas astonished his roommates by memorizing telephone numbers from the New York City telephone directory (why he would want to do this is not clear). All their techniques are based on the principle that in order to remember a new piece of information it must be associated with something you already know in *some ridiculous way*. Since digits are intangible, they are difficult to remember. Thus it is necessary to transform the numbers into pictures that correspond to the digits. Lorayne and Lucas suggest the following system:

Digit	*Sound*
1	*t* or *d* (a small *t* has one downstroke)
2	*n* (has two downstrokes)
3	*m* (has three downstrokes)
4	*r* (last letter of the word "four")
5	*l* (the five fingers thumb out form an *L*)
6	*j*, *ch* (a 6 and a capital *j* are almost mirror images)
7	*k* (you can make a capital *k* with two 7s)
8	*f* (handwritten *f* and *8* look similar)
9	*p* or *b* (a *p* is a mirror image of a *9*)
0	*z* (first letter in the word zero)

The objective is to transform the digits into words, thereby improving your recall. In this phonetic alphabet, vowels have no meaning (they are only used to make meaningful words), silent letters are disregarded, and double letters as in be*ll*ow are considered one sound. When you have mastered the system, the long number—91852719521—can be transformed into an equivalent phrase "a beautiful naked blond," which is easier to picture and remember.

The *b* in beautiful is a 9. The next consonant sounds are *t* or 1, *f* or 8 and *l* or 5. So far we have 9185. The *n* in naked is a 2, the *k* represents a 7 and the *d* represents a 1. Now we have 9185271. The *b* in blond is a 9, the *l* a 5, the *n* a 2 and the *d* a 1. And there you have it—91852719521.

Each of us has a different capacity for information storage and retrieval. Memory systems can help you index your knowledge so that is is readily available when a problem situation arises.

World-View Constraints

Our view of problems is colored by our educational and business training. Dearborn and Simon asked a group of twenty-three executives enrolled in a management training program to read a case entitled the "Castengo Steel Company."[2][8] The departmental affiliations of the executives were as follows: sales (six), production (five), accounting (four), and miscellaneous (eight). Before the group discussion, each executive prepared a written statement describing the most serious problem facing the company. Sales problems were mentioned by five of the six sales executives (83 percent). In contrast, only five of the remaining seventeen executives (29 percent) mentioned sales. Organizational problems were mentioned by four of five production executives (80 percent), whereas only four of the remaining eighteen executives (22 percent) mentioned organizational problems. Only three executives mentioned human relations problems. Interestingly, the three managers were in public relations, industrial relations, and the medical departments.

Normally, managers faced with a problem select for emphasis those aspects that relate to their field of training; psychologists label this "functional myopia." Your view of a problem is *hampered* by your training in a discipline. When you develop depth in a functional field, you begin to focus selectively on certain related aspects of a complex problem, disregarding others. It is as if you were wearing functional blinders.

Functional myopia is based on the perceptual principle of selective sensitization. When you view the world, there are a maximum number of objects that you can perceive. Individuals selectively focus on some objects, and blur others. Similarly, when faced with a problem situation you selectively focus on those aspects of the problem that relate to your training.

The perception of a problem situation is based on the set, or expectancy, that is the result of your educational training. Perceptual set is a long-established principle in physiological perception. When the drawing in Exhibit 2-8 is included in a series of two-digit numbers, subjects view the figure as a "13." When the drawing is included in a series of alphabetic characters, subjects view the figure as a "B." In the first case the subjects acquired an expectancy set for numbers, and in the second instance they acquired an expectancy set for letters.

Exhibit 2-8: Name this picture!

Likewise, training in a discipline provides a set for how you view problems. Without selective sensitization and set, the world would surely be chaotic; however, set can cause myopia and thereby ineffective problem solving.

An effective method of circumventing world-view constraints is the crossfunctional team approach. Each member brings different skills, training, and world-views to the problem-solving team. In the process of defining the problem, functional myopia is minimized by the continual interaction of the team members. The team approach can be a broadening experience for its members and has been frequently used in industry to groom generalists for upper-management positions.

Functional Constraints

The impact of functional constraints on effective problem solving has been studied by Norman Maier and his associates.[29]

Functional constraints can be demonstrated in the following problem: Imagine you are brought into a room and there are two strings hanging from the ceiling as shown in Exhibit 2-9. You are told that the object is to tie string *a* and string *b*

Exhibit 2-9: Can you tie the strings together?

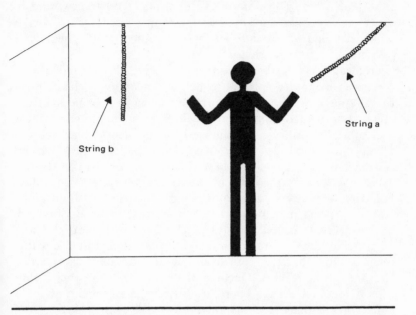

String a

String b

together. However, while holding *a* you cannot reach *b*. Try to solve the problem before you read on.

One way to solve the problem is to use your shoe as a weight, attach it to string *b* and turn string *b* into a pendulum. Now string *b* will swing within reach while you are holding string *a*. Many people fail to solve this problem because they have imposed a functional constraint on the object "shoe." A shoe is something to wear, and many fail to recognize that a shoe has weight and can be used to construct a pendulum.

Maier was the first to suggest that individuals who fail to solve the pendulum problem are *solution-minded* in that they hope to achieve solutions without spending time exploring the problem. Those subjects who are successful are *problem-minded* in that they diagnose the situation before attacking the problem (shades of the Japanese decision maker). The ability to be problem-minded may be related to the ability to withstand ambiguity—a personal constraint considered earlier in the chapter.

Functional constraints impose unnecessary barriers to problem solving. These can be circumvented by creativity techniques such as brainstorming and synectics. In brainstorming we circumvent the functional constraint by generating ideas *without* evaluating them. The idea is to generate many ideas so quickly that there is no time to evaluate each idea. There are situations where logic imposes functional constraints, and in order to circumvent a constraint we must circumvent logic. A more detailed discussion of brainstorming and synectics is presented in the next chapter.

In dealing with the energy crisis facing the United States, American ingenuity appears to be circumventing a classic functional constraint. For years garbage was viewed as an unsightly mess to be hauled away for landfill. With no end in sight to the fuel shortage, utility companies are taking a long, hard look at turning the nation's trash into a national treasury. Several approaches are being evaluated to squeeze BTUs (British Thermal Unit—a quantity of heat) from refuse. The Union Electric Company of St. Louis is experimenting with an incineration process in which garbage is burned to create fuel oil. The process is called pyrolysis. The garbage is heated under pressure in the absence of oxygen, a procedure called destructive distillation. The pyrolysis plant operated by Garrett Research, a division of Occidental Petroleum, can process four tons of garbage a day. There are, in fact, many techniques for converting garbage to fuel oil or low-BTU gas. The Stanford Research Institute estimates that refuse could furnish 10 percent of the fuel needed by American electric utilities. What all of these conversion techniques have in common is the circumvention of functional constraints associated with garbage. An interesting side-benefit of the conversion process is that it may help solve another national problem, namely, garbage disposal. The traditional means of solid waste disposal are landfills, incinerators, and composting. These facilities are limited, and as the nation's garbage piles grow, additional disposal techniques will have to be developed. Conceptually, what is simpler than developing solid waste disposal systems that eliminate refuse (solving problem 1) while recovering energy (solving problem 2)?

Imposed Constraints

In 1943 General MacArthur's staff figured it would take ten years to drive the Japanese from the bases they had acquired after Pearl Harbor. The staff estimated that it would take more planes, ships, and divisions than we had to capture the garrison on the island of Rabaul—and this was only the first in a long series of Japanese strongholds. MacArthur's reply to his staff was, "Let's not take the island." The strategy of bypassing Japanese strongholds, isolating them, and letting them "die on the vine" was developed. Although in warfare the strategy had always been to meet and defeat the enemy, MacArthur was not constrained by previous military strategies.

Often problem solvers impose constraints on themselves that do not really exist. Let me illustrate this with Exhibit 2-10: you are required to (a) connect all nine dots, (b) with four straight lines, (c) without lifting the pencil from the paper, and (d) without retracing any line. Try to solve the problem before reading on.

Exhibit 2-10: Nine-dots problem

Most people fail to solve this problem because they *believe* they must stay within the perimeter of the nine dots. The problem as stated imposes no such constraints. Reread the problem. Indeed, to solve the problem, one of the lines must be extended beyond the perimeter. The solution is shown in Exhibit 2-11. Without the self-imposed constraint the problem is easily solved.

Exhibit 2-11: Nine-dots problem solved

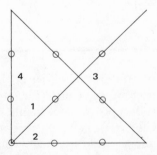

Now that you no longer impose constraints, redo the nine dots problem, except this time connect the nine dots with three straight lines (again without lifting your pencil from the paper or retracing a line). Try it before reading on. You'll find the solution in Exhibit 2-12.

Exhibit 2-12: Nine-dots problem revisited

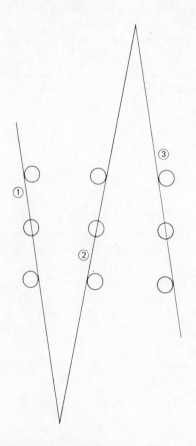

Who said that the dots couldn't be bigger or that the line had to pass through the center of each dot? If you have successfully overcome all your self-imposed constraints, try to solve the problem with a single line.

The nine dots problem would be an amusing party trick were it not for the fact that managers impose constraints on themselves in business problem solving, much as they do in solving the puzzle. In Chapter 1 you were introduced to the manager who, in attempting to cut operating costs, self-imposed constraints on the solution. That manager failed to consider any proposals outside the four walls of the plant. Four walls—nine dots—it's all the same.

Problem-Solving Language Constraints

Sometimes we cannot solve a problem because we choose the wrong problem-solving language. In the past, business educators have relied too heavily on verbal language and not enough on mathematical and visual language (especially the latter). While mathematics has worked its way into most business curriculums, when was the last time you saw a required art course?

There are times when, by merely changing your problem-solving language, an insolvable problem becomes solvable. Let's illustrate this idea with the following puzzle:

> One morning, exactly at sunrise, a Buddhist monk began to climb a mountain. A narrow path spiraled around the mountain to a temple at the summit. The monk ascended at varying rates of speed, stopping along the way to eat. He reached the temple shortly before sunset. Several days later he began his journey back down the mountain. His average speed descending was greater than his average speed climbing.
>
> Prove that there is a point along the path that the monk will occupy on both trips at precisely the same time of day.

Before reading on, try solving this problem.

If you tried to solve the problem using verbal language, by this time you are probably convinced that the problem is unsolvable. Mathematical language won't work since there are not enough quantitative data to develop a set of equations. However, visual language is a natural for this problem.

Close your eyes and visualize the mountain with its spiraled path. Now, instead of one monk on two different days, imagine or visualize two monks on the same day. (It makes no difference.) One monk starts at the bottom, the other starts at the summit. Now *watch* them as they proceed. They are getting closer and closer to one another, and at some time during the day the two monks will meet at one point on the path. You have just solved the puzzle by utilizing visual language.

When you are having difficulty solving a problem, try being multilingual; if one language won't work, try another.

Summary

In this chapter we have discussed the major cultural, organizational, managerial, and individual constraints that keep us from being effective problem solvers. The major cultural constraints are:

1. Bias against diagnosis.
2. The occidental-oriental differing views of time.
3. Bias against change.
4. The sanctity of the scientific method.

Organizations act as catalysts or barriers to effective individual problem solving. While there is little that a manager can do to change his or her environment, the idea of venture groups is suggested as a means of institutionalizing innovation and change in stable organizations.

Problem solving usually deteriorates during crisis conditions. Several problem-solving pathologies have been discussed, and suggestions for minimizing these problems are offered. Perhaps the easiest to implement is a time-management program.

Under managerial constraints we posed the question, "Is there one best leadership style?" The answer is a resounding NO. The best leadership style depends on the characteristics of the problem, and a leadership-style selection tree diagram is suggested for your use.

Finally individual constraints to effective problem solving were discussed. Pogo was correct when he said we are often our own worst enemy. Eight individual constraints have been identified:

1. Stereotyped thinking.
2. Lack of a questioning attitude.
3. Risk of failure.
4. Memory constraints.
5. World-view constraints.
6. Functional constraints.
7. Self-imposed constraints.
8. Problem-solving language constraints.

FOOTNOTES

1. Moshe F. Rubinstein, *Patterns of Problem Solving* (Englewood Cliffs, New Jersey, Prentice-Hall, Inc., 1975), p. 1.

2. James L. Adams, *Conceptual Blockbusting* (San Francisco, W.H. Freeman, 1974), p. 32.

3. Ina Telberg, "They Don't Do It Our Way," *Courier*, Vol. 3, No. 4 (1950).

4. Peter F. Drucker, "What We Can Learn from Japanese Management," *Harvard Business Review*, March-April 1971, pp. 110-122.

5. Ibid.

6. Russell L. Ackoff, *The Art of Problem Solving* (New York, Wiley Interscience, 1978).

7. Michael Aiken and Robert R. Alford, "Community Structure and Innovation: The Case of Urban Renewal," *American Sociological Review*, August 1970, pp. 650-665.

8. Ibid.

9. Michael Aiken and Jerald Hage, "The Organic Organization and Innovation," *Sociology*, January 1971, pp. 63-82.

10. Ibid.

11. Herbert A. Shepard, "Innovation-Resisting and Innovation-Producing Organizations," *The Journal of Business*, October 1967, pp. 470-477.

12. Gene W. Dalton, "Influence and Organizational Change," in Anant R. Negandhi and Joseph P. Schwitter, eds., *Organizational Behavior Models*, Comparative Administration Research Institute, Series No. 2 (Kent, Ohio, Kent State University, 1970).

13. Rollo May, *The Courage to Create* (New York, Norton, 1975).

14. Carolyne Smart and Ilan Vertinsky, "Designs for Crisis Decision Units," *Administrative Science Quarterly*, December 1977, pp. 640-657.

15. Irving L. Janis, *Victims of Groupthink* (Boston, Houghton-Mifflin Co., 1972).

16. Carroll L. Shartle, *Executive Performance and Leadership* (Englewood Cliffs, New Jersey, Prentice-Hall, Inc., 1956), p. 82.

17. Irvin Choran, "The Manager of the Small Company," (Unpublished MBA thesis, McGill University, 1969).

18. Henry Mintzberg, *The Nature of Managerial Work* (New York, Harper & Row, 1973).

19. Thomas V. Bonoma and Dennis P. Slevin, *Executive Survival Manual* (Boston, CVI Publishing Co., 1978).

20. Victor H. Vroom and Philip W. Yetton, *Leadership and Decision Making* (Pittsburgh, University of Pittsburgh Press, 1973).

21. Adapted with permission from Victor H. Vroom and Arthur G. Jago, "Decision Making As a Social Process: Normative and Descriptive Models of Leader Behavior," *Decision Sciences*, October 1974, p. 750.

22. Mason Haire and Willa F. Grunes, "Perceptual Defenses: Processes Protecting an Organized Perception of Another Personality," *Human Relations*, November 1950, pp. 403-412.

23. Russell L. Ackoff, *The Art of Problem Solving* (New York, Wiley Interscience, 1978).

24. J.P. Guilford et al., "The Relations of Creative Thinking Aptitudes to Non-Aptitute Personality Traits," *Representative Psychology*, Lab. No. 20, U.S.C., 1959.

25. Harvey J. Brightman and Thomas F. Urban, "Problem Solving and Managerial Performance," *Atlanta Economic Review*, July-August 1978, pp. 23-26.

26. George A. Miller, "The Magical Number Seven, Plus or Minus Two: Some Limits on Our Capacity for Processing Information," *Psychological Review*, March 1956, pp. 81-98.

27. Harry Lorayne and Jerry Lucas, *The Memory Book* (New York, Stein and Day, 1974).

28. DeWitt C. Dearborn and Herbert A. Simon, "Selective Perception: A Note on the Departmental Identifications of Executives," *Sociometry*, Vol. 21 (1958), pp. 140-144.

29. Norman R.F. Maier, *Psychology in Industrial Organizations* (Boston, Houghton-Mifflin Co., 1973).

3
Overcoming Problem-Solving Constraints

In the previous chapter we focused on four constraints that confront problem solvers. There is little that the individual can do about the cultural constraints except to cope with them in the best way possible. In this chapter we will direct our attention to overcoming the organizational, managerial, and individual constraints that bind us.

"We have met the enemy and we is they."
—POGO

"Assumption is the mother of all foul-ups."
—TYLK'S LAW

How can managers make decisions effectively under crisis conditions? In the last chapter we reported on a set of prescriptions for overcoming the organizational pathologies of premature consensus, communication distortion, groupthink, and overutilization of SOPs. Beyond these we suggested that organizations should seek individuals who can deal with crisis-induced stress.

How do managers react to stress? Cardiologists tell us that there are two distinct types of behavioral responses to stress classified as type A and type B. To control stressful events that are perceived as threats to their sense of control or mastery over the situation, type A individuals exert greater effort than type B individuals. When the stress demands of a job are extreme—as in crisis decision making—type A individuals commonly react as follows:

- They are competitive.
- They strive to achieve.
- They feel rushed.
- They exhibit hostility or aggression.
- They suppress feelings of fatigue.
- They are impatient with delays.
- They attempt to assert and maintain control over the stressors.

Since managers may have little or no control over the stress sources (customers, governmental agencies, higher level management within the organization), type A's eventually realize that they cannot control the stressors, and they begin to show signs of helplessness. Although type B individuals perceive the same degree of stress, they react differently—they are easygoing, relaxed, and not easily irritated. In the short run, type A's may appear to adjust well to crisis conditions, but when they are unable to maintain the hectic pace they demand of themselves, their problem-solving performance deteriorates.

Long-term problem-solving ineffectiveness is only the "tip of the iceberg." Cardiologists believe that type A behavior is a *contributing factor* to coronary heart disease (CHD). (Whether an individual develops CHD also depends on other factors, including genetics, smoking, and elevated serum cholesterol levels.) There are two manifestations of CHD: (1) angina pectoris and (2) myocardial infarction, more commonly called a heart attack. The former is usually precipitated by physical or psychological stress and rarely results in permanent damage to the heart tissue. In the most important study to date, a group of 1,500 type A's and 1,500 type B's were tracked for eight and one-half years.[1] Researchers found that type A's were two and one-half times more likely to develop CHD than were type B's. Further, of those who had coronary heart disease, type A's were five times more likely to have a heart attack.[2] Not only is a type A coping style ineffective in problem solving, it may be injurious to your health.

Are you a type A or type B individual? You can find out by completing the rating scale shown in Exhibit 3-1. Please take a few minutes to answer the seven questions. You can then determine your behavioral pattern by inserting your scores in column 1 of Exhibit 3-2 and completing the table.

The lower your total score, the more you exhibit type A behavior. As with all psychological tests, one cannot attach too much significance to a single test result. It is only meant to be

Exhibit 3-1: The type A behavior rating scale

Place an "X" on the line that best reflects your behavior:

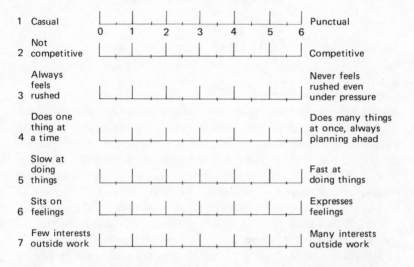

1 Casual — Punctual
2 Not competitive — Competitive
3 Always feels rushed — Never feels rushed even under pressure
4 Does one thing at a time — Does many things at once, always planning ahead
5 Slow at doing things — Fast at doing things
6 Sits on feelings — Expresses feelings
7 Few interests outside work — Many interests outside work

Source: Adapted from Rayman W. Bortner, "A Short Rating Scale As a Potential Measure of Pattern A Behavior," *Journal of Chronic Diseases*, July 1969, pp. 87-91.

Exhibit 3-2: Scoring table for type A behavior rating scale

Question	(1) Score	(2) Weighting factor	(1) x (2)
1		−.1424	
2		−.1420	
3		+.1156	
4		−.1840	
5		−.1960	
6		−.0548	
7		+.0576	
			4.57
		Total score*	

*Add score for all seven questions to get total score.

used as a "quick and dirty" measure of type A behavior. As such, its limitations are obvious.

The interpretation of the score is as follows:

Less than 1.95	A+
1.95-2.149	A
2.15-2.349	A−
2.35-2.549	B+
Greater than 2.55	B

Besides coronary heart disease, physicians know that emotional stress can cause skin and respiratory diseases and trigger asthma attacks. Perhaps the most common symptom of stress is "nervous stomach." In a most unusual study Joseph Brady of the Walter Reed Army Institute of Research demonstrated how stress causes ulcers.[3] He studied pairs of monkeys placed in restraining chairs where they could move their limbs and heads but not their bodies. Both monkeys were given brief electrical shocks at regular 20-second intervals. One of the pair—called Executive Monkey—could prevent the shock to himself and his partner by pressing a lever. The control monkey's lever was a dummy. Initially, both animals were shocked. Then each started pressing its lever to avoid the shock. Of course, both animals avoided shock only when Executive Monkey pressed his lever. After a while, the control monkey lost interest in pressing the lever, but Executive Monkey kept on pressing. Although both monkeys were under the same physical stress (both were restrained and given the same number of shocks), only Executive Monkey was under the additional *psychological* stress of having to press the lever to avoid the shock. After a while, Executive Monkey developed an ulcer and died; the control monkey was unaffected.

The moral isn't "don't press levers"; rather, it is that psychological stress may be more serious than physical stress. Since a manager's world is psychologically stressful, he must learn to cope with stress.

There is little one can do to eliminate stressful situations. As a result, cardiologists, psychologists, and, yes, even "quacks," have peddled a variety of schemes to teach you how to cope with stress. These schemes range from pharmacology or drug-induced therapies to biofeedback and transcendental meditation (TM). Whether any of these can correct the pathological lifestyle of the type A individual is still an open question. Two approaches appear fruitful.

The Cardiac Stress Management Program (CSMP) is designed

to teach type A individuals simple relaxation techniques while encouraging them to substitute type B behavior patterns. Although CSMP appears to cause (or at least be associated with) a drop in serum cholesterol levels, researchers have not yet found corresponding behavioral changes.[4] More research is needed in this area.

Herbert Benson has proposed a relaxation therapy that can be best described as TM without the religious trappings.[5] Its greatest strength is its simplicity. Benson suggests the following four principles:

1. Find a quiet environment.

2. Close your eyes and relax your muscles deeply. Begin at the feet and relax each part of your body.

3. Breathe through your nose. Become aware of your breathing. As you breathe out, say the word "one" silently to yourself. ("One" is your mantra.)

4. Continue for 20 minutes. When you finish, sit quietly for several minutes with your eyes closed, then with your eyes opened.

That's all there is to it. Don't worry if you aren't successful in achieving deep relaxation—just do it. Be passive. Even if it doesn't help you cope with stress (and it may not), it certainly can't hurt you.

If you can't change a manager's dominant coping style, it seems reasonable that you might want to prescreen potential managers for type A/type B behavior patterns. Obviously, the seven-item self-reporting scale is too simplistic for this purpose. The standardized stress interview developed by cardiologists Friedman and Rosenman and the Jenkins Self-Administered Questionnaire have been found to be reliable and valid approaches.[6] Such screening tools would permit you to match the individual manager to the organizational environment.

Fortunately, managers do not tangle with crises every day; but they do have to solve problems daily. In the remainder of the chapter we will focus on overcoming the managerial and personal constraints that prevent us from becoming effective problem solvers.

On Becoming a Consensus Leader or How to Lead a Consensus Problem-Solving Conference

Flexibility in leadership style is an important trait of the effective manager. In Chapter 2 we suggested that the Vroom and Yetton leadership-style decision tree should be used to match managerial style to the problem characteristics. Generally, when a problem is ill-structured, the consensus-leadership style is recommended. When the manager has a proven problem-solving track record and can implement a solution with little help from his or her subordinates, an autocratic leadership style is acceptable. Being an autocratic leader is simple; it is part of our human nature. Being a consensus leader—now that is something else.

How can you become an effective consensus leader? Fortunately, there are general principles to guide you. Remember that a consensus leader shares the problem with his or her subordinates. Together you generate and evaluate alternatives. Your role is to coordinate the discussion and keep it focused on critical issues. You do not attempt to impose your pet solutions on the group.

The general principles of consensus leadership were first suggested by Norman Maier.[7] These principles will probably seem strange at first, but work at them. You should follow the advice of a New Yorker, who when asked how to get to Carnegie Hall replied, "*Practice*, *practice*, and *practice*." These are the principles—

PRINCIPLE 1: Overcome barriers by stressing the possible.

Don't waste time on side-issues; keep the group focused on the problem. Where are we? Where do we want to be? What are the barriers that separate us from where we want to be? Anything else is superfluous. At least initially you should focus on controllable actions and not on uncontrollable events (Remember these terms from Chapter 1?). When facing a problem, don't seek solutions you cannot implement; rather, focus on those factors under your control. If your group doesn't have the necessary authority, convene a group that does.

PRINCIPLE 2: Don't reinvent the wheel—all problems are not alike.

Don't treat new problems as old problems. Solutions that worked twenty years ago probably will fail today because the circumstances are different. As group leader, you must direct the group away from "I remember back in 1955" thinking and into exploring interesting and creative avenues of attack.

PRINCIPLE 3: What's in a name?—encourage multiple definitions of the problem.

Guide your group to generate multiple definitions of the problem. Once a problem is defined, we begin to solve that problem oblivious to the possibility that alternative definitions exist. A problem of "how to reduce conflict in this department" can also be defined as "how to channel the conflict for the good of the department." Urge the group (or allow the group) to explore different problem definitions.

PRINCIPLE 4: Be problem-minded—not solution-minded.

Keep the group (and yourself) from premature closure. Encourage alternative problem definitions or solutions. Groups, like individuals, do not like the uncomfortable feelings associated with an unsolved problem. But we know that solution effectiveness increases if the need for premature closure is overcome.

PRINCIPLE 5: Encourage creative discontent.

Discontent can lead to hard feelings or innovative behavior. The key is how the discontent is channeled. Is it toward individuals (personal) or the problem (professional)? A group in which discontent is submerged is susceptible to the groupthink pathology. You should encourage minority opinions and protect those who see the problem differently. Avoid the tyranny of the majority!

PRINCIPLE 6: Separate idea generation from idea evaluation.

Good ideas are often strangled before they have a chance to develop. Discourage the evaluation of ideas during the initial phases of the problem-solving session. Eventually, it will be necessary to evaluate the suggestions, but to do so prematurely is to be solution-minded, not problem-minded.

PRINCIPLE 7: Don't let a single member dominate the discussion.

Make all members feel wanted. Don't let one person monopolize the conversation. (By the way, that includes you.) In acceptance problems (where there is no objectively best solution) the *feelings* of the participants are valid considerations; they must not be devalued because they are not *facts*.

PRINCIPLE 8: Problems should be viewed as choice situations.

Since people generally do not like the ambiguity associated with a problem, they have a tendency to go with their first solution. You should encourage the group to generate at least two possible solutions—that is, turn the problem into a choice situation. The competition of solutions should improve the chances of solving the problem.

PRINCIPLE 9: Choice situations should be viewed as problems.

If at one stage the discussion has narrowed to one or two solutions, it may be appropriate to reexamine the problem and redefine it. Instead of voting on either solution A or solution B, encourage the group to take another look at the problem. A new problem definition might generate solutions C, D, E.

PRINCIPLE 10: No power trips.

Everyone in a problem-solving group is equal; however, as leader, you are more equal than others. You have more power, and therefore your suggestions will tend to be given more weight, irrespective of their quality. Therefore it is important that you do not enter the session with preconceived solutions. On the other hand, you should not abdicate your responsibility as a professional problem solver. If you do not participate, the group may lose an effective resource. Thus, you should view your job as that of problem solver *and* facilitator. Under no circumstances are you to adopt the old adage "if you can't convince them, confuse them."

Knowing these ten principles does not ensure that you will be able to execute them. However, Maier has found that a procedure called multiple-role playing (MRP) is an effective way to practice consensus problem-solving leadership principles.[8] This technique permits a group of managers to simultaneously role-play a manager and his or her subordinates. While giving you the opportunity to practice the ten principles, MRP can help you gain insight on how your subordinates might react. By switching roles, you can learn what is necessary in successful group problem solving, both as a leader and as a participant.

Once you've mastered the consensus-leadership principles, you should be able to direct a group's problem-solving effort. However, even in a consensus conference, you must be a problem solver as well as a facilitator. Are you an effective problem solver? If not, it is because the individual constraints that we discussed in the previous chapter keep you from realizing your potential.

Techniques for Overcoming Individual Constraints

The basis for overcoming individual constraints to effective problem solving was first suggested in the science fiction short story entitled "The Noise Level."[9] A group of scientists are brought together and presented with proof of an antigravity device. The scientists are shown film clips of the inventor flying without any apparent means of support. Corroborating witnesses are paraded before the group. The evidence is conclusive: An antigravity device has been invented. Unfortunately, the inventor died in one of the test runs, and, since he had not kept records, the government cannot duplicate the antigravity device. The scientists are therefore asked to reinvent the device. The group is taken to the inventor's home where they find a well-equipped physics laboratory and a large collection of books on mysticism. Some of the scientists simply refuse to believe that an antigravity device is possible and leave the project. In the end, those that stay eventually develop the antigravity device.

The project coordinator then informs the group that the original evidence was fabricated—that there had been no inventor or invention. The coordinator suggests that if the group had been brought together to develop an antigravity device, the members' immediate response would have been to dismiss the idea as absurd. So an elaborate hoax was developed to present an antigravity device as a *fait accompli*. To stimulate thinking on this problem, the group was given a confusing description of the inventor. While he was a highly qualified scientist, as witnessed by the elaborate laboratory facilities, he also dabbled in the occult. These contradictions forced the scientists to take a fresh look at the problem, and in the end they were successful.

Many of the problem-solving techniques that will be presented here are based on the same premise that was employed in the short story. In order to solve a difficult problem, we have to break the mental set or habit and take a really new look at the problem. While you may never invent an antigravity device, you may become a more effective problem solver. All the techniques possess one common thread: They stress the creative or left-handed side of problem solving. The first technique we will consider is problem restructuring.

Problem Restructuring

Picture a glass partially filled with water. Is the glass half-empty or half-filled? Actually both statements are correct. Does it make any difference which statement we accept as true? In this case, probably no. But if we change the context to an unresolved problem, *restructuring* or *redefining* a problem may provide a new view of an old problem that may overcome the obstacles blocking successful problem resolution. Restructuring is a basic problem-solving technique and can be done by (1) changing your viewpoint or (2) rearranging the factors in the problem environment to provide alternatives that were not apparent in the original problem definition.

Changing Your Viewpoint: After the Battle of Gettysburg, Meade's army of 80,000 faced Lee's army of 60,000 soldiers. Meade wished to attack Lee's position and consolidate the Union victory. His problem was simple. According to the German rules of warfare, in order to attack a fortified position, a commander needed a ratio of three offensive troops to every two troops on defense. Thus Meade demanded that President Lincoln find him an additional 10,000 troops. What would you have done if you had been the President?

Lincoln could have accepted Meade's viewpoint and attempted to find the additional troops. Lincoln, however, was a problem solver par excellence, and *he chose not to accept* Meade's view of the situation. Lincoln told Meade that his troops should assume a defensive position. According to the rules, Meade then needed only 40,000 troops to defend the area against Lee's 60,000 soldiers. He could use the "additional" 40,000 troops to harass the enemy. The rest is history.

During the French revolution, a commander was given the task of clearing a town square. He was told not to use force unless absolutely necessary. He could have shot over the townspeople's heads, but this might have led to a panic or worse. Instead, he came up with a brilliant idea. He announced to the crowd that he had been ordered to clear the square of the rabble, but that he could see there were many fine citizens interspersed among the crowd. He suggested that if all of the fine citizens would leave the square, he could disperse the rabble. In two minutes the square was cleared.

What is the common thread in the two examples? In both cases, the problem was solved by changing the viewpoint. Lincoln turned the problem inside-out. Meade saw Meade on offense; Lincoln saw Meade on defense. The French commander viewed the situation from the crowd's viewpoint. If you consider people as rabble they will act accordingly. But if given an opportunity to disassociate themselves from the rabble, basically honest citizens will do so. Changing your viewpoint requires that you find another framework that fits the facts of a problem equally well. Perhaps a new framework will provide you with fresh insights into an unresolved problem.

There are several approaches to changing your viewpoint:

1. View the problem as others might see it.

How would your subordinates see the problem? Your superiors? This approach forces you to step out of your skin. This is not always easy to do.

Imagine you are in the fourth grade and you are given the following puzzle:

OTTFFSSENTETTFFSSENTT

What is the next letter in the sequence? Remember, you are only nine or ten years old. I recall that when I tried this puzzle, I searched for patterns in the letter sequence, forgetting that a nine-year-old would not (or could not) do this. Seeing a problem from another's viewpoint is not an easy task. If you still haven't guessed the correct solution, what are the first letters of the digits 1 through 21?

2. Turn the problem upside-down.

If a problem seems unsolvable, redefine it. After all, a definition is not carved in stone. For many years, traffic officials in the state of New York had worked to reduce traffic fatalities. Their strategy was to regulate drivers by banning unsafe drivers from the highways. When Averell Harriman became governor, he redefined the problem as "how can we build safer cars?" In a sense he focused on regulating cars, not drivers. In order to solve that problem, both definitions were needed. However, each definition opened different vistas for problem attack.

3. Change the scope of your problem (the systems approach).

This past year I bought an aquarium and stocked it with angelfish. Although the fish were healthy, they were lethargic. I wondered how I could get them to be more active. Finally, I decided to add some predators to the tank in hopes of arousing my angelfish. It worked extremely well (until the predators ate the angelfish).

When problems frustrate us, it may be time to add something to the problem environment. Perhaps we have been myopic in our problem definition and, like my fish tank, something must be added to enlarge the system under study. Frequently, we think of narrowing a problem; sometimes we may have to enlarge it. When you have failed to solve a departmental problem, perhaps it is time to look to the divisional level. It may be that forces at the division level restrict your actions and to solve the problem you must widen its scope. Problem-solving action taken at the wrong level is worse than no action because it can easily lead to frustration.

This is best illustrated in an incident involving Alex Bavelas, a distinguished social psychologist, who was called in as a consultant for a toy firm.[10] A painting operation had recently been reengineered as follows:

> . . . the eight girls who did the painting sat in a line by an endless chain of hooks. These hooks were in continuous motion, past the line of girls and into a long horizontal oven. Each girl sat at her own painting booth so designed as to carry away fumes and to backstop excess paint. The girl would take a toy from the tray beside her, position it in a jig inside the painting cubicle, spray on the color according to a pattern, then release the toy and hang it on the hook passing by. The rate at which the hooks moved had been calculated by the engineers so that each girl, when fully trained, would be able to hang a painted toy on each hook before it passed beyond her reach.

The introduction of change in the painting operation was

accompanied by chaos. Management expected this and was not alarmed initially. However, after six months of continued chaos, they hired Bavelas.

Bavelas met with the foreman and the workers. The one significant factor that emerged was that the workers wanted to have control over the speed of the conveyor belt. This was done and immediately morale improved, absenteeism decreased, and the average speed of the conveyor actually *increased*. Sounds ideal, doesn't it? So what's the problem?

The increased production from the painting room caused serious disruptions (excessive stockpiling) in the production flow in the rest of the plant. This problem was more serious than the original one. In the end, management threw out the consultant's recommendations which, in turn, led to mass resignations in the department.

The moral of the story is that for problem solving to be effective it must be directed to the right level. For years, this has been the sermon preached by systems analysts; they were correct all along.

4. Think about implicit assumptions you might have made.

Remember the nine-dots exercise in the previous chapter? All of us make assumptions; effective problem solvers *make their assumptions explicit*. Let's see if you have learned anything from the nine-dots puzzle.

Imagine that you wish to plant four trees equal distances from each other. How would you do this? You might try planting the four trees at the corners of a square like this:

But as you can see, that will not work—the trees are not equidistant diagonally. Although not shown here, drawing a circle and placing the four trees on the perimeter will not work either.

What assumptions have you been making in trying to solve this problem? Take a minute or two and list them. Have you been assuming that the land must be flat? If so, you will never solve the problem. Visualize an equilateral triangular prism (a pyramid-shaped hill) with trees planted at the three corners and at the apex of the hill:

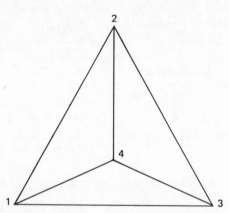

5. Shift your emphasis from one part of a problem to another.

Inside every large, ill-structured problem is a series of smaller subproblems struggling to get out. When a problem has you stymied, decompose the problem. If none of the subproblems lead anywhere, further decompose the problem and try again. Let's see how problem decomposition works: How many tennis matches must be played in a single elimination tournament with 500 competitors before a winner will be declared? Try solving the problem before reading on.

Would it be helpful to decompose the problem into a series of smaller problems? Instead of 500 players, change the problem to 4 players. Now you can solve the problem easily; it will take 3 matches. For 8 players you can easily verify that it will take 7 matches. Thus by decomposing the problem into a series of small tractable problems, the answer to the original problem is 499 matches. Once you've solved the problem by decomposition, you'll probably notice what should have been obvious all along—in a single elimination tournament of 500 players there must be 1 winner and 499 losers, and it will take 499 matches to determine all the losers.

How might we decompose the problem to acquire or not to acquire a firm? We could initially break down the problem into the following two subproblems: (1) Do we wish to acquire firm X? and (2) What should the financial package look like? (The second subproblem need not be addressed until the first subproblem is favorably resolved.) Important factors in the first subproblem include:

1. Potential for growth from the combination.
2. Potential for synergy.
3. Reputation of firm X's senior management, and so on.

While some of this information will be necessary in determining the final financial package, much of the information for each subproblem is unique. Thus problem-solving effectiveness may be enhanced by decomposing the acquisition decision into two distinct subproblems, each with its own intelligence and data-gathering activities.[11]

If problem decomposition fails, shift your focus from controllable to noncontrollable (or vice versa) factors. Were factors you considered noncontrollable really controllable? If so, rediagnose the problem.

Is it possible to shift your focus from one part of a problem to another? While it is difficult, we know that with training it can be done. The visual analog to this problem-solving behavior is shown in Exhibit 3-3. When most people first look at the picture, they see either a vase or two persons staring at each other. By concentrating, they are able to shift their focus away from one figure to the other. Likewise, effective problem solvers are capable of emotionally disengaging themselves from a problem focus that is leading nowhere.

Exhibit 3-3: What do you see?

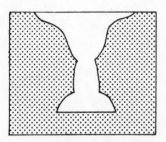

6. Can the problem be structured differently?

How we view a problem limits our problem attack. We could view all problems as operating problems in which we attempt to determine the cause(s) of a deviation; would it be useful to consider operating problems as though they were strategic? Instead of trying to correct a deviation, we might use the opportunity for strategic problem solving to reach a never-before-attainable goal.

We said earlier that problems should be viewed as choice situations and choice situations should be viewed as problems. Here we shift from one structure to another in hopes that we may obtain new insights into a difficult problem.

The restructuring principle can be demonstrated in the following game called "fifteen finesse." The rules are simple. Two players will take turns placing quarters on a series of numbers one through nine. The winner of the game is the one who is first to cover any three different numbers that add to fifteen. Once a number is covered, it cannot be played again. The winner takes all.

Let's watch a typical game:

Player A	Player B	Comments
7	8	
2	6	B blocks A by covering the 6 (since $7 + 2 + 6 = 15$)
1	4	A blocks B by covering the 1 (since $8 + 6 + 1 = 15$)
5	3	A blocks B by covering the 5 (since $6 + 4 + 5 = 15$)

B wins because $8 + 4 + 3 = 15$

Player B has a system that guarantees at least a tie in every game. Can you figure out how player B outwits his opponents by restructuring the game to resemble a more common parlor game?

Forgetting the numbers for the moment, what game requires the winner to obtain a string of three "things" before the opponent does and also permits blocking? If you think about it, you will realize that this game bears a striking resemblance to tic-tac-toe. The equivalence is established by way of *lo-sho*, the well known 3 x 3 magic square that was first discovered in ancient China (Exhibit 3-4).

Note that the three rows, columns, and two main diagonals sum to 15. While player A was trying to select numbers that sum to 15 and simultaneously block his opponent, player B was playing tic-tac-toe. You may wish to instant-replay the previous game and use the magic square. Player B's strategy is now obvious. Restructuring simplified the game and also suggested fruitful lines of attack.

In addition to changing your viewpoint, problem restructuring can be accomplished by shuffling the problem elements.

Exhibit 3-4: The magic square

4	9	2
3	5	7
8	1	6

Problem Rearrangement: It was Polya, the Polish mathematician, who first suggested that *decomposing* and *recombining* problem elements is an effective problem-solving technique.

As an illustration of this technique, imagine that you are a division manager. You have received several complaints from subordinates about two supervisors. You could fire these supervisors, but you know they are competent. Can you recombine the elements of this problem? There are three elements—the supervisors, the workers, and the job. Since job content is identical in both departments, let's focus on the supervisors and the workers. You notice that only younger workers complain about supervisor X and only older workers complain about supervisor Y. You hypothesize that the style of supervision preferred by the workers may be related to age. Perhaps by assigning subordinates to supervisors on the basis of age, the number of complaints will drop. You do this and the complaints cease.

You have just decomposed and recombined the elements of a problem and an unsolvable problem has been solved.

Let's see how the principle works. Form one word from the anagram:

DRY OXTAIL IN REAR

While you work on the puzzle, ask a co-worker to form one word from the following fifteen letters. All we have done is decompose the anagram and rearrange the letters:

AA D E II L N O RRR T X Y

It has been our experience that persons who are given the latter presentation solve the problem quicker. Problem decomposition and arrangement help us overcome our constraints. Did you guess that the solution was the word "extraordinarily"?

First, you decompose the elements and then rearrange them. Hopefully, this arrangement will help you see the problem in a new light. It is important to be able to visualize the elements. While this may not always be possible in a business problem, visual problem-solving language is an important tool. This is demonstrated in the following diagram. You are required to determine the length of line A without measuring it. All that you know is that the radius of the circle is .70″. Try it before looking at the solution:

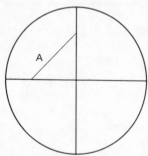

If you haven't been able to solve the problem, try rearranging the lines. Here is the solution:

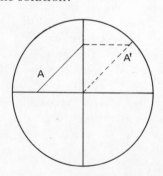

With a small amount of rearranging, we can now see that line A is in fact the same length as the radius. Thus, the answer is .70".

Problem restructuring is a powerful technique for overcoming individual barriers to effective problem solving. It is, however, only one of the techniques presented by Edward De Bono in his book *Lateral Thinking*.[1][2]

Lateral Thinking or Overcoming the Tyranny of Habit

For many years Dr. De Bono has espoused the virtues of lateral thinking. He defines *vertical thinking* as careful, logical analysis that concentrates on arriving at the correct answer. By way of contrast, *lateral thinking* is mind-expanding and encourages exploration and curiosity. De Bono likens vertical thinking to "digging one deep hole" and lateral thinking to "digging many shallow holes." In our culture, vertical thinking is considered good, effective, and scientific; lateral thinking is considered effeminate and soft. Even with all the strikes against lateral thinking, Dr. De Bono argues that it is a desirable and teachable skill. His goal is not to replace vertical thinking with lateral thinking; rather, he views lateral thinking as a complementary technique. Both vertical and lateral thinking are important.

The purpose of lateral thinking is to increase the likelihood of insight restructuring by changing points of view, patterns, and the way things are put together. In other words, lateral thinking is based on the premise that problems should be viewed from many angles.

Differences Between Lateral and Vertical Thinking: What does it mean when we say that the goal of lateral thinking is to dig "many shallow holes"? Dr. De Bono contrasts the two thinking modes as follows:

1. Vertical thinking is sequential; lateral thinking is simultaneous.

2. Vertical thinking is logical; lateral thinking is provocative.

3. In vertical thinking, categories are labeled as fixed; in lateral thinking, they are not (a rose by any other name . . .).

4. Vertical thinking is goal directed; lateral thinking is geared away from the status quo.

5. With vertical thinking, one has to be correct at each step; with lateral thinking, one need only be correct at the final stage.

6. Vertical thinking follows the most logical paths; lateral thinking explores any paths (the more unlikely, the better).

7. With vertical thinking, one excludes what is (considered) irrelevant; with lateral thinking, one welcomes side-trips (you never know where you'll end up).

8. Vertical thinking is right-handed; lateral thinking is left-handed.

Is three half of eight? If you are thinking vertically, then it most certainly is not. Any child knows that half of eight is four. However, if you are thinking laterally, then half of an eight is a three (slice an 8 in half and you get a 3).

In *Lateral Thinking*, De Bono proposes over fifteen separate techniques for becoming a lateral thinker. While a complete discussion would be beyond the scope of this book, several of his techniques are presented here. You will discover that many of the approaches we have already discussed are part of De Bono's stable of techniques.

Challenging Assumptions: Maintaining implicit assumptions about a problem is a fatal weakness. We already know that we must state our assumptions clearly and then judge by the light of day whether they are real or self-imposed. Although we have challenged you with several mind-twisters, the constraint of implicit assumptions is so devastating that another problem is warranted:

> A man works in a skyscraper. Each morning he boards the elevator, presses the tenth floor button, gets out, and walks to the fifteenth floor where he works. At closing time, he boards the elevator on the fifteenth floor, pushes the ground floor button, and gets out. What is the man up to?

After you've generated several solutions, can you infer what assumption(s) you made in solving the puzzle? Take a moment and list your answers.

Typical answers include: (1) the man likes to exercise in the morning, (2) the elevator operates only between floors one through ten in the morning, and (3) the man is an oddball. What is the common thread running through all these answers? It is that the man is normal and his behavior is abnormal. Could it be the other way around? If you start with the assumption that the man is abnormal, you are likely to conclude that the man is extremely short (and cannot reach the fifteenth floor button). A different assumption opens up alternative views of the same facts. Beyond this, it is impossible to challenge your assumptions if they remain hidden.

When you reach an impasse, *list* or, if you are visually-oriented, *draw* a picture of *all your assumptions*. This is extremely difficult because we sometimes don't realize that we have been making assumptions. Yet, in the business world assumptions are always being made about subordinates, suppliers, or customers; we need to verbalize them.

This skill is especially crucial in strategic planning. One approach to selecting the best strategic plan is called the dialectical process.[1][3] For this technique to work, the long-range planning group begins with two sets of assumptions about the future of the firm and develops two strategic plans. Each plan is analyzed with regard to its strengths and weaknesses as well as to the reasonableness of its fundamental assumptions. A final plan is synthesized from the strengths of the competing contenders. Although this is not yet a common practice in industry, the dialectical process is gaining acceptance, and the key to success is making the assumptions explicit.

The Reversal Method: This is a variation of the problem-restructuring technique discussed earlier. Here the problem is turned inside-out, back to front. Does reversing the problem lead to a provocative arrangement of information with more possibilities than the original problem definition?

Suppose you initially define a problem as "How can I structure my job to permit me the time to control my workers?" If this problem definition is not productive, how about reversing the problem to "How can I structure my workers' jobs so that control is unnecessary?" Or "How can I structure their jobs so that they control themselves?" Or "How can I structure their jobs so that they control me?" At best, these provocative reversals may solve the problem; at worst they may help you overcome initial problem-solving inertia.

The purpose of the reversal method is to (1) escape the tyranny of viewing a problem in the usual way, (2) bypass a problem definition that is leading you nowhere, and (3) help you rearrange the information in a provocative way. The goal is not necessarily to solve the problem but to remove the blinders that have stymied your progress. Remember that in lateral thinking the goal is to move away from the status quo. Once you have moved, you can then see what happens. At least you now have a path to explore.

Here is an example of the reversal method: A soldier is in the desert and stumbles across an oasis. There he finds a deep watering hole. The water level is too low for him to drink without falling in. Of course, he can't swim. He wonders how he can get to the water. After several minutes, he reverses the problem and solves it quickly. How did he do it? Instead of defining the problem as "How can I get to the water?" he redefined the problem as "Can I get the water to come to me?" Once the problem was reversed, he saw that if he rolled a boulder into the hole, the water level would rise.

The Analogy Method—Synectics: Analogy is a powerful problem-solving tool. When an impasse occurs, can you develop and pursue an analogy, and then transfer the resulting insights from the analogy to the original problem? The analogy need not fit all the facts of the problem. However, it is crucial that the analogy be concrete and rich in relationships that might be transferable to the problem. As in lateral thinking, the analogy is used to get things moving even when we are not sure that the movement will lead anywhere.

Analogies may be direct, personal, or fantasy. Drawing on analogies from nature can be highly profitable. An architectural team was given the job of designing a roof capable of absorbing heat in the winter and reflecting heat in the summer. Initial attempts failed. Then one of the members asked, "What in nature changes colors?" The group thought of chameleons, but was unable to exploit the analogy. After several dead ends, the leader noted that the flounder changes colors by expanding sacs of black pigment. When these sacs are expanded, the flounder is black; when they are contracted, the flounder is white. The group was then able to take that idea and transfer it back to their design problem. They impregnated an all-black roof with white plastic balls. Under the summer heat, the balls would expand, changing the roof surface to heat-reflecting white. In the winter, the roof color would remain black and thus would absorb heat.

The concept of using analogies to solve problems is the basis for synectics, a technique developed by William J.J. Gordon, one of the founders of Synectics, Inc.[14] Gordon is a most interesting character. After receiving his A.B. degree from Harvard, he decided to forsake his training in philosophy and history and breed pigs. The outcome was "a lot of bone, not much bacon, but the fastest pigs in the East." Gordon has worked as a salvage diver, ambulance driver, ski instructor, and school teacher. While serving with an acoustic torpedo research group, Gordon became interested in the creative design process.

Analogies are used to broaden the scope of the search for relevant facts. The objective of synectics is to utilize an individual's total life experiences in solving a problem. Through the use of analogies, synectics can produce new perspectives on a problem and "make the familiar strange."

Unlike leaders of most techniques, the synectics group leader must be specially trained. A synectics session is highly structured. The phases of the session will be discussed in the context of the following problem, namely, how to bring up samples of oil-saturated rock from beneath a reservoir—

Problem As Given (PAG): This is simply a statement of the problem. The problem was initially stated as, "How do we determine the oil saturation in reservoir rock?"

Analysis and Suggestions: An expert in the field is asked to brief the problem-solving group on the details. The purpose is to answer any questions the group may have, demonstrate that "obvious" solutions will not work, and give the group an opportunity to exorcise any remaining traces of *vertical* thinking.

Goals As Understood (GAU): Each participant generates the goal(s) as he or she understands them. There is no need for consensus. The goals may be factual or wishful thinking—they may violate the physical laws of the universe. For example, in developing alternative sources of energy, a goal could be to violate the law of gravity. Developing goals gives the members the broadest definition of the problem. In the reservoir problem, two GAUs were "How to make the rock tell the truth" and "How to have the oil tell me how crowded it is in the rock."

Mental Gymnastics: At this point the leader asks the group to develop an analogy that may be useful based on one of the goals. The analogy may be taken directly from nature (as in the roof design problem); it may be a personal analogy (how would you feel if you were a virus?); or it may be a fantasy analogy (demons and elves). The leader forces the group to forget the oil-reservoir problem as an analogy is pursued. Factual information concerning the analogy is developed. Even if the factual material is incorrect, no harm is done. During this stage, the problem and goals are quietly forgotten as the analogy takes on a life of its own. In the reservoir problem, the group explored the direct analogy of a crowded virus culture.

Force Fit and Solution: When the leader thinks that the group is ready, he announces that it is time to take the well-developed analogy and force it to be useful in solving the original problem. This can be done in several ways. First, it may simply happen that the analogy fits nicely and the problem is solved (as with the roof design problem). Alternatively, the leader may select one of the properties of the analogy and ask a member to run with it. Finally, the leader may use the "get fired" technique and ask a member to generate a solution that is so absurd that he or she would be fired for incompetence. When force fit works, it is because the group has forgotten the problem and all of its constraints. If force fit fails, the leader may ask for new analogies or goal statements and the process is repeated.

In *The Art of Problem Solving*, Edward Hodnett tells of a burglar who had phenomenal success in discovering hidden cash in the houses he robbed.[15] After he was captured, he explained that he had watched where his wife hid their money. At its least creative level, solving problems through analogy forces you to look for points of resemblance to past problems and solutions. Beware, however, of superficial similarities; otherwise, you might view all problems as instant replays of previous problems. At its most creative level, analogies (to the world of nature, and so forth) may provide new insights into your problems.

Of the remaining approaches to lateral thinking, one technique stands out. It has been used more often than any other, but not always with success.

Brainstorming: Is it Mental Popcorn?: We are all creatures of habit, and one of our worst habits is an overpowering urge to criticize an idea (our own to a lesser degree) before it has been fully developed. Not only is that idea stillborn, but all the other ideas that one idea might have originated are lost forever. In the forties, Alex Osborn developed the brainstorming technique based on one very simple idea—*the principle of deferred judgment.*[16] Osborn argued that idea generation should be a separate activity from critical evaluation. Critical evaluation is absolutely necessary, but only *after* the brainstorming.

Osborn suggested that there are five conditions necessary for a successful brainstorming session:

1. Rule out criticism.

Subjecting ideas to the critical gristmill stifles creativity. A mutually supportive atmosphere is the most important ingredient for a successful session.

2. Welcome freewheeling.

The wilder the idea, the better it is. The leader, as well as the participants, should encourage imaginative or provocative ideas. Although many ideas will eventually end up on the "cutting-room floor," an unusual idea may cause another participant to develop a good solution.

3. Generate many ideas.

The goal is to generate a great number of ideas. Studies have shown that as more ideas are generated, the number of original suggestions increases.

4. Seek combination and improvement of ideas.

Piggybacking of ideas should be encouraged. Good suggestions frequently result from joining two previously stated ideas.

5. Define the problem properly.

A proper definition requires that the problem be stated simply and focused on a single target. Instead of "how to design a house," which is too complex and fuzzy, we might consider a subproblem such as "how to design the living room or family room." Another approach is to change directions 180° and state the problem in much broader terms to allow for innovative approaches. Thus, instead of "redesigning a living room," we might consider "alternatives to living in a house."

A typical session should begin with a two-minute warm-up session to loosen up the participants. Ideally, the six to fifteen participants should have received a general statement of the problem at least a week before the session. This would permit them to start thinking about the problem. They may wish to write down some of their solutions. At the end of the warm-up session, the leader should restate the problem and offer at least two possible solutions. These can come from the participants' solution lists or from the leader's own list.

The formal session should begin with the leader restating the principle of deferred judgment. Then the session should be opened up. If the discussion gets bogged down, the leader should introduce his or her own ideas or utilize some idea-spurring questions focusing on the goals.[17] Let's apply some of the idea-spurring questions to designing a family room:

Idea-spurring suggestions	*Examples*
1. Magnify	Great room
2. Minify	Eliminate it
3. Alter	Two living rooms or no walls
4. Rearrange	Place in rear of house or outside of house
5. Combine	Living-dining room
6. Distort	Make circular

Participants are usually emotionally drained after thirty minutes. A follow-up session a day or two later using the same participants is a good way to pick up all of the afterthoughts. Once the ideas have been generated, they must be subjected to critical analysis.

Brainstorming can be used in all phases of problem solving. However, it is most useful in generating hypotheses in operating problem solving and alternative solutions in strategic problem solving (this is probably the best use of the technique). Supporters of the technique argue that brainstorming is simple to learn, easy to use, and successful. Its detractors think otherwise.

Some of the pitfalls of brainstorming were recognized by Osborn. These include:

1. Failure to describe the problem accurately—either too specifically or too broadly.

2. Failure to warn the participants not to be discouraged because many initial ideas are, frankly, lousy.

3. Failure to distinguish between a freewheeling atmosphere and sheer chaos.

4. Failure to keep from overselling the technique.

5. Failure to subsequently evaluate and criticize the ideas.[18]

Beyond these, Osborn pointed out that brainstorming should be viewed as a supplement, not a replacement, for vertical thinking.

Some researchers have concluded that brainstorming is nothing more than "mental popcorn" and that it does more harm than good. Studies have shown that the principle of deferred judgment does not aid creative problem solving, that individuals are more creative when alone than when in groups, and that despite instructions, individuals find it difficult not to criticize each other's ideas.[19] While the criticisms are justified, on balance, brainstorming is probably more effective than a nonstructured group meeting in generating alternative solutions.

Morphology or "One from Column A and One from Column B"

Here is a foolproof alternative-generating scheme developed by Fritz Zwicky, an astrophysicist.[20] For our living room design problem, it would work this way:

1. List the attributes of the situation (or the goals of the problem)—

> location
> building materials
> shape
> number of levels

2. Below each attribute, list as many ideas as you can. Brainstorming may be used to generate alternatives. (Instead of piggybacking ideas, we are piggybacking techniques. How's that for a creative twist?) See Exhibit 3-5.

Exhibit 3-5: Generating alternatives by brainstorming

Location	Building materials	Shape	Number of levels
in front of house	wood	cube	one
in rear of house	paper	cylindrical	two
on second floor	concrete	triangular prism	three
outside of house		trapizoidal prism	more than three
			none (no floor)

3. Make several random runs through the columns and then assemble your combination of factors into an alternative.

Our first alternative is to build a cylindrical living room out of concrete. The room contains two levels, is outside of the house, and is connected by a covered walkway. The house and living room would look like this:

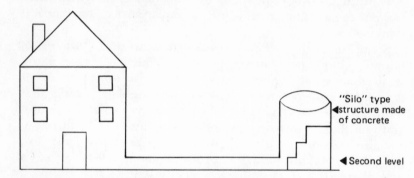

The advantage of using a systematic approach is that with only a few dimensions there are many possible combinations. In our design problem, we had 4 x 3 x 4 x 5 = 240 combinations. By using an exhaustive (and exhausting) strategy, the problem solver can formulate alternatives with little likelihood of neglecting important elements in the problem. While it is true that many of the alternatives are nonsense, it only takes one novel idea to justify the expenditure of time.

Problem Solving: What To Do and What Not To Do

What lessons can we draw from the last two chapters? Are there general principles that can help us improve our problem solving? We think that the answer is YES. We believe that these principles are useful for all types of problems, but we cannot be dogmatic about it (after all, then we would be ineffective problem solvers).

1. Be a professional skeptic.

Don't accept facts or assumptions without challenging them. Never accept someone else's definition of a problem. Make the problem your own. Be a "whys-guy."

2. Defer judgment.

Let a problem stir around in your mind. Don't opt for premature closure. Be "problem-minded," not "solution-minded." Above all else, diagnose the problem before trying to solve it.

3. Exhibit leadership flexibility.

There is no such thing as the "best" leadership style. It depends on you, your subordinates, and most importantly, on the characteristics of the problem.

4. Exhibit flexible or lateral thinking.

Restructure unsolved problems. Never settle, at least initially, for a single problem definition. During diagnosis, many of your sentences should start with "how would it be if we looked at the problem from this viewpoint." Don't impose constraints on yourself that don't exist in the problem environment.

5. Listen and question.

You can't solve problems if you don't know what's being currently done. That means shut up and listen. (This idea is best expressed as "when you are up to your nose in it, keep your mouth shut.") After you know what's being done, think about it critically and, of course, in a professional manner, attack the problem.

FOOTNOTES

1. Ray H. Rosenman et al., "Coronary Heart Disease in the Western Collaborative Group Study: Final Follow-Up Experience of 8½ Years," *Journal of the American Medical Association*, August 1975, pp. 872-877.

2. David C. Glass, *Behavior Patterns, Stress, and Coronary Disease* (Hillsdale, New Jersey, Laurance Erlbaum Associates, 1977).

3. Joseph V. Brady, "Ulcers in Executive Monkeys," *Scientific American*, October 1958, pp. 95-100.

4. Richard M. Suinn, "The Cardiac Stress Management Program for Type A Patients," *Cardiac Rehabilitation*, Vol. 5 (1975), pp. 13-15; Richard M. Suinn, Loring Brock, and Cecil A. Edie, "Behavior Therapy for Type A Patients," *American Journal of Cardiology*, August 1975, pp. 269-270.

5. Herbert Benson, "Your Innate Asset for Combating Stress," *Harvard Business Review*, July-August 1974, pp. 49-60.

6. Meyer Friedman and Ray H. Rosenman, *Type A Behavior and Your Heart* (New York, Knopf, Inc., 1974); C. David Jenkins, Ray H. Rosenman, and Meyer Friedman, "Development of an Objective Psychological Test for the Determination of the Coronary-Prone Behavior Pattern in Employed Men," *Journal of Chronic Diseases*, November 1967, pp. 371-379.

7. Norman R.F. Maier, *Psychology in Industrial Organizations* (Boston, Houghton-Mifflin Co., 1973).

8. Ibid.

9. R. Jones, "The Noise Level," in Kingsley Amis and Robert Conquest, eds., *Spectrum V: A Science Fiction Anthology* (New York, Harcourt, Brace and World, 1966).

10. Alex Bavelas and George Strauss, "Group Dynamics and Intergroup Relations," in William F. Whyte et al., *Money and Motivation* (New York, Harper & Row, 1955), pp. 90-91.

11. Bruce Blaylock et al., "Successful Marriages of the Third Kind," *Business*, January-February 1979, pp. 35-40.

12. Edward De Bono, *Lateral Thinking* (New York, Harper & Row, 1970).

13. Richard O. Mason, "A Dialectical Approach to Strategic Planning," *Management Science*, April 1969, pp. B403-B414.

14. William J.J. Gordon, *Synectics* (New York, Harper & Row, 1961).

15. Edward Hodnett, *The Art of Problem Solving* (New York, Harper Trade Books, Harper & Row, 1955).

16. Alex Osborn, *Applied Imagination* (New York, Charles Scribner's Sons, 1953).

17. *Group Brainstorming Manual* (Chicago, University of Chicago Press, Industrial Relations Center), p. 6.

18. Ibid., p. 13.

19. Edith Weisskopf-Joelson and Thomas S. Eliseo, "An Experimental Study of the Effectiveness of Brainstorming," *Journal of Applied Psychology*, February 1961, pp. 45-49; Donald W. Taylor, Paul C. Berry, and Clifford H. Block, "Does Group Participation When Using Brainstorming Facilitate or Inhibit Creative Thinking?" *Administrative Science Quarterly*, June 1958, pp. 23-47; Marvin D. Dunnette, John Campbell, and Kay Jaastad, "The Effect of Group Participation on Brainstorming Effectiveness for Two Industrial Samples," *Journal of Applied Psychology*, February 1963, pp. 30-37.

20. Fritz Zwicky, *Discovery, Invention, Research Through the Morphological Approach* (New York, Macmillan Co., 1969).

4
Diagnosing Operating Problems

In the last two chapters we focused on constraints to problem solving and how to overcome them. In this chapter we turn to solving operating problems, which are defined as deviations from a standard of performance or a norm. The John Dewey experential problem-solving model, which incorporates a diagnosis, analysis, and solution phase, is used to solve operating problems. In this chapter we will focus on the art and science of problem diagnosis.

"No problem is so large or so complex that it can't be run away from."
— CHARLIE BROWN

"In any decision situation, the amount of relevant information is inversely proportional to the importance of the situation."
— COOKE'S LAW

"What really matters is the name you succeed in imposing on facts, not the facts themselves."
— COHEN'S LAW

"I know you believe you understand what you think I said, but I am not sure you realize what you heard is not what I meant."
— ANON

"Ambiguity is the cardinal sin of problem solving."
— EDWARD HODNETT

Joe Simpson has been working in the same department of a manufacturing company for ten years. His record is exceptional, and recently he was promoted to senior utility man. Several weeks following the promotion, the foreman noticed that Joe's work had deteriorated and that he had had several shouting matches with his co-workers. The foreman discussed Joe's problem with several other supervisors and concluded that Joe was merely experiencing "new job jitters." All agreed that once Joe adjusted to his new responsibility everything would be calm again. Now, two months later, the problem is worse. Some of the other foremen believe that Joe's promotion has gone to his head; others feel that new plant-wide production standards are causing Joe's unusual behavior. Joe's foreman rejects the latter explanation since Joe was a member of the committee that had developed the new standards. What should the foreman do?

Joe is an example of an ill-structured operating problem. Operating problems are deviations from expected or historic performance levels. In this chapter we will focus on operating problems that are fuzzy messes—namely, those that have never occurred before in your organization. Typical examples of ill-structured operating problems are a *sudden* increase in absenteeism, a major breakdown on a *new* production line, or a trusted employee who becomes surly and withdrawn.

A problem that is not properly diagnosed cannot be solved. We have already noted the overpowering urge to be solution-minded and not problem-minded. A symptom is mistaken for the problem itself. Because a problem is an uncomfortable feeling, just "doing something" may be mistaken for progress.

General Principles in an Effective Diagnosis

Before we present two methods for diagnosing operating problems (and return to Joe Simpson's unusual behavior), we need to establish certain general principles that are crucial to an effective diagnosis. These general principles, combined with specific diagnostic methods, provide a powerful framework for diagnosing ill-structured operating problems.

Be skeptical of the language used to describe a problem situation.

In diagnosing a problem we generally rely on others to describe a problem situation. And that's the dilemma. The language people use to explain events reflects not only what happened but also indicates their cultural and individual biases.

The words may tell us more about the reporter than about the news story. This problem of semantic confusion was first discussed by the authors of the Old Testament:

> All the earth had the same language and the same words. And as men migrated from the east, they came upon a valley in the land of Shinar and settled there. . . . Come, let us build us a city and a tower with its top in the sky, to make a name for ourselves; else we shall be scattered all over the world. The Lord came down to look at the city and tower which man had built, and the Lord said, "If, as one people with one language for all, this is how they have begun to act, then nothing that they propose to do will be out of their reach. Let us, then, go down and confound their speech there, so that they shall not understand one another's speech." . . . This is why it is called Babel, because there the Lord confounded the speech of the whole earth; and from there the Lord scattered them over the face of the whole earth.
>
> —Genesis 11:1-9

The representation of events by language is called *encoding*. Encoding is a tricky process because it depends on cultural and total-life-experience factors. Even within a single culture there is no guarantee that "what is seen is what is sent." Robert Krauss reported on his own Tower of Babel.[1] He paired off four-year-olds and separated them by a screen. Each child was given a set of blocks; each block had a different design. One child (the encoder) was told to describe the designs to the other child (the decoder). All went well until the first child came across the numeral "3." He kept referring to it as *sheet*. Of course, the second child never could guess the design. When Krauss asked the encoding child why he called the number three a sheet, the child responded: "Have you ever noticed that when you get up in the morning, the bed sheet is all wrinkled? Well, sometimes it looks like this."

In order for the proper meaning to be transmitted, the receiver and transmitter must be on the same wavelength; that is, they must encode events in compatible form. If they don't, we have noise, not communication. As a professional problem solver, you need to understand and cope with the encoding process; for remember, nobody translates anything with total accuracy.

When a problem-solving team is composed of members from

several cultures, the encoding/decoding process is further confused. While Americans have only one word for snow, Eskimos have many. Since their lives depend on it, snow is not snow is not snow. Rather, each word takes on subtle but important distinctions that can mean the difference between life and death. It gets worse. *Burro* means "butter" in Italian and "ass" in Spanish. Imagine the confusion that could cause! *Billion* in the United States and France means a thousand millions (10^9), but in England it means a million millions (10^{12}). Is a *democracy* the same as a "people's democracy?" Wilhelm Von Humboldt once remarked that different languages are not so many designations of the same thing; they are different views of it. Clearly, language, even within one culture, not only conveys information but also expresses world views and biases.

Moshe Rubinstein notes that different cultures even have different divisions of the color spectrum.[2] In Bassa, a language spoken in Liberia, the color spectrum is divided into two: (1) purple, blue, and green are represented by a single word and (2) yellow, orange, and red by another word (Exhibit 4-1). Imagine trying to convey the distinction between a purple chair and a green chair to a Liberian who speaks Bassa! You would surely think him stupid because he could not grasp what is readily obvious to anyone.

Remember, words are not the events themselves; rather, they are a translation of the events into language. No translation is perfect. In diagnosing a problem, be skeptical of words—inquire into their real meaning. *Beware the translator!*

Question all "facts"; don't assume anything.

In diagnosing a problem it is crucial that you distinguish *fact* from *opinion*. Facts are based on objective evidence; opinion is mere assertion. Often opinions are stated as facts. Two examples come to mind. An assistant to a vice-president reports that there is a serious morale problem in the field. The vice-president does not investigate the assertion but accepts it as fact. The

Exhibit 4-1: Comparison of color spectrum

PURPLE BLUE GREEN	YELLOW ORANGE RED	English
I	II	Bassa

next day at an executive committee meeting he reports the "morale problem." Because of its potentially serious consequences, the executive committee sets up a study group to investigate the problem. Note that no one has yet questioned if in fact there is any problem in the field—morale or otherwise. What started off as an assertion is now being treated as gospel.

Similarly, a large mailroom is confronted by a crisis. The manager of the mailroom states that all of the printing plates have worn out and must be replaced. As there are only a few new plates in stock, the operation will have to be shut down until new plates can be ordered and installed. The mailroom manager convenes a problem-solving meeting. The discussion is summarized below:

1. The mailroom manager holds up a plate that has worn down by .002″. He indicates that the plate will not hold steady in the guide rails, which causes the printing machine to jam.

2. The general manager states that he has never felt really comfortable with the new mailroom process. He believes that the crisis vindicates his initial objections.

3. The sales manager deplores the situation and demands to know how this crisis could have occurred without any forewarning. He complains that the potential impact on sales will be great.

4. The purchasing manager states that, with some arm-twisting and cashing in of IOUs, he can get a shipment of new printing plates in four days.

Besides violating all of the principles of a consensus problem-solving session, what we see here is opinion being taken for fact. Note that at no time has anyone established that the worn-out plates are causing the slippage. True, the plates are worn down and slippage is occurring. But have cause and effect been established? The answer is, of course, that they have not!

The absurdity of the situation can be clearly demonstrated by shifting cultures and moving back in time. Three thousand years ago the Chinese believed that they could cause an eclipse to disappear merely by banging gongs and cymbals. When an eclipse occurred, they would bang their gongs, and indeed the eclipse would disappear. Was the mailroom manager any less absurd than the ancient Chinese? Neither demonstrated that their assertions were factual. Indeed, neither ever considered their assertions as anything but facts. We'll return to the worn-out plates later in the chapter and diagnose the problem correctly.

These techniques are all based on the inductive inference procedure. Briefly, we are drawing an inductive inference when we take a sample of evidence and jump to a general conclusion. Inductive inference is going beyond the known into the unknown. However, as demonstrated in the following story, it is easy to draw incorrect inferences:

> An experimental psychologist has trained a cockroach to jump on command. He demonstrates this by placing the roach on the table and shouting "jump!" The roach jumps. He then surgically removes one of its legs and again shouts "jump!" Again the roach jumps. In time, he removes all of the legs. He then places the roach on the table and shouts "jump!" This time the roach remains stationary. Drawing an inductive inference, the experimental psychologist notes in his journal that when you remove all the legs of a cockroach, it becomes deaf.

Corny jokes aside, inductive inference is crucial to testing assertions. Unfortunately, there are no guarantees when drawing inductive inferences.

In diagnosing a problem, don't mistake opinions for facts. Opinions are assertions (more technically called hypotheses) and must be subjected to verification. An effective problem solver painstakingly answers the questions: What have I assumed? Is it true? How do I know it? What if I am wrong? What other assumptions might be true? Remember, the first three letters of the word *ass*ume tell it all.

Search for problem causes, not blame.

In the case of the worn-out plates, we saw little problem-solving behavior. Instead, everyone adopted a "PYA" strategy (also known as protecting your flank). This is problem solving at its worst. Searching for problem causes requires a strategy similar to that used in brainstorming—namely, *diagnosis now, criticism later*. Can you imagine a pilot in a crippled aircraft looking for someone to blame? Common sense tells us that the pilot first better get out of the aircraft, then, when safely back on the ground, determine who or what was at fault. Here's another example:

> A company has an extremely poor track record in developing and marketing new products. The chief executive officer convenes a problem-solving meeting.

Immediately, the vice-president of marketing accuses the research and development group of being "ivory tower" and ignoring customer wants. The vice-president for research replies that the marketing department has historically failed to sell its inventions. A shouting match ensues.

Again, what we see here is the antithesis of effective problem-solving behavior.

Effective problem solvers are able to overcome the concept of "original sin"—the overpowering need to blame *someone*. We need to suspend value judgments and learn to be Sherlock Holmes. Instead of looking for fall-guys, we need to inquire into what and how—not who.

Anticipate multiple causality.

Frequently, problem solvers assume (there's that word again) that every problem has a single cause. This is not always true. As effective problem solvers, we should search for combinations of factors, rather than assume that a problem is due to a single cause. Two cases should bring home the point. Both cases illustrate ill-structured operating problems (deviations from expected performance); however, the first is production-oriented and the second is people-oriented.

The Case of the Blackened Filament

The first problem occurred about forty years ago in a large, well-managed plant making plastic filament for textiles.[3] There were six machines in the plant, and each extruded viscose raw material along channels into an acid-hardening bath where the viscose streams became plastic strands of filament. On each machine 480 strands of filament were formed and collected in spinning take-up buckets. The centrifugal force of the take-up buckets threw the strands of filament against the sides of the buckets and thus built up layers of filament from the outsides toward the centers of the buckets. Every eight hours the cake of filament in each bucket had to be emptied. It took a worker one minute to empty the bucket and place it back on-line. Thus one worker could service all 480 buckets of a machine in an eight-hour shift.

One day a serious problem suddenly occurred. When the operator on machine number 1 emptied bucket number 232, he noticed that the last filament strands (nearest the center of the filament cake) were black instead of the normal translucent color. In emptying the next several buckets, he noticed that more strands were black. He asked his relief man to get the plant superintendent. When the operator reached bucket number 243, he noticed that the last strands to enter the bucket were again translucent. Whatever the problem had been, it had disappeared. However, since no one had taken measures to correct the problem, the superintendent knew that the situation might occur again.

What made this problem so difficult was that blackened filament had never occurred in this plant. Here we have a typical example of the ill-structured operating problem.

By doing some very good detective work, the superintendent was able to determine that the blackening agent was carbon. But that was strange because there was no source of carbon within the plant. The superintendent (using the Kepner-Tregoe Diagnostic Worksheet) was able to determine that the carbon was caused by a steam locomotive that had cleared its smoke-stacks while parked on a siding outside the plant. He deduced that the carbon had infiltrated the plant via the acid-bath exhaust system that removed acid fumes from the acid-hardening bath. But how had carbon outside the plant infiltrated the exhaust system? Investigation revealed that the exhaust fan had been out of order for some time; instead of drawing acid fumes out of the plant, it had permitted carbon to enter the plant. *Multiple causality*—a carbon source outside *and* a faulty exhaust fan were the causes of the blackened filament.

The blackened-filament problem was actually a fortunate one. Because of it, the company averted the more serious problem of continual exposure of workers to acid-fumes that could have caused serious employee health problems. Interestingly, some workers had complained of nausea and light-headedness, but the superintendent had thought that the workers were merely complaining as usual.

The Case of the Erring Mechanic

In the second case we focus on a people-oriented problem.[4] Titus Nolan was foreman and service manager for the Thomas Motor Company. His technical ability was widely respected. The other mechanics were Bob, Jim, Ralph, and Dexter. Bob and Jim had worked for the company for ten years. Dexter, an apprentice, had been at Thomas Motor Company for one year.

Ralph Turner had previously worked as a serviceman for his father's fleet. About fifteen months earlier, it was decided that in exchange for Ralph working for Thomas Motor, the senior Turner would send all his truck repairs to the company. Initially, Ralph worked exclusively on his father's trucks. After several months, it was decided for efficiency reasons that this practice would stop. Ralph agreed.

In this repair shop it was an unwritten law that if a serviceman were ahead with his job, he could take an informal coffee break in the morning and afternoon. Bob and Jim, being the fastest repairmen, always went. Ralph was rarely able to go.

Suddenly Ralph began making serious mistakes. Foreman Nolan told Ralph to slow down and Ralph agreed. Yet the mistakes continued. Ralph told his father that the other mechanics were unfriendly, kept their work stations dirty, and played the radio loud just to disturb him. The situation grew worse. Ralph's helper—Dexter—began to complain that he could never take a coffee break because Ralph was so slow. Nolan's only response was to admonish Ralph to work slower so that he wouldn't make mistakes.

Nolan had failed to analyze properly the causes of Ralph's poor performance. Nolan *ass*umed that by merely telling Ralph to slow down, the problem would be corrected. Beyond the superficiality of this solution, Nolan violated the diagnostic principle of searching for multiple causality. A systematic diagnosis of Ralph's behavior would have revealed that his sloppy work was caused by many factors: his expectations of the job, the changing work procedure, the pressures of the new job at Thomas Motor Company, and the real or imagined reactions of his co-workers. Regardless of the problem, expect multiple causality.

A good diagnosis requires a tight problem specification.

Never diagnose a problem as "the problem is how to . . . ." This statement suggests that you already know what is causing the problem and you are ready to take corrective action. When the mailroom manager stated that "the problem is how we can coerce our suppliers into sending us new printing plates within four days," the problem definition was an implied solution. These types of problem definitions are to be avoided.

Rather, a proper diagnosis requires that the boundaries of the problem be tightly specified. We must be sure to differentiate problems from their symptoms. In the textile company case, merely stating the problem as blackened filament is unacceptable. Rather, we must state the *what*, *when* and *where* of the problem: What is the problem? When is it occurring? Where is it occurring? In answering those questions you should avoid adjectives like the plague, for adjectives are imprecise. Thus, rather than stating that the problem is blackened filament, you should determine what the blackening agent is and whether it occurred on (or in) the filament. Further, you should determine if the filament became black at the machine, the acid bath, or the take-up bucket. A proper diagnosis reduces the problem-solution search area. For example, once it was determined that only the filament on machine number 1 had become blackened, the manager could focus his problem-solving search in the physical area of machine number 1. Or once he knew that the blackening agent was carbon, he could begin to search for carbon, rather than lead or other blackening agent sources. A tight problem specification is like a magnet drawing the problem solver toward a solution.

In accusing Ralph Turner of working too fast, Titus Nolan offered an implied solution. If only Ralph would slow down, everything would be all right. Can't you see that Nolan had not really diagnosed the problem? Rather, he had attempted to solve it before he had answered the what, when, and where diagnostic questions (Nolan is obviously solution-minded, not problem-minded).

In summary, an ill-structured operating problem is a deviation from expected or historical performance. The solution or cause(s) of the deviation cannot be determined until we have a tight diagnostic specification. To aid the diagnostic process, two models—one behavioral and one analytical—will be presented.

In diagnosing an operating problem, an effective problem solver must:

1. Be skeptical of the language used to describe the problem.
2. Question all "facts" and verify all assertions.
3. Search for problem causes and not be concerned with placing blame.
4. Anticipate multiple causality.
5. Develop a tight problem specification.

Behavioral Models for Diagnosis

Since many of the problems managers face involve people, we

need to understand human behavior. The behavioral models that we will discuss are not formal diagnostic techniques. Rather, they are general frameworks that aid in analyzing and interpreting human motivation and behavior in a problem environment. We will present two behavioral models; one focuses on the individual, and the other treats the individual as a member of a small group. Each model provides different insights into human behavior.

Individual Behavior Models

We can never get inside individuals to know how they really feel or what really motivates them. All we can see is their outward behavior, and from that we must infer what is going on inside. The term used in systems engineering to describe our inability to understand what goes on inside the individual is "black box." During World War II the Americans were able to capture Japanese decoder machines, but they could not open them because they were booby-trapped. The Americans had to infer the decoding process by feeding in message streams and then studying the decoded versions of the message streams—a difficult and time-consuming job. So too, with understanding human behavior.

Douglas McGregor in *The Human Side of Enterprise* offered two distinctive behavioral models of man—Theory X and Theory Y. While the theories dealt with management philosophy, each was derived from a set of behavioral assumptions. Theory X, the conventional (carrot and stick) management view, made the following implicit assumptions regarding human nature and motivation:

1. Employees are basically lazy and do as little as possible to survive on the job.

2. Employees have little ambition, avoid responsibility, and mind their own business.

3. Employees are self-centered and unconcerned with the goals for the organization. Their motto is best expressed as "me, myself, and I."

4. Employees prefer the status quo and are resistant to change.[5]

Given these assumptions, it was logical to advocate that management must motivate, control, and modify employee behavior to suit the requirements of the firm. Theory X mandated that people can and must be manipulated. The four assumptions underlying Theory X were themselves based on even more fundamental assumptions about human needs and motivation.

Although he was not the first to recognize that needs organize human behavior, Abraham Maslow's Hierarchial Theory of Motivation was an important contribution to human psychology.[6] He suggested that people act as they do in an attempt to satisfy a hierarchy of needs: physiological, safety, love, esteem, and self-actualization.

Physiological and safety needs are basic to survival and include such things as food, drink, warmth, and shelter. While it may be true that man does not live by bread alone, until he has bread he really isn't concerned with much else. Once the two basic needs are at least partially satisfied, the love needs become dominant. These include affection and a sense of belongingness. The individual strives for his place in the group. He not only wants to receive love; he wants to give it to others.

According to McGregor, a Theory X management style satisfies only the physiological and safety needs and, to a lesser extent, the love needs. Theory Y operates under the assumption that workers do strive to achieve the higher-level needs of esteem and self-actualization.

Self-confidence, independence, achievement, and respect of others are all part of the esteem needs. To fulfill esteem needs, people must develop a reality-based evaluation of their own worth. And according to Theory Y, an organization should act as a catalyst to insure that achieving the esteem needs is possible within the context of the firm. Once this need has been partially fulfilled, a person naturally strives to reach his or her fullest potential.

Self-actualization needs are at the top of the needs hierarchy and can be best expressed as "what a man can be, he must be." McGregor believed that only a Theory Y management style, which assumes workers are desirous of autonomy and responsibility, would permit individuals to reach the top of the needs hierarchy.

Contrary to popular belief, Maslow never said that the needs hierarchy is fixed. Actually, some people may strive for self esteem before the love needs have even been addressed. Further, Maslow never stated that higher-order needs emerge only when lower-order needs are satisfied. Rather, he suggested that higher-order needs gradually become important as lower needs are partially satisfied. What was crucial to Maslow's theory was the fact that the *five needs organize or control human behavior*, and if you want to understand human behavior, look to the needs hierarchy, for that is where you will gain insight into what drives people to be the way they are.

But, of course, no man is an island unto himself. Therefore we now turn to an examination of the behavior of individuals in group settings.

Group Behavior Models

The basic premise here is that the individual is not the sole determiner of his behavior. Although needs do direct the individual's behavior, when someone becomes a member of an organization, there are others who have a vested interest in his or her behavior, and these others have power over the individual. Thus behavior on the job is a dual function of the employee's own desires and needs and the desires and needs of those around him.

The term *group dynamics* has been invented to describe the nature of groups, how they develop, and their effect on individual behavior. This definition is not accepted by everyone. Malcolm Bradbury, writing in the English magazine *Punch*, defines group dynamics as:

> a way of getting people out of toilets without anyone hearing the flush. In larger situations, it is called "How to Keep People Waiting for Four Days in a Fog and Make Them Like It" . . . . Group dynamics is based upon a discovery that the reason why people disagree with one another is that they are different and they have perceived a simple solution which will abolish all conflict: you make all people the same.[7]

Bradbury's definition aside, the emergence of the group-dynamics school has furthered our understanding of individual behavior in groups. Although several models have been marketed, the *role dynamics* model developed by Robert Kahn and his associates is the richest and yet simplest to understand.[8] Three concepts are fundamental to the role dynamics model: the *focal person*, his or her *role set*, and his or her *role behavior*.

Suppose we want to understand a foreman's behavior on the job. He is designated the focal person. His job is interwoven with others in the organization by virtue of the work flow, technology, or the authority structure. These "others" have a vested interest in the focal person's behavior, and because of this they attempt, whenever possible, to influence his behavior. The "others" constitute the focal person's role set. Whereas all jobs within an organization are usually interconnected, the role set constitutes those people who are *directly* affected by the focal person's behavior. It's like picking up a fishnet and pulling it taut. While all the knots of the fishnet would be affected, only those closest to the point where the net was pulled taut would move substantially. A diagram of a foreman's role set is shown in Exhibit 4-2.

In our example, the foreman's role set includes his manager, the foreman from the preceding and succeeding departments, and his subordinates. It could, of course, include other people within, and even outside of, the organization. Each role-set member can be thought of as a focal person with his or her own role set that, in turn, provides us with an interesting view of an organization. However, the purpose of our analysis is to understand the determinants of human behavior on the job.

Our foreman's role-set members depend on his performance and thus develop expectations about what he should or should not do on the job. The role-set members share their expectations with the focal person and attempt to influence that individual's behavior. How are these expectations developed? Development depends on three factors: organizational considerations, the role-set members' personalities, and the outcomes of previous influence attempts. Clearly, the expectations held by role-set members result from factors such as their rank and status as well as from the profitability and growth rate of the

Exhibit 4-2: A foreman's typical role set

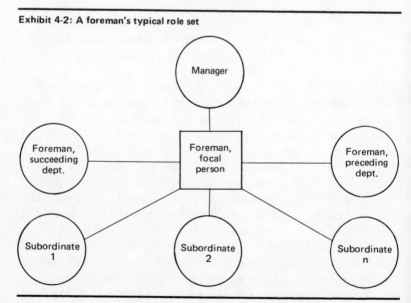

organization. Too, the expectations are, in part, determined by their needs, wants, and desires. Finally, role expectations are tempered as the result of previous successful and not-so-successful attempts to control the focal person's behavior.

In addition to influencing the focal person's behavior, role-set members evaluate his response to their pressures. To the extent that the focal person fails to conform, additional pressure will be brought to bear. These multiple pressures to conform account for what Kahn calls *role conflict*. Since we cannot expect that all role-set members have the same expectations, no matter how well the focal person performs, somebody will find his behavior unacceptable (it's like Catch-22). Kahn tells of a foreman who experienced unusual amounts of role conflict because of the firm's promotion and demotion policies:

Q: From the things you said, you want to keep on goods terms with the men?

A: That's the truth. The reason I'm saying this is that, as you know, I've been broken four or five times . . . (many foremen are temporarily demoted during periods of heavy lay-offs). The shop steward has already said, "I'll remember when you come back down to production." We have to be okayed by the union in order to get back to our job again, so you're in the middle there and you don't know what you are going to do.[9]

This foreman is faced with two sets of role members (his superior and his subordinates) who demand incompatible things, and both have considerable power over him. What will he do? Whatever he does, it's important to recognize that had we focused solely on the foreman, our analysis would have fallen far short. But why focus on the individual at all if his role-set members affect his behavior? The reason is simple. Each focal person is also a self-sender of pressure and information and his behavior is the result of both sets of forces.

Beyond diagnosing human behavior in an organization, the role-dynamics model is useful in understanding the implementation process—namely, how we implement solutions to people problems. Suppose that a manager concludes that in order to solve a problem, person A must change his behavior on the job. From the role-dynamics model, we know that in order to *promote and maintain* behavioral change in a focal person we must also change his role-set members' expectations; for unless they change, the focal person will find it difficult to maintain any change. If he changes and they do not, then he will experience role conflict that he will attempt to avoid. He may revert to his old behavior simply to reduce the level of role conflict. And when he has reverted, the manager will probably say, "See Jones—he'll never change."

When implementing behavioral solutions to problems, the unit of analysis should be the focal person's role set. (See Chapter 3, "Problem Restructuring.") Remember that outward behavior can best be understood in terms of the individual and those around him or her who have a stake in his or her performance.

An Analytical Model for Problem Diagnosis

An operating problem is defined as a deviation from expected, standard, or historic performance levels. A rise in customer complaints, a drop in absenteeism, or an increase in the number of cases of polio—these are all examples of ill-structured operating problems. They can be represented as follows:

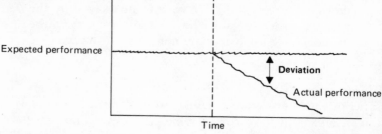

The function of diagnosis is to develop a tight problem specification by *polarizing* the situation. According to Kepner and Tregoe, polarizing is accomplished by answering the following four diagnostic questions:

1. *WHAT IS* the deviation versus what it *IS NOT*?
2. *WHERE IS* the deviation occurring versus where it *IS NOT* occurring?
3. *WHEN IS* the deviation occurring versus when it *IS NOT* occurring?
4. *TO WHAT EXTENT IS* the deviation occurring versus to what extent it *IS NOT* occurring?[10]

The questions are used to help the problem solver fill in the Kepner-Tregoe problem-diagnosis worksheet shown in Exhibit 4-3. In specifying the problem, the boundary between the *Is*

Exhibit 4-3: Diagnostic worksheet

	Is	Is not	Any distinctions of the Is?	Any changes?
WHAT				
WHERE				
WHEN				
TO WHAT EXTENT				

and *Is not* should be as tight as possible. As such, adjectives are unacceptable because adjectives are vague terms (big, small, or black as in the blackened filament). The last two columns will be discussed in Chapter 5 because they are useful only after the problem has been diagnosed.

We will use the diagnostic worksheet to specify four different problems. These range from fairly trivial personal problems to serious manufacturing crises. The amount of time spent on diagnosis, while large, is necessary, for as trivial as it may sound, a problem that has been properly diagnosed is half-solved.

The Case of the Underexposed Color Slides

Back in Chapter 1, I shared with you a problem that happened to me several years ago. Now I'd like to tell you how I diagnosed and solved it. A friend, using my camera and flash unit, took 35-mm color slides at my surprise party. When the film was processed, all the slides were underexposed (not enough light had reached the film). I accused my friend of being incompetent. Two weeks later I shot a roll of 35-mm color slides outdoors, and when all the slides turned out to be perfectly exposed, I was sure my friend had ruined my party pictures. About a month later I shot a third roll of color slides at my daughter's indoor birthday party. As always, I used my flash unit when shooting indoors. All the slides were again underexposed. Of course I immediately apologized to my friend.

The problem appeared simple. Since the problem only occurred indoors, I immediately ASSumed that the flash unit was the culprit, and I had it serviced. Well, twenty-five dollars and one roll of indoor color slides later, I was still getting underexposed pictures. Beyond throwing twenty-five dollars down the drain, I had violated every principle of problem solving in this book.

Then I remembered the Kepner-Tregoe Diagnostic Worksheet. (Since this was a personal and not a professional problem, I forgot to use the techniques I would normally have used in the business world. Talk about myopia!) In reviewing the conditions column, I thought about *what* the deviation was, *where* it was occurring, *when* it was occurring, and to *what extent* it was occurring. I filled in the worksheet with all the information I had (Exhibit 4-4).

I thought some more about the specification. Then it dawned on me that I had used the adjective "underexposed" in the specification and that I needed to specify the degree of underexposure. More specifically, I had not yet completed the *To what extent* row of the worksheet. When I reexamined all the questionable slides, I noticed that they all seemed to be underexposed by just over one f-stop (the amount of light reaching the film was about one half the amount required to properly expose the film). After I inserted the information into the worksheet, I began to look for an explanation/solution to account for the differences in the *Is* and *Is not* columns.

Then it hit me. In December I had bought a polarizing filter that is used in outdoor photography. It reduces the light hitting the film by just over one f-stop. What had happened was that I had forgotten to remove the filter when shooting indoors. Of course, when I shot outdoors the light meter of my 35-mm single-lens reflex camera automatically adjusted for the reduced light; indoors the light-meter system is disengaged and the camera had no way of knowing that less than one half of the necessary light was reaching the film. When I checked the camera, the polarizing filter was there. Did I feel stupid!

In the next example, we diagnose the *real* cause of the worn-out plates. Recall that at the problem-solving session, more heat than light had been shed on the problem. Let's pick up the action right after the meeting was adjourned.

Exhibit 4-4: The underexposed color slide worksheet

	Is	*Is not*
WHAT	35-mm slides underexposed	Other film defects—overexposure, blurring, etc.
WHERE	Indoors	Outdoors
WHEN	After February 15	Before February 15
TO WHAT EXTENT	*All* slides of two different rolls underexposed	Some of both rolls underexposed

The Case of the Worn-Out Plates

After the meeting adjourned, the vice-president was told of the crisis. Being an effective problem solver, he immediately recognized that no one had questioned the mailroom manager's assertion that the plates were causing the jamming. The vice-president obtained several new plates (recall there were some new plates in stock) and had them installed in the machines. Within fifteen minutes the new plates were also slipping and jamming. So he concluded that whatever was causing the slippage, it was not the worn-out plates. Fortunately, he was able to reach the purchasing manager before additional plates were ordered.

At this point, the vice-president knew that the worn-out plates were *not* causing the slippage, but he still had no idea what was. Instead of generating more solutions, he decided that a complete diagnosis was needed. Using the diagnostic worksheet, he jotted down some questions he would need answered. Were all the plates slipping or just some of them? When had the slippage begun? Did it happen every day? With the answers to these questions he began to fill in the worksheet (Exhibit 4-5).

As soon as he had filled in the information, he realized that the worn-out plates could not have caused the jamming for two reasons: First, while the jamming had begun only three days ago, he was sure that some of the older plates had worn by more than .002″ long before then; second, if the plates were causing the slippage, then why were *all* the machines jamming? Not all of the plates had worn by .002″. He had not at that point been able to obtain any *where* information. He decided to call another division that also had a printing shop. He found out that they were not experiencing any slippage problems. And they never had, even though they were using plates that were worn by more than .002″. Under the *Is* column he wrote "our

Exhibit 4-5: The slipping plates worksheet

	Is	Is not
WHAT	Plates jamming in guiderails	Other defects
WHERE	?	?
WHEN	Began three days ago; every day	Before three days ago; selected days
TO WHAT EXTENT	All machines jamming	Some machines jamming

division"; under the *Is not* column he wrote "division Y." Now he was beginning to get a handle on the problem. Whatever was causing the slippage was unique to his division, had begun three days ago, and was occurring daily on *all* the machines. Certainly this was a better diagnosis than the mailroom manager's.

With some good detective work (and some additional techniques that will be discussed in the next chapter when we take a final look at this problem), he was able to trace the slippage to a recent decision to change ink suppliers. The purchasing department had switched ink suppliers several months ago because of potential cost saving. After the old ink supplies were exhausted, the mailroom had switched over to the new ink. This had been done about three and one-half days ago. When the vice president asked the purchasing manager why he didn't know about the ink switchover, he replied, "Hell, I knew about it—I was the one who made the final decision on the ink. However, I didn't think it was related to the slippage problem since the mailroom manager had assured us that the plates were causing the slippage."

The vice-president immediately ordered the mailroom to switch back to the original type of ink, and the problem disappeared. As a result of the snafu, he also ordered a change in organizational procedure so that whenever a production change was contemplated, it would be tested before implementation and all affected parties would be notified. In doing this, the vice-president hoped to prevent future crises.

In our next example, we examine a problem where the pre-implementation findings don't jive with the results when the production process is finally implemented.

The Case of the Droopy Eyeglasses

Many years ago, the Worldwide Optical Company reintroduced a 14-K gold eyeglass frame. Because it had been thirty years since they had produced them, no one knew how to manufacture them. The major problem was that 14-K gold is very brittle and easily cracks. In order to shape the temples of the frame (the part that fits behind the ears), the temples had to be softened so they could be machine-stamped to shape. So far, no problem. The difficulty was to harden them after stamping so that they would not easily bend out of shape in use.

The metallurgy lab experimented with different temperatures and times. The objective was to harden the temples to B-98 Rockwell hardness since this would ensure that the temples would not bend out of shape. (The Rockwell number is a numerical expression of the degree of hardness of a metal, and is named after Stanley Rockwell, a twentieth century American metallurgist.) After much trial and error, the lab was able to harden the temples successfully.

The operation was then ready for full-scale production. However, when the first batch of 14-K temples were heat-treated in the production facilities, the temples were too soft. Indeed, it appeared that the temples had not hardened at all. Yet the temples had been heat-treated according to the time and temperature predetermined by the tests. So what went wrong?

As the lab geared up to attack the problem, the diagnostic worksheet was utilized (see Exhibit 4-6). The following questions were generated: How soft? Soft over the entire frame? All frames or some of them? Within several hours enough information was available to make an initial attempt at a diagnosis.

In the next chapter, we will solve this problem by utilizing the last two columns of the diagnostic worksheet, *Any distinctions of the Is?* and *Any changes?* (see Exhibit 4-3). These help the problem solver generate *likely* solutions and also provide a vehicle for testing his or her solutions.

In our final case, we return, as promised, to Joe Simpson and his unusual behavior. This time we will use all of our diagnostic tools to determine what is upsetting Joe.

The Case of the Surly Worker

Joe Simpson's behavior was puzzling. Normally steady and

Exhibit 4-6: The 14-K disaster worksheet

	Is	Is not
WHAT	Temples at B-28 rather than B-98	Other defects; other B-Rockwell number after hardening
WHERE	In production area	In metallurgy area
	Over entire temple; hardness tested at 3 places	Nondifferential hardness over the temple
WHEN	First production run	Before production run in metallurgy lab
TO WHAT EXTENT	All temples of first production batch at B-28 (softer than before hardening operation)	Some temples at B-28
		Temples at same B-Rockwell number as before hardening process

reliable, Joe's productivity had dropped, and he had recently engaged in several shouting matches with the men. Most of the other foremen believed that Joe's recent promotion was responsible and that once he got over the new job jitters all would be okay. Two months later, the problem was worse. What should the foreman do?

Now it is time to diagnose the problem. The foreman needed a tighter problem specification than "Joe is grumpy." Further, the specification should focus on problem diagnosis and not on the implied solution as expressed by the other foremen—"new job jitters."

With the diagnostic worksheet in mind, Joe's foreman began his diagnosis. Joe's work had begun deteriorating about the first of July. How much had it dropped? Did it occur every day? On all his jobs? (As senior utility man, Joe rotated work stations daily.) Again, note that the worksheet helps the problem solver generate a set of relevant questions. Based on his investigation, Joe's foreman was able to develop an initial problem statement (Exhibit 4-7).

In light of the diagnostic worksheet, let's examine the initial solutions offered. If Joe is experiencing new job jitters, why is it that Joe's performance is poor only on Monday and Friday? While this may be *part* of the problem, there is more. Furthermore, the new plant-wide production standards and Joe's concern over getting a major promotion failed to agree with the evidence from the worksheet.

After Joe's foreman had developed the worksheet, he decided to pursue the *When* portion of the specification; specifically,

Exhibit 4-7: Joe Simpson's worksheet

	Is	*Is not*
WHAT	Average productivity for the week dropped to 90% from 100% of standard	Other behavioral problems
WHERE	On all his jobs	Some of his jobs
WHEN	Since July 1	Before July 1
	Monday and Friday	Tuesday through Thursday
TO WHAT EXTENT	Not every day	Every day
	Monday, Friday—productivity about 75% of standard	75% every day

Note: On Tuesday through Thursday Joe's productivity remained about 100% of standard. On Monday and Friday it dropped to 75% of standard. Thus over the entire week Joe's average productivity was 90% ([75 + 100 + 100 + 100 + 75] ÷ 5).

the Monday-Friday/Tuesday-Thursday patterns. The foreman began to wonder what was happening on the weekend that might account for Joe's unusual behavior on Fridays and Mondays. As Joe wasn't a talkative person, no one in the plant had any idea what was bugging him. One day the foreman finally asked Joe if he was having any personal problems. At first, Joe didn't want to discuss it, but with some coaxing, the story came out.

Joe had been having marital problems for some time. After Joe had been promoted, the extra pressures from the job had made the problems worse, and his wife had decided on a trial separation. She had moved back to her home town about thirty miles away. Each weekend Joe visited his wife to dicuss their problems. At that point, the foreman realized why Joe's work had suffered on Mondays and Fridays. The foreman decided to give Joe some time off so that he could resolve his marital problems without the additional pressures from the job. Within two weeks Joe and his wife were reunited, and although their problems hadn't been solved, both were again committed to the marriage. Immediately, Joe's productivity increased and his surliness decreased.

Earlier in the chapter, we warned you to consider multiple causality and not look for a single (or simple) reason; behavior is much too complicated for simplistic causality. Beyond that, we saw that the other foremen's diagnoses were implied solutions—another no-no in problem diagnosis. In fact, they violated all of the general principles of an effective diagnosis.

This case also demonstrates that a focal person's role set can include individuals outside of the work environment. Joe's wife was certainly a member of the role set because her behavior affected his on-the-job performance. It is important that we not take too myopic a view of a role set; otherwise, we may misinterpret an individual's behavior.

Conclusion

Americans are notorious for skipping the diagnostic phase in problem solving. In this chapter we have presented several models to assist you in this important area of problem solving. Different models were necessary because, as the old saying goes, "if the only tool you have is a hammer, everything begins to look like a nail."

In order to utilize the diagnostic techniques effectively, five general principles were presented. These include:

1. Be skeptical of the language used to describe a problem—a rose is not always a rose.

2. Assume nothing.

3. Search for causes—scapegoating is counterproductive.

4. Anticipate multiple causality.

5. Develop a tight problem specification.

FOOTNOTES

1. Robert M. Krauss, "Language as a Symbolic Process in Communication," *American Scientist*, Autumn 1968, pp. 265-278.

2. Moshe F. Rubinstein, *Patterns of Problem Solving* (Englewood Cliffs, New Jersey, Prentice-Hall, Inc., 1975), p. 43.

3. Charles H. Kepner and Benjamin B. Tregoe, *The Rational Manager* (New York, McGraw-Hill, 1965), pp. 73-87.

4. Austin Grimshaw and John W. Hennessey, Jr., *Organizational Behavior* (New York, McGraw-Hill, 1960).

5. Douglas McGregor, *The Human Side of Enterprise* (New York, McGraw-Hill, 1960).

6. A.H. Maslow, "A Theory of Human Motivation," *Psychological Review*, July 1943, pp. 370-396.

7. Malcolm Bradbury, "The Institutional Joneses," *Punch*, February 10, 1960.

8. Robert L. Kahn et al., *Organizational Stress* (New York, John Wiley, 1964).

9. Ibid., p. 61.

10. Kepner and Tregoe, *The Rational Manager*.

5
Solving
Operating Problems

In the last chapter we focused on the art and science of problem diagnosis. A problem that is diagnosed is already half-solved. In this chapter we continue with the John Dewey experiential problem-solving model, but focus on the analysis and solution phases.

"If enough data are collected, anything may be solved by statistical methods."

—WILLIAMS AND HOLLAND'S LAW

"The number of different hypotheses erected to explain a given phenomenon is inversely related to the available information."

—ANON

"My mind is made up—I don't want to be confused by the facts."

—ANON

"The number of rational hypotheses that can explain a given phenomenon is infinite."

—PERSIG'S LAW

Once a problem has been diagnosed, we are ready to analyze and solve it.

Analysis Phase

What is a hypothesis? It is a tentative solution that can be accepted or disproved. It is an informed guess that has a reasonable chance of being correct. It is an operating assumption that has yet to be proved. It is a plan of attack; it is alternative routes to a solution; it is the beginning of wisdom.

During most motor vehicle license examinations, you are required to park a car between two fifty-five-gallon drums. As you may know, it is not an easy task. Can hypotheses or tentative parking strategies (such as those found under "good driving tips" in a driver-education manual) help you solve the parking problem? Yes! Even if a strategy fails, you may learn from your failure and develop a parking strategy that works.

The important point is that *failure can be informative* when failure suggests certain new and promising paths to explore. Let's demonstrate this idea.

Toward the end of the eighteenth century, Allessandro Volta set out to prove that Luigi Galvani's hypotheses on animal magnetism were correct. Although Volta's experiments utterly refuted Galvani's work, these "failures" led to the invention of the electric battery.

Is any hunch a hypothesis? No! To qualify as a hypothesis, the hunch must be formulated so that deductions can be tested. If there is no evidence that might cause the problem solver to reject a tentative solution, then it is not a hypothesis but a dogmatic assertion; effective problem solvers do not entertain dogmatic assertions.

Let's examine how a hypothesis could be formulated and tested in a simple experimental setting. Suppose that a large number of poker chips, each bearing a number, are placed in a bag. Two chips are selected. The first chip bears the number 8 and the second bears the number 16.

If we believe that there is a pattern to the numbers being drawn, we should generate as many hypotheses as possible to explain the first two draws of the experiment. Although your algebra may be rusty, at least five different hypotheses can be generated. In each hypothesis, the letter n denotes the number of the draw:

H_1: $8n$
H_2: $2^n + 2$
H_3: $n^2 + 5n + 2$
H_4: $2^n + 6n$
H_5: $n^3 + n + 6$

For values $n = 1$ and $n = 2$, the five hypotheses will all yield 8 and 16 on the first two draws respectively. Take a minute and verify this. Thus, at this point, all five hypotheses are still contenders. Before we actually draw the third chip, let's generate some deductions for the third draw for each of the five hypotheses (Exhibit 5-1).

Suppose that the third chip bears the number 26. All the hypotheses except H_3 and H_4 would be eliminated. We would continue to predict the chip numbers until only one hypothesis remained. It is, of course, possible that neither H_3 nor H_4 would correctly predict the chip value for the fourth draw. This would mean that the correct hypothesis had not been included in the original five hypotheses. And so we have already learned one important lesson:

LESSON 1—Generate as many hypotheses as you can. The more you generate, the more likely you are to solve the problem.

Let's continue the experiment. Up to this point only H_3 and H_4 remain viable contenders; the others have been disproved. Suppose that the fourth chip bears the number 38. What could we conclude? Hypothesis H_3 correctly predicts that the fourth chip will be 38 ($4^2 + 5(4) + 2 = 38$), whereas the H_4 hypothesis incorrectly predicts that the number will be 40 ($2^4 + 6(4) = 40$). So it's obvious that H_3 is the correct answer. *Wrong!* Technically, we can never be certain that a hypothesis is correct, for it is possible to find some hypothesis other than H_3 (not included in the original five) that might account for the sequence of draws. And so the second important lesson is:

LESSON 2—There is no such thing as a proven hypothesis. A hypothesis is accepted when its assertions are established beyond a reasonable shadow of doubt (the so-called reasonable-man rule).

Suppose that after the third draw the experimenter misplaces

Exhibit 5-1: Logical consequences of the five hypotheses for draw number 3

Contender	Calculation	What we anticipate if hypothesis is correct
H_1	$8n = 8(3)$	Third chip will bear the number 24.
H_2	$2^n + 2 = 2^3 + 2$	Third chip will bear the number 32.
H_3	$n^2 + 5n + 2 = 3^2 + 5(3) + 2$	Third chip will bear the number 26.
H_4	$2^n + 6n = 2^3 + 6(3)$	Third chip will bear the number 26.
H_5	$n^3 + n + 6 = 3^3 + 3 + 6$	Third chip will bear the number 36.

n = Number of the draw.

the bag of chips. Then both H_3 and H_4 are plausible, but both cannot be correct since they generate different possible consequences for draws 4, 5, and successive draws (we have already demonstrated this for draw 4). Which hypothesis should we select?

The outcomes of scientific revolutions have hinged on which of two competing hypotheses was accepted. Scientists have been influenced by an obscure Franciscan scholar of the fourteenth century—William of Occam—who first suggested that "it is vain to do with more what can be done with less." Thinkers of a later age interpreted that to mean that if a simple explanation will do, it is worthless to seek a complex one. This concept became known as Occam's razor.

One of the early tests of Occam's razor occurred in the sixteenth century. A young Polish cleric was ready to challenge the 1500-year-old Ptolemaic (geocentric) theory of the universe. According to the geocentric theory, Earth was at the center of the universe, and the sun and the planets revolved around it. Now in order to explain the apparent motion of the stars, it was necessary for Claudius Ptolemy to propose that the stars exhibited a bewildering complexity of epicyclical movements. (For example, imagine a stationary tractor tire. Rolling along the circumference of the tractor tire is a much smaller car tire. A nail is protruding from the car tire. If we trace the curve made by the nail as the car tire rolls along the circumference of the tractor tire we would have an epicyclical curve. An intricate curve indeed!) When Nicolaus Copernicus looked at the same heavens, he rejected the geocentric theory for a heliocentric theory that placed the sun at the center and the planets in a circular orbit revolving around the sun. Copernicus argued that the heliocentric theory eliminated the need for complex trigonometric curves to explain the motions in the heavens. While there were still discrepancies between heliocentric theory and the heavenly motions (these would be eventually resolved when Johannes Kepler replaced the circular orbits with elliptical ones), the simplicity of the Copernican theory eventually won the day. Thus:

LESSON 3—Simple hypotheses should drive out complex hypotheses, or keep it simple (a "KIS" strategy).

Unfortunately, to many individuals simplicity is not a virtue. This is dramatically demonstrated by an experiment conducted by Alex Bavelas, noted consultant in small-group interaction.[1]

Subjects A and B are shown medical slides of healthy and sick cells and told they must learn to differentiate them. Each time a slide is projected the subjects must respond, whereupon they are told if they are correct or not.

Subject A gets true feedback; that is, he is told whether his guess is right or wrong. Most subject A's learn to correctly distinguish healthy cells from sick cells about 80 percent of the time.

Subject B's feedback is not based on his own guesses, but on A's guesses. It does not matter what B responds; B is told "right" if A guessed right, "wrong" if A guessed wrong. Of course, subject B does not know that his feedback does not depend on his responses.

Both subjects are eventually asked to discuss the rules they have developed for distinguishing between healthy and sick cells. Subject A's explanation is simple and correct; subject B's explanation is of necessity very subtle and complex—after all he had to develop his hypothesis on the basis of very confusing information.

What is interesting is that subject A is truly impressed by the "brilliance" of subject B's explanation. Subject A tends to feel inferior because his explanation (which is correct) is pedestrian and lacks complexity. When asked who will do better on a second set of slides, all B's and most A's say that B will.

Lesson 3 is not easy to accept. While other lessons await, it is now time to turn our attention to techniques for generating hypotheses.

Generating Hypotheses, or How to Design Alternative Paths to a Solution

Techniques for generating hypotheses range from very formal approaches, such as the Kepner-Tregoe system, brainstorming, and synectics to the less formal approaches of analogy and WAGS (wild-guesses). Whatever technique is used, the hypotheses must be capable of verification.

Kepner-Tregoe Diagnostic Worksheet: In diagnosing operating problems in Chapter 4, we used the first two columns of the diagnostic worksheet; in generating hypotheses we will utilize the last two columns. These are shown in Exhibit 5-2. Since an operating problem is defined as a deviation from the expected, the last two columns direct the manager to search for explanations that will differentiate between the *Is* and the *Is not*

Exhibit 5-2: Diagnostic worksheet—hypotheses generation columns

	Any distinctions of the Is?	Any changes?
WHAT		
WHERE		
WHEN		
TO WHAT EXTENT		

columns in the diagnosis. The manager must ask, "What distinguishes a fact in the *Is* column from its counterfact in the *Is not* column?" Further, if a deviation has occurred, something in the environment must have changed to cause the problem. The last column prompts the manager to search for such changes. In searching for changes, the manager must ask, "What is new or different? What has changed that could explain the distinctions generated in column 3 of the diagnostic worksheet?" Once the two columns have been completed, the manager should generate multiple hypotheses (Lesson 1) to explain the distinctions or changes. Then by a process of elimination, or by techniques discussed later in this chapter, hopefully only one hypothesis will stand the test of verification.

In the Case of the Droopy Eyeglasses, the manager had completed the first two columns of the diagnostic worksheet. Now it was necessary to complete the remaining two columns (Exhibit 5-3). What was distinctive between the production area and the lab? Different personnel and different equipment. The manager noted, however, that there had been no recent changes in either the production personnel or the factory hardening equipment. The fact that the temples were uniformly soft tended to rule out problems with the 14-K gold material itself. In reviewing the possible distinctions for the *Extent* row of the worksheet, the fact that the temples were softer than before hardening suggested that perhaps too much heat had been applied to the temples, causing them to "overharden" or become soft again. After completing the worksheet, the manager generated two hypotheses:

H_1: *Personnel in production area at fault; temples hardened too long (too much heat).*

H_2: *Production equipment differs from lab equipment; applies too much heat to temples.*

Both hypotheses seemed reasonable. However, the first hypoth-

Exhibit 5-3: Droopy eyeglasses worksheet revisited

	Is	Is not	Any distinctions of the Is?	Any changes?
WHAT	Temples at B28 rather than B98	Other defects	Suggests problem is in hardening process	
WHERE	In production area	In metallurgy area	Different equipment; different personnel	No changes lately here!
	Over entire temple; hardness tested at three places	Same hardness over temple		
WHEN	First production run	In lab	Upgrading from pilot to full-blown operation	Different equipment? Different personnel?
TO WHAT EXTENT	All temples of first batch at B28 (softer than before hardening)	Some temples at B28 Temples at same Rockwell B hardness as before hardening	Softer than before hardening	Temples receiving too much heat?

esis was rejected because, according to the automatic readout instruments, the factory personnel had set the time-temperature settings correctly. This also seemed to rule out H_2 since the settings were identical to those used in the lab.

The manager reconsidered the distinctions (or differences) between the two temple-hardening facilities. The equipment in the lab was scaled for research work, whereas the production facilities were large enough to meet the daily manufacturing requirements. The manager decided to inspect the production facilities. He quickly discovered that one major difference in the production facilities was a blower fan used to insure that the heat in the heat-treating chamber was uniform. A fan was unnecessary in the smaller lab. The manager then realized that the fan in the production facilities was delivering more heat to the surface of the temples than was the still air found in the lab equipment. The extra heat transfer at the surface caused the temples to overharden and soften. By adjusting the time-temperature conditions in the production heat-treating facility, the problem was solved. Scaling up from a pilot operation is not always an easy process.

If you find it difficult to develop "distinctions" from a problem specification, it probably means that your original specification is too loose. Eliminate the adjectives and replace them with nouns! Do some more detective work! Now you will probably be able to generate distinctions and, thereby, legitimate hypotheses.

Let's take another look at the Case of the Worn-Out Plates. Recall that the vice-president had proven that the worn-out plates were not causing the machines to jam. As we pick up the action, the vice-president has completed the first two columns of the diagnostic worksheet (Exhibit 5-4) and is developing the hypotheses. The vice-president asked, "What differentiates the data in the *Is* column from the data in the *Is not* column?" He reasoned that whatever the problem was, it was happening on all the machines. This tended to rule out the plates, since not all the plates were worn .002", yet all the machines were jamming. He also noted that the problem was confined to his division, although division Y reported that their plates had worn down by more than .002". Thus the jamming could not be caused by the plates. He knew, of course, that the two divisions were run as separate companies, each with its own line and staff functions, and were physically located in different cities. At this point the information did not seem to lead anywhere; he, however, reasoned that since the slippage was occurring every day, the cause of the problem was always present.

The vice-president then began to consider what changes in the division could account for the distinctions he had specified. There had been no recent changes in the print shop personnel. Anyway, that would not account for all the machines jamming. The vice-president wondered, "What is common to all the

Exhibit 5-4: Slipping plates worksheet revisited

	Is	Is not	Any distinctions of the Is?	Any changes?
WHAT	Plates jamming	Other defects	Forces attention to guide rails where plates jam	
WHERE	Our division	Division Y	Decentralized operations: geographic differences	
WHEN	Three days ago; every day	Before then; selected days	A continuous problem	Look for something that happened three days ago only in our division
TO WHAT EXTENT	All machines jamming	Some machines jamming	Problem is common to all machines	

machines that might have permanently changed about three days ago?" Electricity, temperature in the printshop, humidity, and ink—all were reasonable hypotheses.

He thought that a change in the electrical voltage might have caused slippage of the plates, but a quick call to the electric company revealed no unusual and sustained power surges during the previous three-day period. Temperature and humidity were ruled out since (1) they had not appreciably changed within the past three days and (2) the temperature-humidity index was similar to that experienced in division Y's printshop.

This left the ink-supply hypothesis. The vice-president asked the mailroom manager if the printshop had recently switched ink suppliers. The mailroom manager said that, as far as he knew, they were still using the same ink supplier. This seemed to disprove the ink-source hypothesis. And yet it seemed to be the best hypothesis, for it matched the diagnostic worksheet specification. If it were the ink supply, then all the machines would jam because the ink was supplied by one vendor. Since each division had its own purchasing agent, the two divisions could have been using different ink vendors, which could account for the differences in the *Where* row of the worksheet. The vice-president decided to pursue this hypothesis. He contacted the purchasing agent who confirmed that there had been a recent change in ink vendors (the vice-president later proved that the ink was causing the slippage by the method of difference, a verification technique discussed later in this chapter). The switch had been motivated by huge potential cost savings. When asked why purchasing had not notified the mailroom manager, the purchasing manager's response was classic: "Why was it necessary? His job is to meet production . . . mine is to save money."

The Kepner-Tregoe worksheet is a powerful tool for diagnosing operating problems and generating potential hypotheses; it is also useful in establishing whether a hypothesis is correct. However, there are several other techniques for generating hypotheses that should be considered.

Analogy: A teacher that I know has an incredible record of catching students in the act of cheating. I once asked him what accounted for his success. He explained that when he was an undergraduate he listened to the cheating exploits of his fraternity brothers and that today's students are still using the same old techniques. That's problem solving by analogy.

An analogy is a likeness between two situations on which a

comparison can be based. For example, a pump is an analogue of a human heart. That analogy helps us grasp a broad, but perhaps inaccurate, mental picture of the workings of the heart. Analogies are a trusted, although imperfect, approach to hypothesis generation.

Let's take a simple example. In the last chapter we met Joe Simpson whose marital problems were affecting his on-the-job performance. Suppose that several months later another worker exhibits the same baffling symptoms. If the supervisor's diagnosis reveals that indeed the two problems are similar, he or she would be justified in exploring with the worker whether there were any outside problems that might be affecting the worker's behavior. That's hypothesis generation by analogy. Of course the worker's actual problem may have nothing to do with outside factors, but it would be a reasonable hypothesis to pursue.

Sometimes an apparent lack of similarity with previous problems makes a problem difficult. The problem may be that we have focused the search area for analogies too narrowly. I suppose it is reasonable to look to previous marketing problems when faced with a new marketing problem. But if you widen the search area, you may find similarities between your present marketing problem and previous production problems. Remember *analogies need not be isomorphic*. Go beyond mere superficial similarities.

Analogies can be used in two very different ways in hypothesis generation. We have already discussed the first approach— namely, searching for similarities between problem situations. While this is useful, there is a danger that all problems may be seen as reincarnations of previous ones, and subtle distinctions may be lost in the shuffle. Clearly, analogy is more useful when a manager is dealing with structured or recurring problems, whereas the Kepner-Tregoe approach is more useful in dealing with novel problems.

Analogies may also be used to overcome obstacles in problem diagnosis. The synectics technique discussed in Chapter 3 helps the manager see the problem differently by pursuing different types of analogies. Because analogies often have lives of their own, they help us bypass the mental barriers that keep us from solving problems.

Hypothesis generation by analogy is an important tool for an effective problem solver. As Francis Bacon said long ago, a good problem solver must have a mind nimble and versatile enough to catch resemblances and steady enough to distinguish differences.

Observation: I was always amazed at Sherlock Holmes' powers of observation. In one of his exploits, he observed a scuff mark on a shoe and then constructed an elaborate hypothesis suggesting that the fellow had recently been discharged from the Bengal Lancers because of an act of cowardice. When Holmes patiently described his reasoning process to Dr. Watson, his logic was flawless.

Seeing, *really* seeing, is done not only with the eyes; it is done with an open mind—a mind willing to explore, to consider novel hypotheses, and to be open to that data. Some of the earlier chapters attempted to overcome your mental barriers by engaging in mind-stretching exercises. If these have been successful you are now truly prepared to see.

The failure to observe was crucial in the Case of the Worn-Out Plates. If the mailroom manager had noticed that there was an ink film along the guide rails that locked the plates to the machines, he might have investigated the ink supply as a potential cause of the problem long before the notorious "unproblem"-solving meeting where all hell broke loose.

Theory: One good theory is worth a thousand random observations. One function of theory is to provide fertile grounds for ideas and the conceptual framework to translate ideas into working hypotheses.

In the Case of the Surly Worker, Joe Simpson's foreman might never have considered the impact of outside influences on Joe's behavior had it not been for the theory of role dynamics. Recall that the role-dynamics model suggested that an individual's role set could extend beyond the immediate work environment. Armed with the model, Joe's foreman was prepared to explore such possibilities. Had no model existed, the hypothesis might never have been generated. Theory is indeed a spawning ground for good hypotheses.

Brainstorming: In Chapter 3 we discussed this technique in detail. It is mentioned here because it is a useful technique for generating a large number of hypotheses in a short period of time. Once these have been generated, they can be screened to ensure that they meet the minimal conditions for hypotheses and are reasonable or legitimate contenders.

Morphological Forced Connection: This technique was also discussed in Chapter 3. It is a somewhat far-out technique and should only be considered when traditional approaches have failed. Again, once hypotheses have been generated, they can be screened and evaluated.

In their amusing book entitled *The Universal Traveler*, Koberg and Bagnall suggest many additional techniques for generating hypotheses.[2] These include the "tell me, stranger" and "get out of town" approaches—their nomenclature is inspired. Although the book is written for architectural students, professional managers will find it useful and fun to read.

How to Use (and Not Use) Hypotheses in Problem Solving

Merely generating hypotheses is not enough; hypotheses must be used properly by the manager in the search for additional evidence to solve the problem. Arthur Elstein and his co-workers investigated the differences between effective and ineffective problem solvers and how they generate and utilize hypotheses.[3] Although the study focuses on physicians in the act of diagnosing a difficult illness, the lessons easily extend to the manager and his or her environment.

Meet Dr. X and Dr. Y. Dr. X is acknowledged by his colleagues to be an ineffective diagnostician. Dr. Y is considered an expert diagnostician. The purpose of the study was to determine *why*.

Both doctors were asked to develop work-ups on the same medical case. In addition to videotaping the work-ups, they were asked to think aloud as they conducted the examination. They could use as many tests as they wished to support their diagnosis. The audio and video tapes thus documented their different approaches to the art and science of medical diagnosis. It was hoped that striking differences would surface to explain the physicians' differential effectiveness. The researchers were not disappointed.

The patient is a 21-year-old female who is brought to the emergency room early one morning paralyzed in both legs. Having gone to bed the night before believing herself well, she is agitated and hysterical over her paralysis. She repeatedly asks questions like, "What is wrong with me? Will the paralysis spread? How long will I be like this?" The patient is single, a college student, and has a boyfriend with whom she is not contemplating marriage. She may possibly be pregnant.

Before Dr. X and Dr. Y examined the patient, the senior medical staff had correctly diagnosed her illness as multiple sclerosis. The senior staff believed that the two most reasonable hypotheses regarding the patient's illness were (1) conversion hysteria (HY)—a psychological disorder and (2) multiple sclerosis (MS)—a neurological disorder. Of course, other hypotheses could be generated during the examination. The senior staff agreed that given the brief personal history of the patient, the HY hypothesis was initially the most promising, for in its more severe forms hysteria can cause a breakdown of the sensory and motor functions.

The staff listed a series of critical findings and important pieces of evidence that could emerge during the examination. They weighted each finding along a five-point scale ($-$ $-$, $-$, 0, $+$, $+$ $+$). The double-negative sign meant that the finding was extremely negative evidence for the medical hypothesis under consideration; the double-positive sign meant that the finding strongly supported the medical hypothesis under consideration. The scoring system was used to trace the medical reasoning and problem-solving behavior of doctors X and Y. The work-ups of the two doctors are presented in Exhibits 5-5 and 5-6.

Let's examine each work-up closely, and then draw some general conclusions. For our purposes, it is unimportant what questions were actually asked; what is important is *how the doctors processed* the patient's responses. Within the first 29 questions, Dr. X generated four possible hypotheses (Exhibit 5-5). The HY hypothesis was supported by two positive critical findings and refuted by one negative critical finding. There was some positive support for the viral infection and trauma hypotheses, and some damaging evidence (negative signs) for the meningitis and MS hypotheses. Within the next 30 ques-

Exhibit 5-5: Dr. X's work-up

Question number	HY	Organic disease	Viral infection	Meningitis	Trauma	MS
				Hypotheses generated		
1-29	Generated 2+ 1−	Generated	Generated 1+	Generated 1−	1+	1−
30-59	1+ 4−	2+	1− Rejected	2− Rejected		5+
60-89	2+ 1−	1+			Generated −1	
90-119	2+				Rejected	
120-137	−1 Accepted					+1

tions, Dr. X's behavior is revealing. Although he found four negative findings and only one positive finding for the HY hypothesis, he did not reject it. Rather, he rejected the viral infection and meningitis hypotheses (for which there was also negative evidence). Also, he obtained five positive critical findings for MS, but apparently he did not consider these important because he never formally generated an MS hypothesis. Later, he formally generated, and subsequently rejected, the trauma hypothesis. Over the last 77 questions he obtained four positive and two negative findings for the hysteria hypothesis. At no time was the MS hypothesis formally considered, even though the positive findings significantly outweighed the meager negative evidence (six pluses versus one minus). After question number 137, Dr. X concluded that the patient was suffering from conversion hysteria. He was wrong.

Dr. Y (Exhibit 5-6) also thought the patient was suffering from hysteria. With the first questions (different questions from those asked by Dr. X) he obtained three positive critical findings supporting the HY hypothesis. During the next 50 questions he generated and rejected the infection hypothesis, generated a vascular condition hypothesis, and found three more positive findings for the HY hypothesis. Finally, given two positive findings for the MS hypothesis, Dr. Y formally considered MS for the first time. In the remaining questions he attempted to utilize tests and ask questions that would differentiate between the HY and MS hypotheses. As you can see, he found ten positive critical findings for MS as well as ten negative

Exhibit 5-6: Dr. Y's work-up

Question number	HY	Infection	Peculiar vascular condition	MS
				Hypotheses generated
1-49	Generated 3+	1−		1−
50-99	3+	Generated Rejected	Generated	
100-149				2+ Generated
150-249	4−			4+
250-299	6−			5+
300-322				1+ Accepted

findings for HY. After 322 questions, he concluded that the patient had multiple sclerosis.

After the diagnoses were completed, Elstein and his co-workers spoke to both doctors in order to gain a better understanding of how they had arrived at their conclusions. The conversations were fascinating and hold important lessons for all problem solvers. Dr. X was asked why he hadn't considered the possibility of multiple sclerosis, especially in light of the positive critical findings. Dr. X responded that he was so sure that the patient was suffering from hysteria that it was difficult for him to seriously consider other possibilities. He told the researchers that although he had initially generated several hypotheses, these were more the result of being videotaped than an honest conviction that these hypotheses were reasonable contenders. Did it not disturb him that there were negative findings for his HY hypothesis? asked the researchers. Dr. X responded that some negative findings were likely, even for the correct hypothesis. He concluded by saying that he was sure that the patient was experiencing severe hysteria.

Dr. Y's conversation was equally informative. He told the researchers that he initially thought the patient was experiencing conversion hysteria. His initial six positive findings tended to confirm this suspicion. However, the patient's response to question number 116 suggested to him that she might have multiple sclerosis, and so he formally generated that possibility. Then he felt he had two reasonable hypotheses and that his plan of attack was to differentiate the two maladies. Over the next 175 questions he was able to rule out the hysteria hypothesis in favor of multiple sclerosis.

If we strip away the medical trappings, we can draw several additional lessons for hypothesis generation (beyond not engaging Dr. X as our personal physician). These amplify and extend the three lessons discussed early in the chapter.

LESSON 4—The proper use of hypotheses is to direct our search for more data. A hypothesis is a beacon in the night, lighting our path to problem solution.

Once Dr. Y had narrowed the search to two legitimate contenders, his plan of attack called for evidence to *differentiate* the two diseases. Basic to his plan of attack was the use of if-then reasoning to establish the likely consequences or evidence if a hypothesis were true. We will have more to say about this form of reasoning in the section discussing that topic.

Furthermore, in order to evaluate his hypotheses properly, Dr. Y asked more than twice as many questions as did Dr. X.

LESSON 5—Generate many hypotheses and allow them to compete in the problem-solving arena. Develop only real contenders—no straw-men hypotheses.

While it would appear that Dr. X generated more hypotheses than Dr. Y, according to Dr. X's own testimony, only the hysteria hypothesis was seriously considered. In problem solving strong conceptual competitors are needed, not straw-men that are paraded out to impress the boss. When Dr. Y generated the MS hypothesis, he treated it as a serious possibility.

Is there any upper limit to the number of hypotheses that can be simultaneously evaluated? Two recent studies suggest that problem solvers are capable of maintaining between four and seven hypotheses at any one time.[4] Now that you know this, you cannot afford to be satisfied with only one hypothesis.

LESSON 6—Don't prematurely commit to a hypothesis. Truly suspend judgment until enough facts are in. Tolerate ambiguity for a while and keep an open mind.

The researchers speculated that Dr. X committed himself to the hysteria hypothesis at an early point because of his inability to tolerate the ambiguity associated with an unresolved diagnosis. They speculated that Dr. X was psychologically unable to cope with the pressures of an unresolved problem, and thus he opted for the HY hypothesis. Is this mere speculation? While broad generalizations are not yet appropriate, I will shortly present some research I conducted on problem-solving effectiveness and intolerance of ambiguity in the business environment. The findings support the contention that managers who cannot tolerate ambiguity tend to be ineffective problem solvers and, incidentally, ineffective managers.

LESSON 7—Don't ignore disconfirming or negative evidence; it is as important as positive evidence.

Dr. X's greatest downfall was his inability to assimilate the negative critical findings for the hysteria hypothesis. There have been many empirical studies demonstrating that problem solvers fail to give adequate weight to negative information.[5] Contemporary psychologists have merely provided experimental evidence of an observation made several centuries ago by Francis Bacon in a discussion of the "idols" (mental weaknesses) of the mind."

> It is the peculiar and perpetual error of the human intellect to be more moved and easily excited by affirmatives than by negatives; whereas it ought properly to hold itself indifferently exposed toward both alike. Indeed in the establishment of any true axiom, the negative instance is the more forcible.[6]

Successful problem solvers must be as open to negative evidence (even when it destroys a pet explanation) as to confirming evidence. There is an apocryphal story told about the prolific inventor Thomas Edison. When asked if he was discouraged because the first 10,000 experiments to perfect the electric light had failed, he responded: "No, now I know 10,000 things that will not work." For the successful problem solver, failure to confirm a pet hypothesis can be informative. Probably Dr. X was unreceptive to the negative evidence because he was psychologically committed to his hypothesis. No matter how much negative evidence he obtained, he discounted its importance.

As a successful problem solver, you must never allow your ego or psychological makeup to close your eyes to negative evidence. Otherwise you may end up as the main character in the following tale:

> Two learned teachers were involved in a deep philosophical discussion. "Since you're so smart," said one, "try to answer this question: Why is it that when a slice of buttered bread falls to the ground, it always falls on the buttered side?" As the second educator was somewhat of a scientist, he decided to run an experiment. He buttered a slice of bread and dropped it, and it landed with its buttered side up. He then shouted triumphantly, "So where is your theory now!" And the first educator responded, "You think you're so smart! You buttered the bread on the wrong side."

Applying Hypothesis Generation Lessons to the Business World

Are individuals who can tolerate ambiguity better problem solvers than those who cannot? Are managers who are superior problem solvers, better managers? Several years ago Tom Urban and I conducted a study to determine the impact of problem-solving attitude and ability on managerial performance.[7]

On the basis of their job evaluations, fifty-one first-line production supervisors of a midwestern manufacturing company were classified as outstanding or average by the division manager. Each supervisor was given a battery of behavioral and intellectual tests to measure problem-solving abilities. The subjects were male and ranged from thirty to sixty years in age. Before administering the tests, the division manager sent a personal letter to each participant explaining the significance of the testing program. The letter also explained that the company wished to determine what factors accounted for supervisory success. The subjects were assured that results from the testing program would not be used in their job evaluations for the upcoming year. The tests, which took two hours, were administered on company time in four sessions composed of approximately thirteen subjects each. The problem-solving measures constituted the independent variables in the study. The dependent variable in the study was the job performance rating of each supervisor.

Blocks to Problem Solving: Although there are several blocks to effective problem solving, only three were chosen for inclusion in this study. Perhaps of prime importance is the *intellectual block*. A manager cannot solve problems with a shortage of intellectual ammunition. We utilized the Watson-Glaser Critical Thinking Appraisal to assess the supervisors' problem-solving capabilities. The appraisal taps the following five dimensions of critical thinking:

1. The ability to define a problem.
2. The ability to select pertinent information for the solution of a problem.
3. The ability to formulate and select relevant and promising hypotheses.
4. The ability to recognize stated and unstated assumptions.
5. The ability to draw conclusions and to judge the validity of inferences.

The *information processing blocks* can restrict data gathering and evaluation. Problem solving can occur only when the problem solver processes the necessary information. Dogmatic individuals reject data that are inconsistent with strongly held beliefs. Consistency of beliefs, rather than data worth, is the rule for accepting or rejecting data. Schulze's Dogmatism Scale, a twenty-item 'instrument, was used to measure the supervisors' levels of dogmatism.[8]

Emotional blocks may interfere with a problem solver's ability to explore and manipulate ideas and concepts. Adams suggests that a common emotional block is the problem solver's inability to tolerate chaos.[9] Because a problem is a state of chaos, and problem solving is a process of transforming ambiguity into clarity, we thought the ability to tolerate moderate levels of ambiguity would be an important behavioral trait of an effective problem solver. Since ineffective problem solvers cannot deal with ambiguity, they cope as best they can.

Coping With Ambiguity: One coping tactic is to stop searching for relevant data and to offer premature solutions—solutions that are frequently incorrect (a solution-minded rather than a problem-minded strategy). Budner's Intolerance of Ambiguity test was used to assess the supervisors' ability to tolerate chaos.[10]

Another coping tactic is problem avoidance. If problems are avoided, anxiety is postponed; and tomorrow the problem may disappear. Clearly supervisors who avoid problems are unlikely to be effective managers. The Edwards B and the Edwards F scales from the Edwards Personality Inventory were used to measure the tendency to avoid problems and liking for set routines, respectively. The test scores for the five measures are presented in Exhibit 5-7.

Managerial Profile: An inspection of Exhibit 5-7 reveals that the supervisors rated as outstanding scored *higher* on the Watson-Glaser Critical Thinking Appraisal and *lower* on the remaining four test instruments than did their average-rated counterparts. Thus a profile of a successful manager emerges: He or she is a superior critical thinker and problem solver, open to new ideas, tolerant of ambiguity, copes effectively in unstructured and fluid situations, and searches for problems.

Exhibit 5-8 is a brief questionnaire that you and your colleagues can answer to determine your openness to new ideas and your ability to tolerate chaos or ambiguity. Please respond to each statement by assigning the number from the following seven-point scale that most closely corresponds to your feelings: (1) strong diagreement, (2) diagreement, (3) mild disagreement, (4) neutral, (5) mild agreement, (6) agreement, (7) strong agreement.

While it is always dangerous to infer too much from a single

Exhibit 5-7: Test scores for problem-solving measures

Block	Measure	Test instrument	Average-rated supervisors (N = 24)		Outstanding-rated supervisors (N = 27)		Score interpretation
			Mean	Variance	Mean	Variance	
Intellectual	Critical thinking	Watson-Glaser Critical Thinking Appraisal Form—YM	66.29	8.79	69.15	8.27	Subjects who score *high are superior* critical thinkers.
Information Processing	Dogmatism	Schulze's Dogmatism Scale	64.38	8.37	58.51	12.34	Subjects who score *low are more open* to new information (less dogmatic).
Emotional	Intolerance of ambiguity (IOA)	Budner's IOA Scale	59.71	9.69	57.29	7.37	Subjects who score *low are more tolerant* of chaos.
	Liking for set routines	Edwards-F Scale	7.67	3.02	4.81	2.58	Subjects who score *low are more effective* in ill-defined and unstructured environments.
	Problem avoidance	Edwards-B Scale	4.96	2.11	4.29	1.58	Subjects who score *low* seek problems.

Exhibit 5-8: Budner's test of intolerance of ambiguity

Statement	Raw score	Converted score*
An expert who doesn't come up with a definite answer probably doesn't know too much.		
*I would like to live in a foreign country for a while.		
There is really no such thing as a problem that can't be solved.		
*People who fit their lives to a schedule probably miss most of the joy of living.		
A good job is one where what is to be done and how it is to be done are always clear.		
*It is more fun to tackle a complicated problem than to solve a simple one.		
In the long run it is possible to get more done by tackling small, simple problems rather than large and complicated ones.		
*Often the most interesting and stimulating people are those who don't mind being different or original.		
What is familiar is always preferable to what is unfamiliar.		
*People who insist upon a yes or no answer just don't know how complicated things really are.		
A person who leads an even, regular life in which few surprises arise really has a lot to be grateful for.		
*Many of our most important decisions are based on insufficient evidence.		
I like parties where I know most of the people more than ones where all or most of the people are complete strangers.		
*Teachers or supervisors who hand out vague assignments give a chance for one to show initiative and originality.		
The sooner we all acquire similar values and ideals the better.		
*A good manager or teacher is one who makes you wonder about the way you look at things.		
Your total score is:		

*For those statements with an asterisk, the converted score is obtained by subtracting your raw score from eight. For non-asterisked statements, the converted score is the same as the raw score.

Source: Adapted from *Measures of Social Psychological Attitudes* by John P. Robinson and Phillip R. Shaver (Ann Arbor, Michigan, Survey Research Center, Institute for Social Research, 1973), p. 401, with permission.

paper and pencil test, this test may provide insight into your problem-solving attitude. Remember, the lower your score the more effectively you deal with ambiguity. How high is high and how low is low? Benchmarks are provided in Exhibit 5-9 for your guidance in interpreting your own score.

Solution Phase

In the solution phase, a problem solver must first determine the consequences of each hypothesis. *If* the patient has multiple sclerosis, *then* she should be blind in one eye; *if* .002" worn-out plates are causing the jamming, *then* new plates should cause the jamming to cease; *if* the cause of Joe Simpson's surliness is new-job jitters, *then* once he has "learned the ropes" the jitters will disappear. We must deduce the consequences of a hypothesis and see if the consequences square with the facts. If the facts do not agree with the consequences, the hypothesis should be rejected.

If-Then Reasoning

Once hypotheses have been generated, successful problem solvers immediately engage in *if-then* reasoning to comprehend the implications of the hypotheses. If-then reasoning guides the problem solver in the search for evidence that will eventually help him or her accept or reject the hypothesis. For if-then reasoning to work, the "then" consequences must be capable of being verified. Better yet, they should be statements that, if

Exhibit 5-9: Useful benchmarks

Sample	Sample size	Score
Outstanding first-line supervisors	27	57.3
Average first-line supervisors	24	59.7
The *mandatory* college freshmen (At most universities unwilling freshmen are used as subjects in psychological experiments.)	50	50.9
Third-year medical students	75	44.3
The author (who may have fudged)	1	36
The author's wife (ditto)	1	57

rejected, lead the problem solver to develop better hypotheses (remember that failure can be informative).

There is no formula that I know of that can make you proficient at sequential if-then reasoning. Like anything else, good if-then reasoning takes training and practice. Here is an exercise to sharpen your skills:

> An employer has three equally qualified candidates for a position—Mr. A, Mr. B, Mr. C. The employer decides to test the three candidates. He tells them: "I have placed a mark on each of your foreheads. Naturally, you cannot see your own mark, but you can see the mark of the other two candidates. The marks are either black or white; when you see a white mark on anybody's forehead, raise your hand. When you know the color of your mark, get up from your seat. *Do not guess.*" All three men raise their hands, but nobody initially gets up. If you were Mr. C, could you determine the color of the mark on your forehead?

Try using if-then reasoning to solve this problem before reading on.

If all the marks were black, then none of the participants would have raised their hands. Since all raised their hands, all the marks cannot be black. Can two of the marks be black? No, for the person with the single white mark would not have raised his hand, and we know that all three participants raised their hands.

Now let's consider one black and two white marks. All three participants would now raise their hands, which agrees with the data. But remember that no participant got up from his seat. Does the evidence square with the two white marks-one black mark hypothesis? Let's draw a picture (it makes no difference for now which participant is shown with the black mark):

A white   B white   C black

If the two white-one black hypothesis were correct, *then* both Mr. A and Mr. B should have immediately known what color mark was on their foreheads. Mr. A should have reasoned that if B raised his hand, it was because either A or C (or both) had white marks on their foreheads. Since C has a black mark, A's mark must be white. Thus Mr. A should have immediately stood up. Similar reasoning can be applied to Mr. B. Mr. C still would not have known what color mark was on his forehead. Thus *if* the two white-one black hypothesis were true, *then* two of the three participants should have immediately stood up. Since no one stood up, this hypothesis is rejected. That leaves only one remaining hypothesis; namely, all three marks must be white and therefore you, as Mr. C, must have a white mark.

If you're still not convinced, let's consider the three white marks hypothesis and examine why the participants did not stand up initially. Let's view the problem from Mr. A's viewpoint. Mr. B raised his hand, which means that Mr. A or Mr. C or both have white marks. Since Mr. C has a white mark, Mr. A cannot be sure of the color of his mark. Similar reasoning applies to Mr. B and Mr. C, which would explain why none of the participants initially stood up.

Now let's revisit the two engineers from Chapter 1 who were trying to improve the production process. You may recall that they had concluded that the process would be improved by installing high-precision bearings. They argued that the same problem had occurred before and that high-precision bearings had solved the problem. Although I did not recognize it at the time, it is now clear that they were not offering a hypothesis or potential solution; rather they were making a dogmatic assertion that, if left unchallenged, would never be evaluated.

By applying if-then reasoning, their dogmatic assertion was transformed into a working hypothesis. I reasoned that *if* high-precision bearings (on order for four months) would improve product quality, *then* inferior bearings would degrade quality. Some cheaper bearings were purchased and installed, and surprisingly the product quality did not deteriorate. Of course the engineers' assertion had not been proven false, but its likelihood was significantly reduced.

After several months product quality was improved, and, as I suspected, it did not involve high-precision bearings. Interestingly, significant cost savings were made by substituting less expensive bearings.

Returning to the world of mind-stretching exercises, you are invited to use if-then reasoning in dealing with the deceitful cabbie:

> One day an emcee of a quiz show got into a cab to
> go to the studio. On the way, the emcee talked

nonstop about his show's popularity and the great following he had. Finally, the driver said, "I'm sorry sir, but I am deaf and my hearing aid has been stolen." At that point the emcee quieted down. After he arrived at the studio, he realized that the cabbie had lied to him. How did he know?[11]

In using if-then reasoning you should beware certain fallacy traps that can snare the unsuspecting. Suppose you reason that *if* hypothesis X is true *then* evidence Y will be found. Suppose that evidence Y is later found. Can you argue that hypothesis X has been proven? Technically no, for you have just committed what logicians refer to as the *fallacy of affirming the consequent*. The statement "hypothesis X is true" is the antecedent, and the statement "evidence Y is present" is the consequent. Remember, in the poker chip example we stated that a single piece of evidence can be the consequence of more than one hypothesis, and therefore to prove that hypothesis X is correct, you must systematically eliminate all other logical contenders that could have accounted for evidence Y. Once this is done, you have verified that hypothesis X is true.

The illogic behind the affirming-the-consequent fallacy can be clearly demonstrated in the following argument:

If I were a Frenchman, then I would be human.
I am human.
So, I am a Frenchman.

Clearly the conclusion is false, even though the preceding statements are true.

It is important to remember that hypotheses are not tested by if-then reasoning; only their consequences are generated.

Another common fallacy trap is called *denying the antecedent*. It goes like this:

If p *then* q.
Not p.
So, not q.

The illogic is demonstrated in the following argument: If my name were John, I would be a male. But my name is not John, so therefore I am not male. Clearly the conclusion is false even though the preceding statements are true. In general, an if-then statement informs us of what will be true if the antecedent is true; it tells us nothing when the antecedent is false.

A successful problem solver avoids these fallacy traps. He or she does not rely on logic alone to test hypotheses. Rather, all hypotheses are subjected, whenever possible, to rigorous verification techniques.

A Side Excursion Into Other Forms of Reasoning

While if-then reasoning is the most useful approach to determine the consequences of a hypothesis, you may find other reasoning techniques useful.

Backwards Reasoning: One of my favorites is backwards reasoning. Normally, when confronted with a problem you start with where you are now and work your way toward a solution (where you want to be). For example, if you plan a trip from Atlanta to Boston, you normally ask yourself, Where will we stop after the first day of driving? After the second day? and so forth. Thinking that starts at the beginning and concludes at the end is logical, reasonable, traditional—and sometimes doesn't work. When you fail to solve a problem with forwards reasoning, reverse the process and begin at the end. In backwards reasoning we focus on the goals or objectives and try to determine the antecedent conditions that, when taken together, will cause us to arrive at our objective. Start at the end or goal and work your way to the beginning. The difference between forwards and backwards reasoning is the difference between finding a needle in a haystack and the needle finding its way out of the haystack.

Try the following problem on your colleagues (you can probably win some money from them):

> Imagine there are ten coins. You and another player will take turns picking up one or two coins at a time. The person who picks up the tenth coin wins the game and all ten coins. Can you devise a strategy so that if you go first, you will always pick up the tenth coin? Remember, think backwards and try to solve the problem before you look at the solution.

If you haven't solved it yet, the solution is shown in Exhibit 5-10.

Your goal is coin 10. In order to select it, you must force your opponent to select either coin 8 or coin 9. If he selects coin 8, you select coins 9 and 10; if he selects coin 9, you select coin 10. In either case you win. In order to force your

Exhibit 5-10: Ten-coin exercise

1	2	3	4	5	6	7	8	9	10
▲			▲			▲			▲
Subgoal 3			Subgoal 2			Subgoal 1			Original goal

opponent to select coin 8 or 9, you must select coin 7. Now the problem is how to get coin 7. If you can force your opponent to select either coin 5 or 6, then coin 7 is yours, and so is the game. By selecting coin 4, you guarantee that you will select coins 7 and 10 and win the game. You can obtain coin 4 by forcing your opponent to take either coins 2 or 3. Thus all you need to do is select coin 1 and the game is over (although your opponent doesn't know it yet).

Reasoning backwards can be a useful approach. Imagine you have just solved your problem, and step back to where you would have had to be so that you would end up at the solution. This one step back becomes a new subgoal (like coin 7). Work your way back until you reach the starting point; that is, the point where you now find yourself. That is backwards reasoning.

Problem Decomposition: Another useful reasoning technique is problem decomposition. This technique requires breaking down a large problem into a series of subproblems. The idea is to replace a difficult problem with a series of simpler subproblems, thus reducing the problem to manageable proportions.

How many single-elimination tennis matches must be played by 1,136 players before a winner is declared? The problem can be reduced to a more manageable size by substituting 3 players for 1,136. Once the decomposed problem is solved, the answer can be rescaled for the original problem. For 3 players, it will take 2 matches. Why? Because 1 player must win while 2 players lose. For 2 players to lose a match, it will take 2 matches. Thus for a tournament with 1,136 players, there must be 1,135 matches and losers.

Now try a more difficult problem. Remember to decompose the problem, solve the decomposed problem, and then rescale the solution to the original problem. The problem, known as the Tower of Hanoi, is shown in Exhibit 5-11. You are required to transfer all eight discs to another pin. You can only move

Exhibit 5-11: Tower of Hanoi exercise

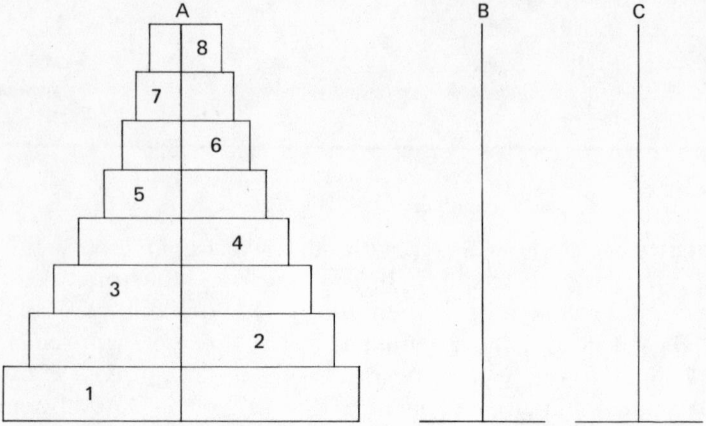

one disc at a time, and a large diameter disc may never rest on a smaller one. What is the minimum number of moves?

Because of the large number of discs, this is a difficult problem. So let's reduce the problem to a more manageable size—say two discs. Move disc 8 to pin C, disc 7 to pin B, and then disc 8 back to pin B. Thus for a two-disc problem, the minimum number of moves is three. How many moves will it take if we enlarge the problem by adding a third disc (disc 6)? In three moves, discs 7 and 8 have been transferred to pin B. Now move disc 6 to pin C—your fourth move. To transfer discs 7 and 8 from pin B to pin C, will take the same number of moves—three—as it did to transfer those two discs originally from pin A to pin B. Thus a three-disc problem requires 3 + 1 + 3 = 7 moves. Enlarge the problem again by disc 5. In seven moves discs 6, 7, and 8 have been transferred to pin C. Move disc 5 from pin A to pin B—your eighth move. To transfer discs 6, 7, and 8 from pin C to pin B will again require seven moves. Thus a four-disc problem requires 7 + 1 + 7 = 15 moves.

Once these smaller problems have been solved, it's time to attack the original problem. The solution is shown in Exhibit 5-12.

Although there are many other reasoning techniques, our side trip must end. For those interested in learning additional techniques, I recommend Wayne Wicklegren's *How to Solve Problems*[12] and Martin Gardner's *Aha! Aha! Insight.*[13]

Exhibit 5-12: Solution to Tower of Hanoi

Number of discs	Solution
2	3
3	3 + 1 + 3 = 7
4	7 + 1 + 7 = 15
5	15 + 1 + 15 = 31
6	31 + 1 + 31 = 63
7	63 + 1 + 63 = 127
8	127 + 1 + 127 = 255

Verification Techniques

Verification is the end of the trail. Verification demonstrates beyond a reasonable shadow of a doubt that a tentative solution is correct. By if-then reasoning we show that if a hypothesis is correct, certain consequences follow. *If* the data are consistent with that hypothesis and no other, *then* the hypothesis is accepted.

But verification does not always follow. However, even failure can be helpful. If hypotheses have been formulated and their consequences reasoned, rejection of a hypothesis is informative because it indicates what is not the cause. Further, the data may suggest certain modifications. This is what happened to Ptolemy's geocentric theory of the solar system. As certain predicted phenomena failed to materialize, additional assumptions and hypotheses were introduced. Because of the excessive number of assumptions necessary to keep the geocentric theory afloat, Copernicus challenged Ptolemy's theory with a simpler, yet more powerful, theory. If hypotheses are used to guide observation, then a failure is informative rather than mere failure.

Managers often commit major errors in verification by jumping to premature conclusions about the cause(s) of a problem. To avoid this error managers need to vigorously test hypotheses. In the Kepner-Tregoe approach, verification is defined as *a process of searching for any exception that can be found to a possible explanation of a problem*. Testing requires determining if a possible cause will precisely produce the evidence found in the *Is* and *Is not* columns in the Diagnostic Worksheet. Ideally, if a potential solution fits all the facts, then it is *probably* the cause of the problem. As was noted earlier, alternative hypotheses not under consideration may also explain the problem symptoms or evidence. Nevertheless, if the hypothesis squares with the facts, it is assumed to be true, and appropriate action is taken.

Inductive Inference: Many years ago I worked for a company that manufactured ophthalmic lenses. The final factory process was the polishing operation to remove pitting and scratches from the lens surface. From experience, the old-timers knew that when the cerium-oxide polishing compound deteriorated (was used beyond one week), the lens quality would drop. One day an operator noticed that the lens quality was unacceptable. He recalled that the polishing compound was over a week old. He therefore reasoned that the cause of the problem was the polishing compound, and he threw it out. Yet, the lens quality failed to improve. What went wrong?

The operator drew an incorrect *inductive inference*. An inductive inference is a logical process by which we draw general conclusions based on sample evidence; it is going one step beyond what is known into the realm of the unknown. Any time you draw a general conclusion, you can be incorrect. Why? Well, the sample may be too small to warrant your general assertion, the sample may not be representative of the population from which you wish to draw an inference, or the data may be consistent with some other hypothesis not presently under consideration.

Consider a classic inductive inference blunder that occurred in the summer of 1936. The *Literary Digest*, a then highly respected periodical, conducted a scientific poll for the upcoming Roosevelt-Landon election. Remember, this was before the advent of the sophisticated sampling techniques now employed by professional pollsters. In an attempt to be scientific, the *Literary Digest* pollsters randomly selected names from telephone books all across the country. Based on their survey, they concluded that Landon would win big. Of course Roosevelt drubbed Landon. In fact, Landon received the electoral votes from only two states—Maine and Vermont. Up to that time, the conventional political wisom was, "As Maine goes, so goes the nation." After the 1936 election, one political pundit rewrote the adage to read, "As Maine goes, so goes Vermont."

Why had the *Literary Digest* been so inaccurate in its prediction? With the 20/20 vision reserved for hindsight, the blunders are obvious. In 1936 the Great Depression was at its worst. The only families that could afford the luxury of owning a telephone were the well-to-do, who tended to vote Republican. Thus the pollsters had primarily surveyed Republicans, and, yes, they were prepared to vote for Landon. Unfortunately for Landon, Democrats outnumbered Republicans by a 2-to-1 margin. So, simply stated, the problem was that the sample chosen was not representative of the voting population.

Now I know what you are thinking—if the inductive-inference process is imperfect, I simply won't use it, and besides, only statisticians and pollsters really use this technique anyway. While it would be ideal to forego inductive inference, it can't be done. Whenever any decision must be made, all the evidence will never be available and therefore, like it or not, you must draw an inductive inference.

Consider a jury trial. The jury listens patiently to the evidence and must decide if the person is guilty or innocent. The jury will never know all of the evidence, because some will be withheld, or some will never be discovered. Therefore the jury's decision is an inductive inference. The outcomes of a judicial inductive inference are presented in Exhibit 5-13.

When a jury makes an incorrect inference, either an innocent person is sent to jail or a guilty person is set free. The judicial system recognizes that a jury can never be absolutely sure of the person's guilt, and that is why the judge will instruct the jury to find the plaintiff innocent or guilty "beyond a reasonable shadow of a doubt."

Similarly, to verify a hypothesis, a manager will often need to draw inductive inferences. Fortunately, there are some techniques that can reduce the chances of drawing incorrect inferences. The methods of induction were developed by John Stuart Mill, a nineteenth-century English philosopher and economist. We shall begin with the most often used (and weakest) technique.

Method of Enumeration (Casual Observation): You're sitting in an office and you notice a leg at the doorway. You immediately

---

Exhibit 5-13: The jury trial as an inductive inference

		THE JURY FINDS THE DEFENDANT:	
		Innocent	*Guilty*
THE DEFENDANT IS TRULY:	Innocent	Correct inference	Incorrect inference: Innocent person sent to jail
	Guilty	Incorrect inference: Guilty person set free	Correct inference

draw an inductive inference that a person will momentarily be walking into your office, just as the operator in the polishing department concluded that the cause of the scratched lenses was the week-old polishing compound. In both instances, inductive inferences were drawn by the method of enumeration. John Stuart Mill defined the method of enumeration as follows:

If event or hypothesis A *and event* B *occur frequently together then* A *is a cause or antecedent of* B.

The process is inferential, for even though we observe only a small sample of events *A* and *B* occurring, we conclude that event *A* is a cause of event *B*.

For many years it was believed that alcohol (event *A*) caused cirrhosis of the liver (event *B*). This inductive inference was based on the method of enumeration diagrammed in the confirmation table shown in Exhibit 5-14.

The symbol $A \longrightarrow B$ means that when we observe an alcoholic (*A*) we simultaneously observe a person with a deteriorating liver (*B*). After finding *n* such people, we draw an inductive inference (*THEREFORE*) that indeed the two factors are related.

In fact, alcohol does not cause cirrhosis. While it is true that some alcoholics do suffer cirrhosis, it is not due to alcohol consumption. Rather, we now know that alcoholics have poor dietary habits, and it is the lack of certain vitamins that affects the liver.

When you saw the leg at your doorway, you reasoned: Every time that I have seen a leg at my doorway (event *A*) it has always had a body attached to it (*B*); therefore I expect to see a person walking through the doorway. That's an inductive inference by the method of enumeration. Similarly, the operator in the polishing department used the method of enumeration to justify throwing out the polishing compound.

Exhibit 5-14: Alcohol/cirrhosis confirmation table

$A_1 \longrightarrow B_1$

$A_2 \longrightarrow B_2$

$\vdots$

$A_n \longrightarrow B_n$

THEREFORE
A (alcohol) causes B (cirrhosis of the liver)

Why we feel compelled to draw inductive inferences is unclear. Perhaps this compulsion is based on our need to reduce the world around us to defined and patterned regularities. Bertrand Russell concluded that even animals use the method of enumeration; he called this method of induction *animal propensity*.[14] He relates an amusing story of a turkey who drew inferences. In September a turkey would hear the noon whistle and see its master approaching. Shortly thereafter the turkey would be fed. This went on for several months. The turkey reasoned as follows: Whenever I have seen my master at noon (event A), I have always been fed (event B). Therefore (and he draws the inductive inference), whenever I see my master at noon I *will always* be fed. On the day before Thanksgiving the turkey paid the price for drawing an incorrect inductive inference.

Enumeration is a simple technique, but it often leads to faulty verification, for it is nothing more than casual observation. The major weaknesses of the method of enumeration are:

1. Leads to overhasty generalizations.

2. Does not consider other factors or hypotheses that could account for the data (event B).

3. Is susceptible to the *post hoc* fallacy trap.

The Latin phrase, *post hoc ergo propter hoc*, means "after this therefore because of this" or because B follows A, A causes B. We fell into this trap when we "proved" that alcohol causes cirrhosis of the liver. For instance, the ancient Chinese were guilty of post-hoc reasoning for they believed that when an eclipse occurred (A), the beating of gongs would cause the eclipse to disappear (B). They "proved" this hypothesis by beating gongs and noting that the eclipse disappeared (B). Later we shall reexamine the ancient Chinese and their beliefs using a more vigorous method of verification.

Although the method of enumeration is useful in *generating* possible hypotheses, it should not be used for verifying them.

Method of Agreement (Systematic Observation): In the method of enumeration we viewed the repeated conjunction of two facts (A and B) and drew an inductive inference. Yet in each instance other facts were present in addition to facts A and B. The method of enumeration simply disregarded these; the method of agreement does not. John Stuart Mill defined the method of agreement as follows:

If event or hypothesis A *is a cause of event* B, *we must*

*demonstrate that the absence or presence of other hypotheses
C, D, E, ... make no difference to the A-B connection.*

Let's use the method of agreement for the following
problem:

> In June the sales manager notices that the actual
> sales for the past several months are below budgeted
> figures (call this event *B*). Based on this knowledge,
> the sales manager generates three possible
> hypotheses:
>
> H_1: Competition may have lowered their price,
> thereby attracting some of the firm's sales.
>
> H_2: Salesmen were not properly compensated or
> motivated, and thus our sales dropped.
>
> H_3: The sales forecast was based on projecting an
> exponential trend that caused us to overestimate
> sales.

The method of agreement requires that all three possible
hypotheses be considered simultaneously. The confirmation
table is shown in Exhibit 5-15.

First, note that we are drawing an inductive inference—based
on only four months of evidence, we are concluding that the
competition's lowered price is a cause of the decline in sales.
How has the method of agreement led us to this conclusion?
Hypothesis two (H_2) cannot be a cause of the sales drop
because in March the firm instituted a new compensation
program (this program could have had nothing to do with the
decline, for as of yet the sales manager was unaware of any
problem), and sales continued to be below the targeted figures.
Of course, motivation could have been the core problem, but
either (1) the new plan did not work or (2) the impact of the
new program will take several months to filter down to the sales
force. These alternative explanations aside, April's data would
tend to eliminate the H_2 hypothesis. The H_3 hypothesis could
not be an explanation since even after the sales forecast was
changed to a more conservative linear trend in February, sales
continued to be under targeted figures.

We can therefore conclude that the H_1 hypothesis is a
probable cause of the unanticipated sales drop, since whenever
H_1 was present, sales were below the targeted figures regardless
of the absence or presence of factors H_2 or H_3. Of course,
another hypothesis not yet considered may actually be the real
cause of the sales drop.

As another example, the family car refuses to start (event B) on some days. The following hypotheses are generated:

H_1: Weak battery
H_2: Clogged fuel line
H_3: Improper timing
H_4: Weak starter
H_5: Carburetor valve sticky

The method of agreement requires that we check to see which of the five hypotheses are present every time the car doesn't start. A typical confirmation table is shown in Exhibit 5-16.

Since H_3 was always present when the car wouldn't start, regardless of the presence or absence of other potential explanations, H_3 is the likely cause of the problem.

Note that it took eleven days to solve the problem because on those days that the car started, there was no need to make systematic observations. Thus, verifying hypotheses by the method of agreement can be a slow process, for like the method of enumeration, the method of agreement is observation-

---

Exhibit 5-15: The sales drop confirmation table

Month	H_1 Present?	H_2 Present?	H_3 Present?	Event B
January	Y	Y	Y	Sales drop
February	Y	Y	N	Sales drop
March	Y	Y	N	Sales drop
April	Y	N	N	Sales drop

THEREFORE
Competitive price cutting (H_1) causes the sales drop

Exhibit 5-16: Confirmation table for the obstinate car

Day	H_1 Present?	H_2 Present?	H_3 Present?	H_4 Present?	H_5 Present?	Event B
1	Y	N	Y	N	Y	Doesn't start
7	Y	Y	Y	Y	N	Doesn't start
9	Y	N	Y	N	N	Doesn't start
11	N	Y	Y	N	Y	Doesn't start

THEREFORE
H_3 (improper timing) causes the car not to start

oriented rather than experimentation-oriented. When an event B occurs (like a car failing to start), all you can do is record the absence or presence of the tentative hypothesis as you construct a confirmation table.

Another major weakness is demonstrated by Max Black's Case of the Logical Lush.[15] A certain habitual drunkard was urged to save himself by abandoning his nightly highball. Being a student of logic, he decided to record what he had drunk in the past several days. The first night he drank rye and soda and got smashed; the second night, rum and soda, the third night, gin and soda; and the fourth night, vodka and soda. Using the method of agreement, he constructed a confirmation table (see Exhibit 5-17).

Since soda water was the only factor that was present every time he got drunk, he concluded, by the method of agreement, that soda water caused his drunkeness. Thus he took a solemn oath that from that day forth he would abstain from soda.

Our logical lush was guilty of two glaring errors. First, the various beverages should have been classified under the generic title of alcohol. Second, the soda water hypothesis is not a reasonable explanation (similarly the glass size—substitute tall glass for soda and you will conclude that tall tumblers cause intoxication). *Hypotheses must always be legitimate contenders!*

In summary, although the method of agreement is an improvement over the method of enumeration, the method of agreement suffers the following weaknesses:

1. Factor misclassification is a potentially dangerous problem.

2. The method can be extremely time consuming.

3. As you can see from the examples, the technique uses the process of elimination and thus is better suited for disproving hypotheses than for confirming them.

Method of Difference (Experimentation Method): Of all the verification techniques, the method of difference is the most rigorous. Factor A, or the hypothesis, is varied while the other factors are held constant, and we determine if event B co-varies. If event B co-varies, then factor A is a cause of event B.

If the ancient Chinese wished to test the gong-banging hypothesis by the method of difference, they could have conducted an *experiment*. When an eclipse occurred, they could have banged the gongs, and, of course, the eclipse would have disappeared. When the *next* eclipse occurred, they would *not* have banged the gongs. Of course, the eclipse still would have disappeared. Therefore they would have proved beyond a shadow of a doubt that banging gongs does not cause an eclipse to disappear (see Exhibit 5-18). If the eclipse had remained when the gongs were not banged, then they would have concluded that the two factors were related.

This method of difference verification technique was used by the vice-president in the Case of the Worn-Out Plates. Recall that the .002″ worn-out plates were thought to cause the slippage. The vice-president reasoned that if worn-out plates were the real cause of the problem, then new plates should stop the slippage problem; that is, he could turn the slippage problem on or off, depending on whether worn-out or new plates were used. When he ran his *confirming experiment* he found that slippage occurred when *both* new and worn-out plates were used. He concluded, by using the method of difference, that the problem wasn't worn-out plates.

Some time later he *hypothesized* that the problem was due to a new ink supplier. He *verified* the hypothesis by the method of difference. He set up two identical machines, both with worn-out (.002″) plates. In one machine he used the old ink, and in the second machine he used the new ink. The same operator was used for both machines. Thus, as far as possible, all the

Exhibit 5-17: Confirmation table for the logical lush

Day	Factor 1	Factor 2	Event B
1	Rye	Soda	Smashed
2	Rum	Soda	Smashed
3	Gin	Soda	Smashed
4	Vodka	Soda	Smashed

THEREFORE
Factor 2 (soda) causes intoxication

Exhibit 5-18: Confirmation table for the gong experiment

Bang gongs	Eclipse disappears
Don't bang gongs	Eclipse still disappears

THEREFORE
The gong-banging hypothesis is rejected

conditions were identical except for the ink. Within fifteen minutes, the plates on the machine using the new ink were slipping, whereas the plates on the other machine were not. By the method of difference, the vice-president concluded that the ink supply was a cause of the slippage problem. He was sure he had solved the problem because *he could turn the problem on or off* merely by changing ink suppliers.

The method of difference is the most powerful technique for verification. To use it, a manager must be able to control the problem environment—such as changing ink sources or not banging gongs. Sometimes managers do not have this amount of control and therefore must substitute observation for experimentation. Given a choice between the systematic observation of the method of agreement or the casual observation of the method of enumeration, the former is preferable.

Conclusion

Although you may not yet be a master craftsman, you should be well on your way to becoming a respected journeyman in the art and science of solving operating problems. The one tool you will need to become a master craftsman is a "SHOVEL." In the following mnemonic "shovel" the lessons of the last two chapters are summarized:

1. **S**pecify the problem using the role-dynamics and Kepner-Tregoe models. A problem that is not specified cannot be solved.

2. **H**ypothesize freely. Don't prematurely commit to a pet hypothesis; be open to disconfirming evidence.

3. **O**riginate novel hypotheses for operating problems, especially the tough problems. Don't fall prey to the "I remember back in . . . " syndrome.

4. **V**erify all hypotheses. If possible use the method of difference; if not, use the method of agreement. Remember, the inductive inference process is laden with pitfalls for the unsuspecting.

5. **E**valuate and **L**earn from your own problem-solving efforts. Do instant replays—use post-mortem sessions—to review your problem-solving process. Which paths were productive? Which were not? By analyzing past successes and failures you will improve your problem-solving batting average.

6. Dig in!

FOOTNOTES

1. Paul Watzlawick, *How Real is Real?* (New York, Random House, 1976), pp. 48-50.

2. Don Koberg and Jim Bagnall, *The Universal Traveler* (Los Altos, California, William Kaufmann, Inc., 1976).

3. Arthur S. Elstein, Norman Kagan, Lee S. Shulman, Hilliard Jason, and Michael J. Loupe, "Methods and Theory in the Study of Medical Inquiry," *Journal of Medical Education*, February 1972, pp. 85-92.

4. Herbert A. Simon, "How Big is a Chunk?" *Science*, February 1974, pp. 482-488; Arthur S. Elstein, Lee S. Shulman, and Sarah Sprafka, *Medical Problem Solving* (Cambridge, Massachusetts, Harvard University Press, 1978).

5. Jerome S. Bruner, Jacqueline J. Goodnow, and George A. Austin, *A Study of Thinking* (New York, John Wiley & Sons, Inc., 1956); Peter C. Wason, "On the Failure to Eliminate Hypotheses," In P.C. Wason and P.N. Johnson-Laird, eds., *Thinking and Reasoning* (Baltimore, Penguin Books, 1968).

6. Francis Bacon, *Novum Organum*, excerpted and retranslated in Charles P. Curtis, Jr. and Ferris Greenslet, *The Practical Cogitator* (Boston, Houghton-Mifflin, 1962).

7. Harvey J. Brightman and Thomas F. Urban, "Problem Solving and Managerial Performance," *Atlanta Economic Review*, July-August 1978, pp. 23-26.

8. John P. Robinson and Phillip R. Shaver, *Measures of Social Psychological Attitudes* (Ann Arbor, Michigan, Survey Research Center, Institute for Social Research, 1973), p. 430.

9. James L. Adams, *Conceptual Blockbusting* (San Francisco, W.H. Freeman, 1974).

10. Robinson and Shaver, *Measures of Social Psychological Attitudes*, p. 401.

11. If the cabbie was deaf, how did he know where the emcee

wanted to go, or how did he know that the emcee had been talking nonstop?

12. Wayne A. Wickelgren, *How to Solve Problems* (San Francisco, W.H. Freeman, 1974).

13. Martin Gardner, *Aha! Aha! Insight* (New York, Scientific American, Inc., 1978).

14. Bertrand Russell, *The Art of Philosophizing and Other Essays* (New York, Philosophical Library, 1968).

15. Max Black, *Critical Thinking* (New York, Prentice-Hall, 1952), p. 297.

6
Diagnosing
Strategic Problems

In the last two chapters we focused on solving operating problems. We now shift our attention to solving strategic problems, or what is more commonly called managerial decision making. We will reintroduce the enriched rational model first presented in Chapter 1 and use it as a vehicle for discussing the art and science of managerial decision making. In this chapter we focus on problem diagnosis, setting objectives, and designing alternative solutions.

"You can observe a lot by just watchin'."
—YOGI BERRA

"It is better to stir up a question without deciding it than decide it without stirring it up."
—JOSEPH JOARBERT

"You ain't learnin' nothin' when you're talkin'."
—LYNDON JOHNSON

"I ask for more information because I am unable to unscrew the inscrutable."
—SAM ERWIN

What are the differences between operating and strategic problems? Operating problems are encountered by an organization on a day-to-day basis and can be characterized as deviations from expected or anticipated performance. When operating problems occur, the manager must diagnose the cause and correct the problem. At the other end of the problem-solving spectrum, managers must deal with strategic problems—problems that are important in terms of actions taken, resources committed, or precedents set. The goals of strategic problem solving are to decide where a department, division, or company should be, and how to get there. Simply stated, solving operating problems is *reactive* and solving strategic problems is *proactive*. Once again we'll follow the model that we discussed in Chapter 1.

Enriched Rational Model Review

The first step is problem awareness (Exhibit 6-1, 1). If a

Exhibit 6-1: The enriched rational model

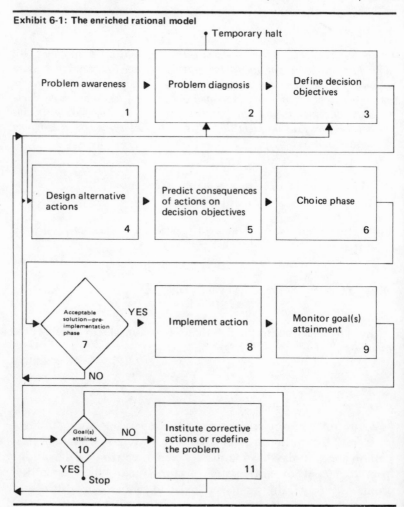

manager is unaware of a problem, then no problem-solving activity can take place. Unlike operating problems that come looking for solutions, strategic problems require that managers seek possibilities for exploitation. Because managers are usually busy solving current operating problems, it is difficult to get them to look for the strategic problems—tomorrow's opportunities.

One way, according to George Steiner, a respected management theorist and practitioner, is for managers to conduct periodic situation audits of their division or firm to identify opportunities, threats, strengths, and weaknesses that might be exploited.[1] A situation audit is used to analyze the trends and forces having the greatest potential significance for the firm. A typical situation audit would include a series of thought-provoking questions focusing on an analysis of customers and markets, an evaluation of the firm's competition, the financial performance of the firm, and the political, technological, social, and legal trends in the industry. Such an audit, if done properly, can make management aware of areas in need of managerial decision making.

Strategic problems uncovered by a situation audit must then be diagnosed or conceptualized (2). The role dynamics and Kepner-Tregoe methods are not appropriate for diagnosing strategic problems. Instead, the decision-science diagnostic method is recommended. This method helps a manager conceptualize a strategic problem by focusing on four important elements: controllable actions, uncontrollable events, interrelationships, and outcomes. Once the problem has been conceptualized, the manager should determine if the costs of solving the problem outweigh the potential benefits. If so, the problem should be temporarily shelved.

If the cost-benefit ratio is acceptable, the manager should then define the decision objectives (3), generate alternative solutions to the problem (4), and tentatively select a solution (5), (6). The manager should generate many alternative solutions, because the final solution can be no better than the original set of choices.

Once an alternative is selected, it should be preimplemented (7). In other words, the manager should attempt to determine if there will be any serious negative consequences to the adoption of the solution. If there will be serious potential problems, the manager might (a) consider more alternative actions, (b) redefine the decision objectives, or (c) redefine the problem itself—that is, take a new look at the problem.

The manager should then implement the solution (8) and monitor whether or not the goals are attained (9). If the goals (10) are not met, then corrective action should be taken (11). If corrective action fails to bring the solution "on track," it may be that the problem was diagnosed incorrectly. In this case the manager must rediagnose the problem and cycle through the process again.

Now, let's focus on each step of the enriched rational decision-making model in greater detail.

Problem Diagnosis and Conceptualization

What is half of eight? Everyone knows that half of eight is four. Or is it? If you bisect the number "8" with a vertical line you get a "3"; if you bisect it with a horizontal line you get a "0." It's all in how you look at the problem.

Similarly, in the business world there is always more than one way to conceptualize a strategic problem. But in the rush to "solve the problem," one may accept an improper diagnosis and thus never solve the real problem. By and large, American managers consider problem diagnosis unnecessary—thus the need for a problem diagnosis phase.[2]

Decision-Science Diagnostic Method

You will find it useful to diagnose strategic problems by using the following four elements:

1. *Controllable actions*—These are actions that are under the manager's control.

2. *Uncontrollable events*—These are events beyond the manager's control that affect the likelihood of attaining the goals or objectives. Uncontrollable events include competitors' actions, governmental policies, etc.

3. *Interrelationships*—These describe how controllable actions and uncontrollable events interact to generate outcomes.

4. *Outcomes*—Outcomes measure the degree to which a manager attains his or her decision objectives. In business decisions, dollar outcomes are paramount.

If you apply these four basic elements to a strategic problem, you will understand the problem before attempting to solve it.

Parking-Meter Roulette Problem: Consider how the four-element decision-science diagnostic method could be used to analyze the following "parking-meter roulette" problem. Pretend you are driving along looking for a parking space on the street. Finally you find an empty space, and now you face a decision. First, what is your decision objective?—to park your car with minimum expense (thus outcomes are measured in terms of dollar outlay). What are the controllable actions?— clearly the alternative actions are "to pay" or "not to pay" the meter. Well, what's the problem?

I think it is clear, even in this trivial decision, that certain events over which you have no control will play an important role—that is, will your car be ticketed by the meter maid? Thus the actual outcome (or dollar outlay) associated with the pay or don't pay alternatives depends on whether the meter maid walks by and tickets the car. The interrelationships between the controllable actions and uncontrollable variables of this problem can be illustrated by a decision-tree diagram (Exhibit 6-2).

Interrelationships should also be specified in written form to provide a permanent record of the problem diagnosis. For the parking-meter roulette problem, the written diagnosis would be as follows: If I pay, then it will cost me fifty cents for sure; if I choose not to pay, then the outcome depends on whether the meter maid happens by, an event I have little or no control over. If she walks by and tickets my car, then it will cost me twenty-five dollars; if she doesn't walk by and ticket my car, it will cost me nothing.

Even for this minor problem, the decision-science diagnostic method forces the decision maker to consider how the controllable actions and uncontrollable events interrelate to determine the dollar outcomes. Once a specification has been developed, the decision maker can reality-test it against the problem environment. In short, the decision-science diagnostic method is a *discipline for making the implicit explicit.*

Exhibit 6-2: Diagnosis of the parking-meter roulette problem using a decision-tree diagram

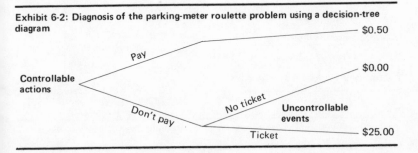

Competitive Market Problem: Let's consider a more realistic strategic problem. A firm operates in a competitive market where price levels are essentially fixed, either by regulation or by industry price leaders.[3] The firm must decide on an optimal production level and an optimal advertising policy for its products. A problem diagnosis developed from the decision-science diagnostic method, using a box diagram, is shown in Exhibit 6-3.

The problem is diagnosed once more using the four basic elements:

1. *Controllable actions*—The actions available to the firm (within the limited context of this problem) are the desired production levels and the desired advertising expenditures. There probably are constraints on the controllable actions—for example, advertising expenditures cannot exceed 2 percent of sales. These constraints must be specified by the decision maker.

2. *Uncontrollable events*—Certain events are beyond the

Exhibit 6-3: Diagnosis of a production and advertising strategic problem using a box diagram

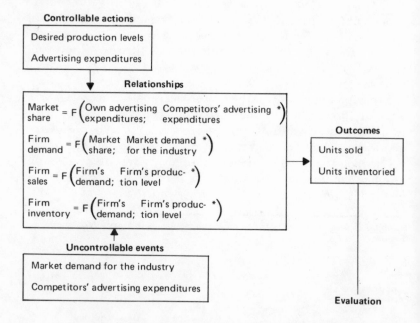

*F (a; b) = Function of variable *a* and variable *b* depends on the level of variables *a* and *b*.

control of the individual firm. We assume that the market demand for the industry depends on the overall economic environment, which cannot be controlled but can be forecast with some degree of accuracy. We also assume that the competitors' advertising expenditures cannot be controlled but may be predicted from past behavior.

3. *Outcomes*—The relevant outcomes are units sold and units inventoried.

4. *Relationships*—The relationships describe how controllable actions and uncontrollable events interrelate to generate outcomes. The following relationships are shown in Exhibit 6-3:

    a. *Market share relationship*—The firm's share of market is assumed to be a known function of the firm's own advertising level relative to its competitors' level of advertising. Based on its history, the higher the firm's advertising expenditures, as compared to competition, the greater will be its share of market.

    b. *Firm demand relationship*—The firm's unit demand is a function of the market share (determined in relationship *a*) and the general market demand for the industry (e.g., *Firm demand = Market share x Market demand for the industry*).

    c. *Firm sales relationship*—The firm's unit sales depend on the firm's demand and the firm's production level (e.g., if demand is greater than production, then sales equal production; if demand is less than production, then sales equal demand).

    d. *Firm inventory relationship*—The firm's inventory level also depends on the firm's demand and the firm's production level (e.g., if demand is greater than production, then units inventoried are zero; if demand is less than production, then inventory equals production less demand).

With this diagnosis in hand, the manager should have a better understanding of the problems and opportunities facing the firm. This will ultimately lead to better solutions.

Why do we *need* to use the decision-science diagnostic method? Simply stated, we are poor diagnosticians; we are all children of Dr. X.

Common Failures in Diagnosis

Based on his extensive problem-solving experience, Russell

Ackoff has compiled the three most common errors made in diagnosing strategic problems.[4]

1. Our view of the actions we can take is unduly constrained.

Company X must reduce the cost of a component it is now producing by 25 percent if the product is to remain competitive. For many months the company has been struggling to reduce this cost by improving the production process but has been unable to reach the 25 percent goal. The corporate managers are discouraged. Actually, the problem is improper diagnosis. The company has not recognized that if the problem were conceptualized as, Can any company produce the product for 25 percent less? (Can we buy the product?), rather than, Can we produce the product for 25 percent less? the goal might have been reached. The "make versus buy" conceptualization of the problem opens up avenues that were never considered because the range of controllable actions was artificially restricted to internal cost-reduction or production-improvement programs.

Why do managers view strategic problems from only one perspective? The reasons are varied. Improper diagnosis may be due to organizational or time constraints. Perhaps this company had solved previous strategic problems within the four walls of the plant. Thus when this problem occurred, managers were inclined to do so again. On the other hand, poor diagnosis may be due to individual constraints. Not everyone is tolerant of ambiguity, open to new ideas, or is a superior critical thinker. These three important constraints were addressed in Chapter 2. However, another reason for an improper diagnosis may be that the manager did not go through the discipline of *making the implicit explicit*. Had the manager developed a formal diagnostic diagram, he or she might have discovered before attacking the problem that the "buy" option had never been considered.

Before attacking a strategic problem, ask yourself, "Have I thought of all the possible controllable actions available to me?" At least initially, do not be constrained by organizational precedent or what others tell you is possible. Remember, the more alternatives you develop, the more likely you are to understand the true scope of a problem. If you enlarge the scope of a problem, does it open up more controllable actions? What happens if you reduce the scope? The way you initially diagnose a problem should not restrict your willingness to explore new definitions or conceptualizations.

2. We often focus on uncontrollable events when we should be focusing on controllable actions (and vice versa).

Several years ago I directed the Small Business Institute Program at Miami University in which graduate students were assigned to local companies in need of financial counseling. One of the firms sold water recreational equipment. Since sales were highly seasonal, the owner asked the students to develop a forecasting technique that could accurately predict fluctuations in sales. While the team was reviewing available techniques, one of the members brought up an interesting point. He wondered, Why focus on better sales forecasting techniques? He argued that the owner should eliminate the highly seasonal sales (a controllable action) rather than attempt to predict the seasonal pattern (an uncontrollable event). The team then recommended that the firm sell winter recreational equipment, which would smooth out the highly fluctuating sales. The firm did that, and the seasonal sales fluctuations were eliminated.

By focusing on more accurate techniques for estimating sales, the owner had improperly conceptualized the problem. The owner had focused on uncontrollable events when he should have been addressing the issue of what he could do about sales fluctuations—namely, controllable actions.

Conversely, failure in diagnosis sometimes results because decision makers focus on controllable actions when they should be considering uncontrollable events. As an example, a small company is about to launch a new product—clearly a strategic decision. The manager is attempting to determine what price should be charged for the product. After several weeks of considering the problem, the manager has arrived at the following diagnosis:

> The sales for the first year will be 10,000 units and will increase by 20 percent per year. The initial selling price will be ten dollars per unit, although I am prepared to examine other alternatives. In subsequent years, the initial price will be increased to reflect the impact of inflation on production costs.

Can you tell from the above diagnosis what implicit assumptions were being made by the manager?

First, it is quite obvious that the manager has focused solely on controllable actions. Indeed, he has even assumed that sales volume is a controllable action; that is, that he can increase sales by 20 percent per year. What about the consumers? Further, he has not considered what the competition will do (an uncontrollable event). While he attempts to increase sales by 20 percent per year, will his competition sit on their hands? If he were to rely on this naive diagnosis and go ahead and introduce the product, the venture would probably end in failure.

3. We view uncontrollable events as if they are forever beyond control.

Uncontrollable events are events over which we have little or no control—*now*. Consider the following example: A firm has experienced many problems because it has only one supplier of an important material. Occasionally, the firm has had to shut down because of delays in delivery. The company has done all it can to alleviate the problem by stockpiling, by searching without success for another supplier, and by looking for an alternative material. The problem remains. Why not attack the source of the problem? Why not acquire the supplier and eliminate the source of uncertainty?

There are many uncontrollable events that we may never be able to control—inflation rate, union demands, etc. But simply because an element in a strategic problem is now uncontrollable does not mean it must remain that way. One of the motivating factors behind recent acquisitions and mergers may be the desire to gain control over the previously uncontrollable—to transform uncertainty to certainty. As you develop your diagnosis, ask yourself, "Must uncontrollable variables remain so, or can I take action to make them controllable?"

Applications of the Decision-Science Diagnostic Method to Selected Strategic Problems

Now that we have introduced the decision-science diagnostic method and warned you about the common failures in diagnosis, you need an opportunity to develop your diagnostic skills. For the following two strategic problems, your mission (should you choose to accept it) is to conceptualize and diagnose the true problem facing the firm, rather than the initial definition of the problem provided by the manager. In short, you are asked to decide if half of eight is four, three, or zero.

The Product-Abandonment Decision: When should a product line be dropped? Far too many firms retain products without ever explicitly making the decision to abandon. Rather, many products overstay their welcome, tying up capital that could be efficiently used in introducing new products. Imagine that you are the marketing manager and you want to develop an explicit procedure for evaluating products and taking action on those that warrant it. Let's diagnose this problem by using the decision-science diagnostic method.

First, decompose the product-abandonment problem into controllable actions and uncontrollable events. Don't be myopic. Brainstorm if you like, for the more variables included in your diagnosis, the more likely you are to see the full implications of the problem. Now stop and, without looking ahead, develop a list of controllable and uncontrollable variables for this problem.

Now, compare your list of variables with the list shown in Exhibit 6-4. Are there any major differences? Does your list include controllable variable 2-alternative options to simply dropping an unattractive product? Did you consider that the firm could take action to make the product profitable again? If you didn't, then you implicitly assumed (there's that word again) that the product-abandonment decision is simply a yes/no decision. By including controllable variable 2 in the diagnosis, an alternative view to product abandonment has been offered. It may turn out that this alternative is not particularly useful. However, it may open up new avenues to explore instead of putting all the effort into determining what is the "best" criterion for retaining or discarding products. Do you see that by including controllable variable 2 in your specification, you must now decide whether to concentrate on product abandonment or product redesign? Regardless of which route you take, the results will be better because you initially explored different possible definitions of the problem. In your specification did

---

Exhibit 6-4: A list of potential variables for product-abandonment decision

Controllable actions	Uncontrollable events
1. Criteria for abandonment: declining sales, declining profit	1. Number of consumer complaints
	2. Declining sales profits
2. Alternative options to abandonment: product design modifications, lower price, new advertising program, market survey, cost cutting, etc.	3. Impact on other products if a product is dropped
	4. Outcome of consumer survey
3. Disposal policy for production equipment	5. Consumer tastes
4. Manufacturing cost	

you consider the impact on the other products if an unattractive product were dropped—the cross elasticity of demand (uncontrollable variable 3)? Frequently problem solvers take too myopic a view of the boundaries of the problem. They forget that a business is a system of interconnected elements, and if one element is altered, its impact causes a ripple effect throughout the organization. In Chapter 3 we suggested that it is often necessary to enlarge your view of the problem; uncontrollable variable 3 certainly does that. Now if you chose the product-abandonment problem definition, and you failed to include uncontrollable variable 3 in your analysis, your diagnosis would be naive and your decision incorrect.

Once a list of variables has been generated, a problem diagnosis diagram helps the problem solver visualize the interrelationships between all of the variables. Since the decision-tree diagram format (Exhibit 6-2) and the four-box format (Exhibit 6-3) have already been utilized, the flowchart format will be used in this problem (Exhibit 6-5).

In turn, each of the boxes could be further decomposed. The "evaluate attractiveness of options" module could be subdivided into a series of submodules involving both controllable actions and uncontrollable events. The purpose of the diagnostic diagram is to ensure that the problem is properly specified and that no important controllable action or uncontrollable event has been omitted in the diagnosis.

"To Drill or Not to Drill?"—That is the Question: Wildcatters Inc. has a serious problem. The company holds an option to

---

Exhibit 6-5: Diagnosis of the product-abandonment decision using a flowchart

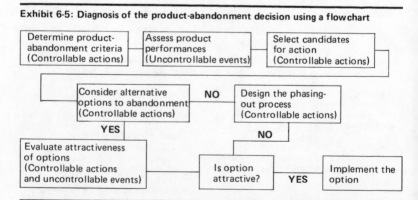

Source: Adapted from *Normative Models in Managerial Decision-Making* by Lawrence A. Gordon, Danny Miller, and Henry Mintzberg (New York, National Association of Accountants, 1975), pp. 50-51.

drill for oil on plot number 2200 in the Midlands Texas Oil Field. Wildcatters Inc. has already signed a firm contract with a major oil company to sell out immediately for one million dollars if they drill and strike oil. The purchaser takes his chances on the amount of oil and gas that will actually be recovered. Let's diagnose the problem facing Wildcatters Inc. What are the controllable actions and uncontrollable events in this decision?

"Why, that's simple," says J. Paul Gitty, president of Wildcatters. "The only controllable action is whether or not to drill for oil on plot number 2200, and the only uncontrollable event is whether oil or gas will be found." Now we could accept Mr. Gitty's diagnosis, but we also know that one of the most common diagnostic faults is that decision makers often fail to consider all the possible actions they can take. Stop here, and before reading on, diagnose the problem facing J. Paul. Do you agree with J. Paul's diagnosis?

Now let's ask J. Paul to review the problem once more. Are there any other controllable actions available? J. Paul recalls that certain geologic tests can be run that may provide a better assessment of the possibilities of gas or oil on the property. Unfortunately, these tests are costly and are not infallible. Sometimes the test results indicate the presence of oil or gas when in fact there is none; sometimes the test results indicate no oil or gas when in fact there is. If J. Paul includes the possibility of conducting or not conducting geologic tests as a controllable action, then an additional uncontrollable event will be generated—namely, the results of this geologic study. The interrelationships between controllable actions and uncontrollable events are shown in Exhibit 6-6.

If a geologic test is conducted, the results will either be favorable or unfavorable, but regardless of the results, since the test is fallible, Wildcatters Inc. must decide whether to drill. If the company chooses to drill, it will either strike oil or gas or come up empty. Is the diagnosis presented in Exhibit 6-6 realistic? We should now show the diagnosis to J. Paul and again ask him to reconsider it. More specifically we should ask him the following questions:

1. If you broaden the scope of the problem by considering the impact of this decision on your *other* lease options, what additional controllable actions and uncontrollable events should be incorporated into your diagnosis?

2. Have you omitted any important controllable and uncontrollable variables?

Exhibit 6-6: Diagnosis of Wildcatters Inc.'s problem using a decision-tree diagram

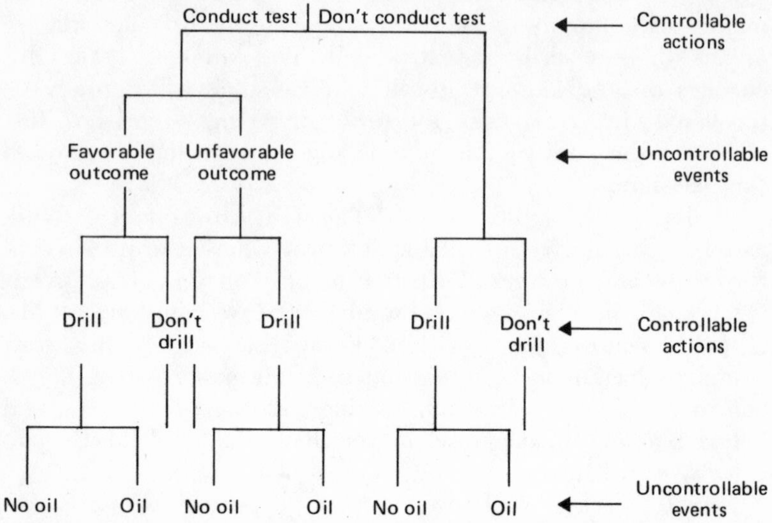

3. Are there any variables now listed as uncontrollable that could be controlled?

4. Have you confused controllable and uncontrollable variables?

By listing all of the variables and portraying their inter-relationships in a diagnostic diagram or flowchart, not only is the diagnosis improved, but the chances of solving the right problem are also enhanced. How a problem is conceptualized has a great bearing on the kinds of alternative solutions generated. An improper diagnosis is fatal in strategic problem solving.

Background on the Booker Industries' Problem

Before continuing with the strategic problem-solving phases, we need to introduce the strategic problem that will serve as a focal point for the remainder of this chapter as well as for Chapter 7: How to generate a sales and profit growth of 15 percent per year (in constant dollars) for the next five years.

Booker Industries has just completed a five-year strategic plan that calls for a sales and profit growth rate of 15 percent per year in constant dollars. Based on an assessment of its present strengths and weaknesses, management is aware that unless new strategies are formulated, there is no way of attaining these corporate objectives—present policies will simply not work. Initially, top management considered two alternative problem definitions. They could concentrate on *internal growth* by developing new product lines and investing heavily in research and development, or they could concentrate on *external growth* by implementing an acquisition program. Based on an assessment of controllable actions (such as cash position of firm, top-management strengths, and degree of acceptable risk) and uncontrollable events (such as the capital markets, general business environment, and stock markets), Booker Industries chose the acquisition route. Now that the initial decision has been made, Booker Industries' management has prepared a diagnostic flowchart outlining the remaining decisions facing the firm (Exhibit 6-7).

In our discussion of the remaining phases of the enriched rational model for decision making, we will focus only on the first two modules in Exhibit 6-7. Once the best acquisition candidates have been determined, a series of additional decisions will have to be made—that is, how much to offer, the financial package, the timing of the acquisition, etc.

Defining Decision Objectives

Simply stated, objectives are desired goals or ends. Decision objectives are derived from the overall goals of an organization and from interest groups that will be affected by the decision. If

Exhibit 6-7: A diagnostic flowchart of the Booker Industries' acquisition problem

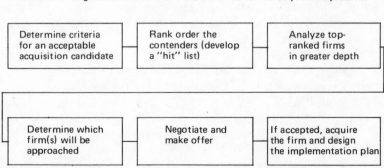

an important interest group's position is omitted in formulating objectives, the resulting decision is likely to create more problems than it solves.

Criteria for Decision Objectives

The properties of acceptable decision objectives are outlined in the following paragraphs in no special order of importance.

Duration: Objectives can be classified as either short-term or long-term. Short-term objectives focus on a one- to three-year time horizon, whereas long-term objectives focus on a three- to seven-year time horizon. Although alternative actions should always be evaluated on their long-term consequences for a firm, we know that greater weight is often given to short-term decision objectives.[5] This is especially true when organizations face crises. To survive an immediate threat, long-term objectives are often devalued.[6] These self-defeating practices should be avoided in managerial decision making; short-term and long-term objectives are equally important.

Measurable: Objectives are not objectives until they have been operationally defined. If a decision objective is to "improve morale," we must define morale so that it can be measured on some scale. We could measure improved morale by (1) the number of grievances filed with the shop steward or (2) the amount of absenteeism. Clearly alternative actions cannot be evaluated unless the objectives are measurable.

Concrete: Objectives should be stated in concrete terms, not vague generalities. "Increase sales to 30,000 units" is superior to "increase sales"; "reduce downtime by 5 percent" is superior to "reduce downtime." Making objectives concrete is especially necessary for the class of objectives called *major objectives* that is discussed below.

Attainable: Objectives must be set realistically; otherwise no alternative actions will be found that meet the objectives, which in turn will lead to frustration. In deciding that downtime must be reduced by 5 percent, the goal must be realistic in terms of the known strengths and weaknesses of the firm.

Flexible: Objectives should not be written in stone. If a large number of alternative solutions look attractive, the objectives should be escalated to levels that will require additional effort to reach them. On the other hand, if no alternatives are found that meet a set of objectives, the objectives should be relaxed.

Priorities: Not all objectives are equally important in attaining organizational goals. Objectives should be ranked in terms of their importance. Later in the chapter a simple procedure for rank-ordering objectives will be presented.

Types of Objectives

Objectives can be classified as *Major or Minor Objectives*. A major objective, or a *must*, is so important that an alternative action that fails to meet that objective is disqualified from further consideration. Major objectives act as filtering devices, for only the alternatives that meet major objectives are considered further. Often major objectives are stated in concrete terms.

Minor objectives, or *wants*, are less important to the organization, and failure to attain these does not warrant automatic rejection of an alternative action. Minor objectives must be rank-ordered in terms of their importance in attaining organizational goals.

Application to the Booker Industries' Problem

Now that Booker Industries has decided on an acquisition program, it must develop a "hit" list of attractive candidates. The hit list will serve to rank order acceptable acquisition candidates.

The setting of decision objectives is a decision itself. Often there are conflicts between powerful groups, and the decision objectives are the result of compromise and consensus. Why do conflicts arise? Managers often take a myopic view of the organization; they view it as a group of fiefdoms rather than as an integrated whole. Given this world view, conflicts as to what is in the best interests of the organization (read here—my area) are likely to arise.

In this problem we are unlikely to have conflict in setting the decision criteria because the CEO and the senior staff are likely to agree on the basic mission of the organization. In a series of meetings they have reached a consensus that alternative acquisition candidates will be evaluated on eight objectives, three major and five minor. The objectives are listed in Exhibit 6-8.

Exhibit 6-8: Booker Industries' decision objectives for potential acquisition candidates

Type	Description	Measure	Duration	Rank/weight
Major				
Product line compatability	The product line of an acquired firm must be consistent with the long-term mission of our firm.	Pass/fail	Long-term	—
Minimum annual sales	The sales of an acquired firm must be at least $50 million. Below this, the acquired firm would be too small to have an impact on our firm.	Pass/fail	Short-term	—
Dilution of earnings per share	In purchasing an acquired firm, our earnings per share must not be diluted by more than 10 percent. Sales price will be estimated based on total market value of the acquired company. Purchase based solely upon issuing common stock.	Pass/fail	Short-term	—
Minor				
Future sales potential	An estimate of the average sales-growth percentage that an acquired firm could sustain over the next five years.	Percentage	Long-term	4.0
Profit/net worth	The ratio of profit to net worth over the past five years.	Ratio	Short-term	1.8
Synergy	The potential for synergy between our firm and an acquired firm in the distribution and warehousing channels. (1 = no synergy; 10 = maximum synergy.)	A scale from 1 to 10	Long-term	3.2
Managerial reputation	An assessment of the strengths and weaknesses of the senior management of an acquired firm. Based on the opinions of the financial community. (1 = weak; 10 = strong.)	A scale from 1 to 10	Long-term	2.0
Legality of combination	The likelihood of a challenge by the Justice Department as to the legality of the acquisition (1 = challenge extremely likely; 10 = no challenge). (By reversing the rating, we have consistency across the board—higher ratings are better than lower ratings.)	A scale from 1 to 10	Short-term	1.0

Rank Ordering Minor Objectives

Once the objectives have been specified, the minor objectives must be rank ordered. Assuming for the moment that there is a single manager and not a group, a straightforward approach is to:

1. Generate all possible pairs of minor objectives.
2. For each pairing, specify which objective is more important.
3. Resolve any inconsistencies in the rank orderings that may result from step 2.

The manager has underlined the most important objectives for all possible pairings:[7]

1. <u>Future Sales Potential</u> (FSP) vs. Profit/Net Worth (P/NW)
2. <u>Future Sales Potential</u> vs. Synergy (SY)
3. <u>Future Sales Potential</u> vs. Reputation (R)
4. <u>Future Sales Potential</u> vs. Legality (L)
5. <u>Profit/Net Worth</u> vs. Synergy
6. <u>Profit/Net Worth</u> vs. Reputation
7. <u>Profit/Net Worth</u> vs. Legality
8. <u>Synergy</u> vs. Reputation
9. <u>Synergy</u> vs. Legality
10. <u>Reputation</u> vs. Legality

Let's check the consistency in the rank ordering implied by the decision-maker's responses. Logic requires that if objective A is more important than objective B and objective B is more important than objective C, then objective A *must be* more important than objective C. This requirement is called transitivity. Intransitivity, or inconsistencies in the rank ordering, can be assessed by diagramming the responses to the pairwise comparisons.

The rank orderings for the first four comparisons are shown here:

In pairwise comparison 5 the decision maker stated that the P/NW ratio was a more important objective than SY. Accordingly, the objectives hierarchy diagram is redrawn:

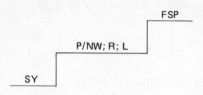

Please insert the responses to the sixth and seventh comparisons and verify that the diagram shown below accurately reflects the decision maker's choices:

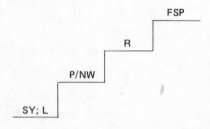

In comparison 8 the decision maker stated that the SY objective was more important than the R objective. Do you see that this is inconsistent with the manager's first seven pairwise comparisons (note in the last diagram that Reputation is a more important objective than Synergy)? Thus we have an intransitivity that must be resolved.

We must ask the manager to reconsider the pairwise comparisons. After much thought the manager again evaluates all possible pairs of minor objectives:

1.	FSP	vs. P/NW		6.	P/NW vs.	R
2.	FSP	vs. SY		7.	P/NW vs.	L
3.	FSP	vs. R		8.	SY	vs. R
4.	FSP	vs. L		9.	SY	vs. L
5.	P/NW	vs. S		10.	R	vs. L

We leave it to you to verify that there are no logical inconsistencies in the rank ordering of objectives implied in these choices.

Based on the pairwise comparisons, the decision maker was able to rank order the five objectives in descending order of importance:

> Future Sales Potential
> Synergy
> Managerial Reputation
> Profit/Net Worth Ratio
> Legality of Combination

Assigning Weights to Minor Objectives

Next, weights must be assigned to each minor objective. This can be done by assigning values to the minor objectives along a scale from 1 to 100. Specifically:

1. The most important objective is assigned a score of 100.

2. The remaining objectives are placed on the scale to reflect their importance with respect to the most important objective.

3. The numerical weight of an objective is then computed by the following ratio:

$$\frac{\textit{Value assigned to an objective}}{\textit{Value assigned to the least important objective}} = \textit{Numerical weight}$$

Let's apply this scaling procedure to the Booker Industries' problem:

Assigning weights to minor objectives

1	10	20	30	40	50	60	70	80	90	100
		L		P/NW R				SY		FSP

The importance of the five minor objectives is summarized in the following objective-weightings table:

Legality of Combination:	25/25	= 1.0
Profit/Net Worth Ratio:	45/25	= 1.8
Managerial Reputation:	50/25	= 2.0
Synergy:	80/25	= 3.2
Future Sales Potential:	100/25	= 4.0

Extensions to Group Decision Making: Nominal Group Technique

In group decision making the weighting procedure has to be modified slightly. Individual members should independently generate their rankings for the minor objectives. Through a round-robin procedure, each group member presents his or her rankings to the group without discussion. All ideas are summarized. After all rankings have been presented, there is discussion. Using a silent, independent voting procedure, the group then develops a final rank ordering for all the minor objectives. Likewise the scaling procedure is modified to permit discussion of the individual weight assignments. The goal is to develop a consensus on the assigned weighting factors.

Generating Alternative Actions

What is rationality in decision making, and how does it affect alternative generation? According to classic economic theory, rationality is embodied in "economic man" who is assumed to know all courses of action and what the outcomes of any action will be. Economic man always selects the best alternative. In short, economic man is omnipotent.

But decision makers are not omnipotent; they live in a world where lack of time, resources, and knowledge are facts of life. In Herbert Simon's view, decision makers can't *maximize*; rather, they *satisfice*—they strive to find alternative actions that are "good enough."[8] Alternatives are generated one at a time and evaluated. If the alternative meets or exceeds all the objectives, the search process ceases and the alternative is implemented. In the enriched rational model we take a middle ground between maximizing and satisficing (is it *maxificing*?). We recommend that *the decision maker generate as many alternative actions as possible within the time and resource constraints, rather than generating alternatives one at a time.*

Of course, not all the constraints are real; some are self-imposed. Information costs fall into the former category. In searching for alternative actions, the benefits from additional search should always outweigh the costs. When information costs more than it is worth, it is time to stop searching for alternatives and proceed with the decision making. Viewed in this light, classic economic rationality that calls for generating all alternative actions would be irrational!

Organizations often constrain alternative actions. When faced with a novel problem, some firms will seek innovative actions, while others prefer actions that are "tried and true"—small modifications of what they are already doing. Back in Chapter 2 we summarized some of the more important organizational barriers to innovation:

1. Highly stable organizational environments.
2. Over-reliance on SOPs.
3. Highly centralized organizations.
4. Preoccupation with status and its associated symbols.

Beyond these sedative forces, Calvin Taylor suggests that if you want to stifle creative solutions to problems you should nurture the following organizational climate:[9]

1. Stress the "one best way" of doing things.
2. React negatively to new concepts.
3. Never reward creative effort.
4. When all else fails, ostracize creative individuals.

Groups also constrain alternative generation. Under conditions first described in Chapter 2, groups are susceptible to the "groupthink" pathology. Groupthink refers to a deterioration in the decision-making capability above and beyond the members' individual problem-solving abilities. The number and type of alternatives considered are carefully monitored by the group. Alternative actions that might cause conflict within the group are squashed. The unthinkable cannot be thought; only alternatives that the entire group can accept are considered. Often the range of alternatives considered is severely limited.

Beyond groupthink, problem-solving groups often restrain creativity. Van De Ven and Delbecq offer a number of reasons:

1. Groups become focused on one train of thought to the exclusion of other alternatives.
2. Individuals participate only to the extent that they view themselves as competent.
3. Subordinates often feel constrained to agree with their superiors even when they have better solutions.
4. More dominant (not expert) individuals monopolize the meeting.
5. Groups devote as much time to the personal needs of their members as they do to generating alternative actions.[10]

To a large degree, many of these problems can be avoided by practicing the consensus leadership skills discussed in Chapter 3.

Problem-solving groups will become effective when they are effectively led.

Finally, individuals constrain alternative actions; we are all Dr. X. In the haste to solve problems, we often stop our search for alternatives long before the costs outweigh the benefits or time becomes a limiting factor. Until we learn to cope with the ambiguity and uncertainty of an unresolved problem, we will remain our worst enemy.

How a strategic problem is perceived and diagnosed has a significant impact on the kind of alternative actions generated. In an interesting study by Richard Norman, decision-making teams reacted to a major reduction in materials requirement for a firm that resulted in a 25 percent reduction in direct manufacturing cost.[11] Each team diagnosed the opportunity differently. Several teams examined the marketing implications, although even here there were striking differences—efficient level of sales versus desired share of market. Other teams focused on developing efficient operation procedures. Because of the different diagnoses, the strategies generated by the teams bore little resemblance to one another.

Decision makers cannot overcome all constraints. Rather, they should strive to overcome the controllable constraints (including themselves and the groups they work within) and not fret about the noncontrollable ones. That is the beginning of wisdom.

Who Generates Alternative Actions?

Who generates the alternative actions in large part depends on the decision maker's leadership style. Autocratic leaders generate alternative actions themselves. Consensus leaders share the decision with their subordinates, and together they generate alternative actions. The leader's function is to act as a coordinator for the group.

In Chapter 2 we argued that a decision maker must be flexible and capable of adopting any of the five leadership styles (Consensus, Consultive Autocrat I-III, Autocrat).

So who generates the alternative actions? While it will change from decision to decision, *it should always depend on the eight problem characteristics and the recommended leadership style from the Vroom and Yetton Leadership Selection Flowchart.*[12]

Generating Alternatives: Search or Design?

There are two schools of thought regarding the generation of alternative actions. Proponents of the systematic school argue that alternative actions are out there waiting to be found and that we need to develop procedures for finding them. They compare alternative generation to finding a needle in a haystack.

Proponents of the creative school disagree. They view alternative generation as a process of design or creation *ex nihilo* — alternatives don't exist but have to be conceived, designed, and constructed. Design proponents liken alternative generation to designing a house. We think both arguments have merit. Generating alternatives is both a search and design process. First we will examine the more common search procedures, and then we will discuss several creative-enhancement techniques for designing alternative actions.

Prospecting for Alternatives

The search procedures are presented in the order of the demands in time and effort they place on the decision maker.

Passive Search: Instead of searching for the needle, we wait for the needle to find us. Passive search is waiting for unsolicited alternatives to appear. In this view not only are organizations searching for alternatives, alternatives are searching for organizations. Passive search is a prevalent alternative-generating approach in acquisition decisions. Firms let it be known to financial intermediaries that they are available for the "dating game" and would like to be introduced to a few, selected acquisition-minded firms.

Alternatives are often looking for problems to solve. Mandatory sentencing or gun control (depending on where you stand) always seem to surface during a crime wave. Some have referred to this phenomenon as the mating approach to search.[13] For example, a worker is killed in a crane accident. Advocates of a new crane-control device seize the opportunity to promote the new device, even though there may be no link between the old control equipment and the accidental death.

Search Generators: This involves putting out feelers—activating "search generators"—to produce alternatives, such as letting suppliers know that the firm is looking for certain equipment or asking investment firms to recommend a few acquisition candidates. A major advantage to this approach is that it opens up the decision process to individuals from outside the organization whose world views may significantly differ from those of management. External search generators can produce innovative alternatives.

Neighborhood Search: Since organizations, like people, wish to avoid drastic change, managers search for alternatives in the neighborhood of what they are already doing. New alternatives are incremental modifications of existing options. While exciting and innovative alternatives are unlikely to be found, they have a high likelihood of being implemented if adopted. Charles Lindblom refers to this search procedure as "muddling through."[14]

Historical Search: The search for alternatives is strongly influenced by past behavior. If in the past alternative A was a reasonably good solution for decision B, then a new problem resembling decision B will generate the same or similar alternatives. This approach might also be called *analogy search*. When faced with a decision, we tend to search for a similar decision we have already made. Solutions generated for the new decision will be modifications of previously successful alternatives. In short, solutions are recycled until they no longer work—the Peter Principle applied to alternative generation.

Divergence Search: The previous four techniques can generate a large number of alternative actions, but they may all be qualitatively similar. Divergence search systematically seeks alternatives that are different from what has been or is now being done. Often outside consultants or colleagues from other departments can suggest alternatives that they have tried but that are novel to your particular situation. As a manager, you should seek their input. After all, a radical solution in one area may be commonplace in another.

You can take some actions on your own to improve the quality of alternative actions. Once you've generated a tentative list of alternative actions, ask yourself, "Given these alternatives, what fundamental assumptions have I made, or what constraints have I self-imposed?" Often, managers do not realize that certain of their world views inhibit the alternatives generated. This was dramatically illustrated in the Pentagon Papers' account of the development of the Vietnam policy. During repeated crises, strikingly similar options emerged from the administration's deliberations. Why weren't really different alternatives ever seriously considered? Apparently because all the options that emerged were based on the fundamental assumption that the "domino theory" was correct. Given this world view, the similarity of the options was a foregone conclusion.

Often we are not even aware of fundamental assumptions. Make them explicit, challenge them, and generate additional alternatives that result from a different world view.

Designing Alternatives

Designing alternatives is a creative, costly, and time-consuming process. When design processes are used to generate alternative actions, we find that fewer options are proposed.[15] The design process is complex and not well understood. As in architecture, the designer begins with an ideal image of what he or she wants the final product to look like (in our context, an alternative that meets or exceeds all the objectives). As an initial alternative crystallizes, the designer gropes along, refining the alternative brick-by-brick, until a fully proposed alternative emerges. The designer may not know what the final alternative will look like until it has been completed. Design, especially the design of alternative solutions, remains an area of vast ignorance.

Two general design procedures have been proposed. They are presented in ascending order of creativity.

Modified Design: The modified design approach is a sequential process. Search techniques are used to generate a stream of ready-made alternatives; then design processes are used to modify them. Practically speaking, this approach reduces the start-up costs associated with design by providing a set of base alternatives from which other alternatives can be designed.

Let's see how this process works. A company wishes to select a data base system. It has used several of the aforementioned search techniques to generate a list of five alternative data base systems. Based on the technology available in the marketplace, the manager develops an image of an ideal data base system, including the appropriate bells and whistles unique to his firm's requirements. The manager will then either resume his search for the ideal alternative or request several firms to submit prototypes that, as far as possible, match the decision maker's concept.

In the modified design approach, design bridges the gap between what is available (ready-made alternatives) and what is desired (the ideal alternative). In this case, design is more like remodeling a home than initially designing it.

Custom-Made: The manager begins with a set of objectives and designs an option(s) that promises to meet the objectives. There is, of course, give and take between the option and the objectives. Constraints are factored into the design process. After much compromise, coercion, and creative insight, a fully designed alternative emerges. As we said earlier, generally only one custom-made option is developed because of cost and time constraints.

Recently, at Georgia State University a new MBA program was proposed. The designers (a group of five faculty members) began by developing a goals statement enumerating the skills and knowledge-base the manager of the eighties and nineties must possess. With this image in mind, they designed a series of educational modules that promised to meet their objectives. In their initial deliberations they operated as if they were not constrained by internal factors (possible parochial attitudes of the department chairman) or external factors (accreditation requirements of the American Assembly of Collegiate Schools of Business). They realized that if they prematurely constrained the design process, they would probably redesign the present program.

The educational modules were then reviewed by administration and faculty. Modifications were made in the modules as well as in the goals. Eventually the modified modules were translated into specific courses. The courses were then subjected to further modification and the program was eventually submitted to the faculty for formal approval. For a variety of reasons, the faculty rejected the program.

We can gain insight into the design process by analyzing why the faculty rejected the MBA program. Perhaps the major reason was that the general faculty felt they had little input to the design process—specifically, in designing the goals statement (the ideal image of an MBA program) and in the initial design of the courses. By the time the general faculty became involved, they felt (rightly or wrongly) that the MBA program was a *fait accompli.* This created an atmosphere in which the design team's motives were questioned.

An important lesson from the rejection of the MBA program is that creativity techniques, such as brainstorming, synectics and lateral thinking, are not sufficient. Design is more than merely creating innovation; it is a communications process, and *one-way* communication is not enough. While the faculty design team was creating the MBA, it kept the general faculty informed on its progress, but this was not enough. What the team should have done (note that Monday-morning quarterbacks are infallible) was to seek or demand input from the general faculty—*two-way* communications—to reality-test the design assumptions and program elements. A design team should not view its job as designing alternative solutions; rather, a team should view itself as a catalyst or venture group whose mission is to *initiate*, *sustain*, and *manage* the design process.

Group Structure

Often a problem requires a consensus leadership style in which subordinates are involved in generating alternatives. In Chapter 3 we focused on *group processes*; that's how a manager ought to direct the group. Now we shift our focus to the issue of *group structure*. Is one group structure more effective than another in generating innovative alternatives?

In a study to evaluate the impact of group structure on creativity, Van De Ven and Delbecq examined three different group structures:[16]

1. An *interacting group* begins with a problem statement and is followed by a group discussion and generation of alternatives.

2. A *nominal group* uses a structured process in which members privately generate alternatives (personal brainstorming or lateral thinking) and then present their ideas to the group in a round-robin fashion. An open discussion ensues in which alternatives are classified and perhaps expanded. Alternatives are then ranked by a silent voting procedure (this last aspect focuses on the choice phase in decision making).

3. A *delphi group* uses a structured procedure in which group members are not permitted to interact and may remain anonymous. The group leader collects individual alternatives, reformulates them, and provides members with the reformulated alternatives. The members then reevaluate their alternatives and the process is repeated. After a number of iterations, agreement as to which alternatives are best emerges.

In the Van De Ven and Delbecq study, the nominal and delphi groups not only generated more alternatives but generated more innovative alternatives. Creative thinking is more likely to flourish when individuals within a group setting work independently of each other. Having more people generating more alternatives does help, but *how* the group operates makes a great deal of difference.

One crucial aspect relating to the generation of alternatives remains to be discussed and that is the degree of closure between the diagnosis and alternative generating phases in strategic problem solving. Closure refers to the linkage or degree of feedback between two phases. High closure means that once a problem has been defined, redefinition should not take place while the decision maker either searches for or designs alternatives. We believe that high closure is counterproductive, for it fails to recognize the simple fact that any problem can be conceptualized in different ways; and if one conceptualization fails to generate workable alternatives, we ought to rethink our diagnosis. To do otherwise is to be dogmatic.

Applications to the Booker Industries' Problem

Using a variety of search procedures, the long-range planning group of Booker Industries generated six potential acquisition candidates for evaluation:

Lancaster Inc.	Continental Numerics Inc.
Crow Technology	Computer Technics
Advance Systems Inc.	Apex Business Equipment

Several alternatives were recommended by an investment banker (search generation); Crow Technology approached the firm (passive search); and the remainder were generated by selecting firms that were either similar to previous acquisitions (historical search) or similar to the present divisions (neighborhood search) within the company.

FOOTNOTES

1. George A. Steiner, *Strategic Planning* (New York, Free Press, 1979).

2. Peter F. Drucker, "What We Can Learn from Japanese Management," *Harvard Business Review*, March-April 1971, pp. 110-122.

3. Marvin H. Berhold and John Y. Coffman, III, "Decision Science Concepts—Foundation for the Future," *Business*, January-February 1979, pp. 9-16.

4. Russell L. Ackoff, *The Art of Problem Solving* (New York, Wiley Interscience, 1978).

5. Allan Easton, *Complex Managerial Decisions Involving Multiple Objectives* (New York, John Wiley & Sons, Inc., 1973).

6. Carolyne Smart and Ilan Vertinsky, "Designs for Crisis Decision Units," *Administrative Science Quarterly*, December 1977, pp. 640-657.

7. If you're wondering why we didn't ask the decision maker to rank order all five objectives at once, it's because psychologists have found that such a procedure can strain the cognitive limits of the decision maker.

8. Herbert A. Simon, *Administrative Behavior*, 3rd Ed. (New York, Free Press, 1976).

9. Calvin W. Taylor, *Climate for Creativity* (New York, Pergamon Press, 1972).

10. Andrew H. Van De Ven and Andre L. Delbecq, "The Effectiveness of Nominal, Delphi, and Interacting Group Decision Making Processes," *Academy of Management Journal*, December 1974, pp. 605-621.

11. Richard A. Norman, "Business Decision Making: A Phenomenological Approach," *California Management Review*, Winter 1967, pp. 59-64.

12. Victor H. Vroom and Philip W. Yetton, *Leadership and Decision Making* (Pittsburgh, Pennsylvania, University of Pittsburgh Press, 1973).

13. Richard M. Cyert and James G. March, *A Behavioral Theory of the Firm* (Englewood Cliffs, New Jersey, Prentice-Hall, 1963).

14. Charles E. Lindblom, "The Science of 'Muddling Through'," *Public Administration Review*, Spring 1959, pp. 79-88.

15. Richard C. Snyder and Glenn D. Paige, "The United States Decision to Resist Aggression in Korea: The Application of an Analytical Scheme," *Administrative Science Quarterly*, 1958, Vol. 3, pp. 341-378.

16. Van De Ven and Delbecq, "Effectiveness of Group Decision Making Processes," pp. 605-621.

7

Solving Strategic Problems

In the previous chapter the diagnosis, decision-objective setting, and alternative-generation phases were discussed. In this chapter we present the remaining phases of the enriched rational model of decision making.

"Logical consequences are the scarecrow of fools and the beacons of wise men."

—THOMAS HUXLEY

"There's small choice in rotten apples."
—SHAKESPEARE

Twixt the optimist and the pessimist
The difference is drole;
The optimist sees the doughnut
The pessimist sees the hole.
—McLANDBURGH WILSON

"If you torture the data long enough, it will confess."
—RONALD COASE

Once the decision objectives have been defined and rank-ordered, and the alternatives have been generated, the decision maker must estimate the consequences of each alternative on all the decision objectives. After this is done, it is a relatively simple process to determine the best alternative.

Estimating Consequences of Alternative Actions

Estimating the consequences of actions on objectives is not a new idea. Its roots can be traced back to Ben Franklin. While Franklin's exploits as a statesman, author, and scientist are well known, he was also an early advocate of systematic decision making. Consider the following letter to Joseph Priestly, the discoverer of oxygen. Priestly was trying to decide whether to accept a new position and sought Franklin's advice. Franklin wrote:

> In affairs of so much importance to you, wherein you ask my advice. I cannot, for want of sufficient premises, counsel you what to determine: but, if you please, I will tell you how.

> When these difficult cases occur, they are difficult, chiefly, because, while we have them under consideration, all the reasons pros and cons are not present to the mind at the same time. Hence the various purposes or inclinations that alternatively prevail, and the uncertainty that perplexes us.

> To get this over, my way is to divide half of a sheet of paper by a line, into two columns: writing over the one "pro" and over the other "con." Then, during three or four days' consideration, I put down under the different heads, short hints of the different motives that at different times occur to me for or against the measure.

> When I have got these together in one view, I endeavour to estimate their respective weights, and, where I find two (one on each side) that seem equal, I strike them both out. If I find a reason "pro" equal to some two reasons "con," I strike out the three reasons. If I judge some two reasons "con" equal to some three reasons "pro" I strike out the five: and thus proceeding, I find, at length, where the balance lies: and if, after a day or two of further consideration, nothing new that is of importance occurs on either side, I come to a determination accordingly.

> And, though the weight of reasons cannot be taken with algebraic quantities, yet, when each is thus considered separately and comparatively, and the whole lies before me, I think I can judge better, and am less liable to make a rash step; in fact, I have

found great advantage from this kind of equation in what may be called *moral or prudential algebra*.

Wishing sincerely that you may determine for the best, I am ever, my dear friend,

Yours most affectionately,

Benjamin Franklin

Generating Consequences

Now what does moral algebra have in common with generating consequences in the enriched rational model? Franklin's moral algebra emphasizes the examination of the consequences of alternative actions: "during three or four days of consideration, I put down under the different heads, short hints of the different motives that at different times occur to me for and against the measure." The remainder of Franklin's letter details a procedure for choosing the best course of action and is similar, in spirit if not detail, to the procedures outlined in the subsequent choice phase.

The goal in this phase of decision making is to estimate the consequences of the alternative actions on the decision objectives and to construct an *alternative-consequence matrix* similar to that shown in Exhibit 7-1.

Exhibit 7-1: Alternative-consequence matrix

							Objectives
Alternatives	O_1	O_2	O_3	$\cdot$	$\cdot$	$\cdot$	O_m
A_1	C_{11}	C_{12}	C_{13}				C_{1m}
A_2	C_{21}	$\cdot$	$\cdot$				$\cdot$
A_3	C_{31}	$\cdot$	$\cdot$				$\cdot$
$\cdot$	$\cdot$	$\cdot$	$\cdot$				$\cdot$
$\cdot$	$\cdot$	$\cdot$	$\cdot$				$\cdot$
$\cdot$	$\cdot$	$\cdot$	$\cdot$				$\cdot$
A_n	C_{n1}	$\cdot$	$\cdot$				C_{nm}

C_{ij} is the consequence of alternative action i (i = 1, 2, 3, . . . n) on objective j (j = 1, 2, 3, . . . m).

The consequences (C_{ij}'s) are the equivalent of Franklin's "pros and cons." Consequences are measured either as pass/fail or by numbers. Major objectives or *musts* are measured on a pass/fail scale. If an alternative action meets or exceeds a *must* objective, it is given a pass; if it fails to meet a *must* objective, it is given a fail. Only those alternatives that pass *all* the *must* objectives are considered further.

The consequences for the minor objectives or *wants* are represented by numbers. Because we often assign numbers without understanding their implications, a brief excursion into the properties of measurement scales is unavoidable.

Consider four departments (A, B, C, and D) with profits of $100,000, $75,000, $50,000 and $25,000, respectively. What can we infer from these numbers? First, Department A made twice as much profit as Department C and four times the profit of Department D. In other words, the ratio of the two numbers is meaningful. We can also say that the difference in profit between Departments A and D is three times larger than the difference in profit between Departments C and D [($100,000 − $25,000) ÷ ($50,000 − $25,000)]. Thus the ratio of the two intervals is meaningful. Finally, we can say that Department A made the greatest profit, Department B made the second largest profit, and so forth. In other words, we can rank-order the departments along a profitability index. Therefore, if the consequences of an objective exhibit the following three properties:

1. the ratio of two *numbers* is meaningful,
2. the ratio of two *intervals* is meaningful, and
3. the *rank ordering* is meaningful, then

the consequences are measurable on a *ratio or cardinal scale*. Time, weight, and dollars exhibit these three properties.

Is temperature measurable on a cardinal scale? Only if the ratio of two temperatures is meaningful. Is 80° F twice as warm as 40° F? No, for if we convert °F to °C (26.66° F; 4.44° C), the ratio is no longer 2:1. Temperature (in °F or °C) is *not* measurable on a ratio scale. Is the ratio of two intervals meaningful? Is the jump from 10° F to 30° F twice as great as the jump from 10° F to 20° F? The ratio is 30 − 10 ÷ 20 − 10 = 2 and will still be two even if we convert °F to °C. Also, we can say that 30° F is warmer than 10° F, which is warmer than 0° F—rank ordering is meaningful. If consequences exhibit the following two properties: (1) the ratio of two intervals is meaningful and (2) rank ordering is meaningful, then the consequences are measurable on an *interval scale*.

One step below the interval scale is the *ordinal scale*. An ordinal scale permits only rank ordering. Ratios of numbers *or* intervals are meaningless. For example, we might decide to rate wines as either lousy, mediocre, amusing, or outstanding. We could assign any four numbers to these categories as long as the numbers preserve rank order (the higher the number, the better the wine). The following sets of numbers could be assigned to the winetasting categories: (1, 2, 3, 4), (−7, −6, 900, 42,107) or (1, 1.5, 800, 200,106,014).

In summary, consequences on the *must* objectives are measured as pass/fail; consequences on the *want* objectives are measured on at least an ordinal scale.

The problems in assessing the consequences of alternatives depend on (1) the degree to which uncontrollable events, such as actions by other parties or factors beyond our control, intervene and make assessment difficult and (2) the manager's knowledge of the decision environment. Under the best of conditions, there are no intervening uncontrollable events, and the decision maker knows the consequences of any action; this situation is called assessing consequences under certainty. Under the worst of conditions, the decision maker does not even know what the important uncontrollable events in the environment are, and assessing consequences is impossible; this situation is called assessing consequences under confusion. Under those circumstances, we recommend that the decision maker rediagnose the problem to obtain a better understanding of its dynamics.

Fortunately, total confusion is rare. Assessing consequences under certainty, uncertainty, and risk are the most common situations in industry.

Assessing Consequences Under Certainty

This is the simplest of all possible worlds. When the consequences of an alternative action on an objective are known with certainty, the assessment procedure is straightforward. For example, when you are looking for a job and are considering several alternatives, one of your objectives is salary. The dollar consequences for each alternative on the salary objective are known because you have firm offers in hand. The salary offers would be inserted into the salary objective column of the alternative-consequence matrix (Exhibit 7-1).

Often the consequences of an alternative can be predicted with certainty by merely doing some detective work. Suppose you are considering purchasing a home, and one of your objectives is the quality of the local school system. You could rate each home (each alternative action) on the effectiveness of the local school system merely by checking with the board of education, talking to parents in the neighborhood, or meeting with the principals. The school ratings would then be inserted into the alternative-consequence matrix.

In the last example we assumed that there were no uncontrollable events that could affect the ratings of the school system. Suppose you discovered that a certain principal was the major reason behind a school's reputation and that he might be transferred in the near future. The consequence, or the rating of the school, would not be known with certainty because it would depend on uncontrollable events—namely, whether the principal was transferred and who replaced him.

Under certainty, the only problems in assessing consequences are time and effort. Additional problems arise when uncontrollable events intervene and make the prediction of consequences difficult.

Under *uncertainty*, the decision maker knows what uncontrollable events affect the consequences but is unwilling or psychologically unable to assign probabilities to the likelihood of their occurrence. Under *risk*, the decision maker is willing or able to assign probabilities.

Assessing Consequences Under Uncertainty

As an example, Joe Williams is faced with a difficult decision. His company has just been awarded a contract to produce ten thousand servocontrols. He has a choice of either machining or stamping the control unit housings. Both processes are experimental, and Joe is not certain that they will work, but those are his only alternatives (at least that is what he maintains). The consequences—expressed as net profit—depend on whether the processes will ultimately be successful. However, before all the uncertainty is resolved, Joe must make a decision to either stamp or machine the parts, for it will take several weeks to set up the production line regardless of which approach he chooses. This mini-decision can be represented by an *alternative-*

uncontrollable-event matrix (not to be confused with an alternative-consequence matrix). See Exhibit 7-2.

What should Joe Williams do? Under uncertainty, Joe is either unwilling or unable to assign probabilities to the uncontrollable event. Two possible strategies (there are more, but these will not be discussed) can be used to resolve Joe's dilemma.

Pessimist Strategy: We would recommend this strategy to Joe if he is an eternal pessimist. Pessimists believe that no matter what action they take, the worst always happens. If they take an umbrella, it doesn't rain; if they don't take an umbrella, it rains. If they purchase 999 out of 1,000 lottery tickets, they lose; and if they purchase all 1,000 tickets, the lottery will be declared illegal. Given this outlook, a pessimist strategy is to select the alternative action that is the *best of the worst*. Let's apply the best-of-the-worst strategy to Joe Williams' dilemma (Exhibit 7-3).

Joe reasons that if he stamps, the process will fail, and he will make a $2,000 profit. If he machines, the process will also fail, and he will lose $20,000. Since these are the worst consequences, Joe should select the best of the worst and choose the stamping process.

Exhibit 7-2: Alternative-uncontrollable-event matrix

		Uncontrollable event
Alternatives	Process successful	Process fails
Stamp	$55,000	$ 2,000*
Machine	70,000	−20,000

*If stamping fails, Joe can subcontract the order to XYZ Company who has the expertise to make this process work.

Exhibit 7-3: Applying a pessimist strategy

	Uncontrollable event		
Alternatives	Process successful	Process fails	Worst consequences
Stamp	$55,000	$ 2,000	$ 2,000 (Best of the worst)
Machine	70,000	−20,000	−20,000

If maximizing profit were the *only* objective, the decision would be made—stamp the housings. However, if there were multiple objectives, the worst consequences ($2,000, −$20,000) must be inserted into the alternative-consequence matrix, and the final decision postponed until the consequences for remaining objectives are assessed.

Optimist Strategy: The antithesis of the pessimist is the optimist; hope forever springs eternal. Given this Norman Vincent Peale outlook on life, an optimist strategy is to select that action that is the *best of the best* (Exhibit 7-4).

Now if maximizing profit were the *only* objective, Joe's decision would be to machine the housings. If there are additional objectives, the best consequences ($55,000, $70,000) must be inserted into the alternative-consequence matrix. Only after the matrix is complete would the final choice be made.

Another common tactic under uncertainty is the in-betweenist strategy (also known as the Hurwicz Alpha Criterion).[1]

Assessing Consequences Under Risk

Under risk, a decision maker is willing or able to assign probabilities to the uncontrollable events. Suppose that Joe Williams' chief engineer evaluates both processes and assigns the following likelihoods:

> *Stamping process: P (successful) = .8, P (failure) = .2*
> *Machine process: P (successful) = .6, P (failure) = .4**

*Note that for events that are exclusive and exhaustive (such as failure and success), the sum of the probabilities must equal 1.

Under risk, a Bayes Strategy (from the same people who brought you Bayes Theorem) is used to select the "best" alter-

---

Exhibit 7-4: Applying an optimist strategy

| | Uncontrollable event | | |
Alternatives	Process successful	Process fails	Best consequences
Stamp	$55,000	$ 2,000	$55,000
Machine	70,000	−20,000	70,000 (Best of the best)

native action. A Bayes Strategy recommends that you select the action that has the highest expected value (EV). An EV is merely a weighted average and is equal to the sum-of-the-consequences multiplied by the respective probabilities:

$$EV = C_1 \cdot P(C_1) + C_2 \cdot P(C_2) + \ldots C_j \cdot P(C_j)$$

Returning to Joe Williams' dilemma, we would compute the EVs for machining and stamping as follows:

$EV\ (stamp) = (\$55,000)\ (.8) + (\$2,000)\ (.2) =$
$\$44,400\ (Highest\ EV)$
$EV\ (machine) = (\$70,000)\ (.6) + (-\$20,000)\ (.4) =$
$\$34,000$

Again, if maximizing profit were the *only* objective, a Bayes Strategy would call for stamping the product. When profit is merely one of many objectives, then the EVs (\$44,400, \$34,000) must be inserted into the alternative-consequence matrix.

Application to the Booker Industries' Problem

Now let's apply the principles of estimating consequences to the Booker Industries' merger-acquisition problem.

Major Objectives: Major objectives act as filters, for only those alternatives that pass all the major objectives are considered further. With the exception of Apex Business Equipment, all of the potential acquisition candidates met or exceeded the requirements specified by the major objectives (Chapter 6, Exhibit 6-8). In analyzing Apex, it was found that the dilution in earnings per share would exceed the maximum 10 percent cutoff. Because it failed on this major objective, Apex was dropped from further consideration.

Minor Objectives: The minor objectives that must be considered are Future Sales Potential, Profit to Net Worth, Synergy, Managerial Reputation, and Legality of the Combination.

1. *Future Sales Potential (FSP)*: This is an estimate of the average sales-growth percentage that an acquired firm could sustain over the next five years. Since the average sales growth depends on uncontrollable events (such as the state of the economy and the possibility of a technological breakthrough in

solid-state research for the industry), *and* because the corporation is able to assign probabilities to those events, we will use a Bayes Strategy. Consequences are measured in average sales-growth percentages adjusted for future anticipated inflation.

For each firm, we need to develop an alternative-uncontrollable event matrix, assign probabilities to the uncontrollable events, compute the EVs and insert them into the alternative-consequence matrix. The consequence assessment for Lancaster Inc. will be shown as an example in Exhibit 7-5.

The average sales-growth percentages are our firm's best estimates as to Lancaster Inc.'s potential, given a risky environment. Probabilities for the four possible events will also have to be assigned. Again, these will be based on the best information about the economic environment and the potential for a technological breakthrough. The only requirement is that the sum of the probabilities for the four events must equal one. (If the probabilities do not sum to one, you ought to (a) ask the probability assessor to reconsider or (b) normalize the probabilities so that they will sum to one. For example, if the probabilities sum to two, divide each probability by two, and then they will sum to one.) Suppose the following probabilities are assigned:

Uncontrollable events	Probability
Weak economy/no breakthrough	.35
Weak economy/breakthrough	.25
Strong economy/no breakthrough	.25
Strong economy/breakthrough	.15

Thus the expected average sales-growth percentage for Lancaster Inc. is 4% (.35) + 12% (.25) + 7% (.25) + 22% (.15) = 9.45%. The 9.45 percent figure is then inserted into Booker Industries' alternative-consequence matrix (see Exhibit 7-6). The expected average sales growth for the remaining acquisition candidates would be similarly determined, although the per-

---

Exhibit 7-5: Impact of uncontrollable events on average sales-growth percentages for Lancaster Inc.

		Uncontrollable event 2	
		No breakthrough	Breakthrough
Uncontrollable event 1	Weak economy	4%	12%
	Strong economy	7	22

Exhibit 7-6: Booker Industries' alternative-consequence matrix

Alternatives	FSP	P/NW	Minor objectives SY	Minor objectives R	Minor objectives L
Lancaster Inc.	9.45%	.125	5	6	2.1
Crow Technology	7.25	.139	7	9	5.2
Advance Systems Inc.	6.89	.107	8	5	6.1
Continental Numerics Inc.	10.24	.078	3	5	7.8
Computer Technics	8.76	.164	4	8	1.9
Objective weightings	4.0	1.8	3.2	2.0	1.0

Note: Which candidate is best? Try to rank-order the candidates before reading the choice process section.

centages, and possibly the probability assignments, might change from firm to firm. For example, an extremely aggressive firm might be able to retain a higher sales-growth percentage than Lancaster Inc., regardless of the uncontrollable events. In that case, the percentages used in Exhibit 7-5 would all be higher than those shown. The probability assignments might change, depending on whether an acquisition candidate could affect the likelihood of a technical breakthrough.

2. *Profit to Net Worth (P/NW)*: This is the average ratio of net profit to net worth over the past five years for each acquisition candidate. As the data are readily available from published sources, the consequences are known with certainty. The average ratio for Lancaster Inc. is .125. The ratios for the remaining firms must also be inserted into the alternative-consequence matrix.

3. *Synergy (SY)*: This objective rates the potential for SY in the distribution channels between Booker Industries and the acquired firm. The potential for SY is measured on a ten-point *interval* scale, where a rating of 1 is equated with no potential and a rating of 10 is equated with maximum potential. The ratings are based on the best analysis of the distribution channels of the acquisition candidates. While the degree of SY attainment could involve uncertainty or risk, we have chosen to treat the potential for SY as if the consequences were known with certainty. The SY rating for Lancaster Inc. is 5. All five SY ratings must be inserted into the Booker Industries' alternative-consequence matrix.

4. *Managerial Reputation (R)*: This objective rates the strength of the present senior management teams of the acquisition candidates. It is not based on the financial data of the company being evaluated; rather, it is based on the opinions of the financial community. Again an *interval* scale of 1 (incompetent) to 10 (extremely competent) is used to rate the acquisition candidates. The R ratings are assumed to be known with certainty. Lancaster Inc.'s senior management was given a rating of 6 by the financial community (a 10 is reserved for Bo Derek).

5. *Legality of the Combination (L)*: This objective measures the potential for a challenge by the Justice Department regarding the legality of the acquisition. Again an *interval* scale from 1 to 10 was used to assess the consequences. Since, for all previous objectives, high scores were preferred to low scores, a score of 1 means that a challenge is inevitable, and a score of 10 means that a challenge is highly unlikely (the preferred consequence). Now, unlike the previous three objectives, the potential for a challenge depends on an uncontrollable event—which political party controls the Justice Department. An analysis of the possible consequences for Lancaster Inc. shows:

	Uncontrollable event 1
Party A	*Party B*
3	1

The ratings are our best estimates of a Justice Department challenge. If party A is in power, the rating is 3 (likely); whereas if party B is in power, it is inevitable that there will be a challenge. Now we must estimate the probability that the two parties will win. Assuming no third parties, the sum of the probabilities must equal one. Thus:

Uncontrollable event	*Probability*
Party A	.55
Party B	.45

According to the pollsters, if the election were held today, the presidential candidate from party A has a 55 percent chance of winning the election. Thus the expected potential of a challenge, should Booker Industries acquire Lancaster Inc., is (3) (.55) + 1 (.45) = 2.1. This value must also be inserted into the alternative-consequence matrix. Of course, for the remaining four firms, the potential for challenge ratings would differ from those of Lancaster Inc. However, the probabilities associated with each party winning the election would not change since they depend on forces over which the individual firms have no control.

Choice Process

Although more has been written about the choice phase than other phases, it is much less important than any of the previous decision-making stages. If the problem is poorly diagnosed, then using a sophisticated procedure to select the "best" alternative is a little like measuring buffalo chips with a mass spectrometer—overkill at its finest. If the alternatives you generate are superficial, then what does it really mean to select the best from a trivial set of actions? Finally, if the consequences are inaccurately estimated, and you use them to choose the best action, then all you have is "GIGO"—garbage in and garbage out.

The goals in the choice phase are to (a) select the best alternative action and (b) rank-order the remaining alternatives. The job is made difficult because rarely is an alternative best on all objectives (a dominant alternative). Review the Booker Industries' alternative-consequence matrix. You will not find a dominant alternative. So now what do you do?

First, an *evaluation procedure* must be developed that will compress the consequences for the five differentially ranked objectives into a single figure of merit (FOM) score. Once this is done, the FOM scores can be used to rank-order the alternatives in terms of their desirability. The simplest procedure, and one you've probably used before, is to sum the product of the objective weights and the consequence scores (C_{ij}'s) and then to select the highest-scoring alternative—it won't work! Let's see why.

Weighted Sum-of-the-Consequences Procedure

Let's take a simple example and see what happens when this evaluation procedure is used. As a result of the free-agent draft, Pete Jackson is trying to decide which of two teams he should sign with—the New York Yankees or the Atlanta Braves. He has stated that he is only concerned about two objectives—money and playing on a championship-caliber team. Both teams have made their best offers, and now Pete must decide which team to sign with. Pete has assigned a weight of two to the money objective and a weight of one to the team-caliber objective. The dollar amounts represent a three-year contract, and Pete has rated the teams on a scale from 1 (the pits) to 100 (a top contender). Consequences for both objectives are known with certainty, for he has the offers in hand and is familiar with the present team rosters. Which team should he sign with? Here is Pete's alternative-consequence matrix:

		Objectives
Alternatives	Money	Team caliber
Atlanta	$2,000,000	5
N.Y.	1,000,000	90
Objective weightings	2	1

Using the weighted sum-of-the-consequences procedure, we obtain the following FOM scores:

FOM (Atlanta) = $2,000,000 (2) + 5 (1) =
$4,000,005 (Maximum)
FOM (N.Y.) = $1,000,000 (2) + 90 (1) = $2,000,090

The choice is simple; Pete should sign with Atlanta. But when the Yankees find out, they ask Pete to reconsider, and they generate the following matrix:

		Objectives
Alternatives	Money (in millions)	Team caliber
Atlanta	2	5
N.Y.	1	90
Objective weightings	2	1

The weighted sum-of-the-consequences procedure now generates the following FOM scores:

$FOM\ (Atlanta) = 2\ (2) + 5\ (1) = 9$

$FOM\ (N.Y.) = 1\ (2) + 90\ (1) = 92\ (Maximum)$

Just by changing the scale on the first objective, the "best" action was reversed. The problem with the sum-of-the-consequences evaluation procedure is that it is susceptible to scale distortions, and thus cannot be used. However, an evaluation procedure that *is* dimensionally sound is the weighted product-of-the-consequences.

Weighted Product-of-the-Consequences Procedure

The FOM scores are determined as follows:

$$FOM = (Consequence_1)^A \cdot (Consequence_2)^B \ldots (Consequence_m)^K$$

where $A, B, \ldots K$ refer to the weights assigned to the objectives. Let's use this procedure for Pete Jackson's decision:

$FOM\ (Atlanta) = (2,000,000^2)\ (5^1) = 2 \cdot 10^{13}$

$FOM\ (N.Y.) = (1,000,000^2)\ (90^1) = 9 \cdot 10^{13}$

The ratio is:

$$\frac{FOM\ (N.Y.)}{FOM\ (Atlanta)} = \frac{9 \cdot 10^{13}}{2 \cdot 10^{13}} = 4.5$$

The rank order and ratio would remain unchanged if the dollar values were rescaled:

$FOM\ (Atlanta) = (2^2)\ (5^1) = 20$

$FOM\ (N.Y.) = (1^2)\ (90^1) = 90\ (Maximum)$

Using this rule, Pete should sign with the New York Yankees (too bad—we really could have used him in Atlanta).

Before applying the weighted product-of-the-consequences procedure to Booker Industries' acquisition alternative-consequence matrix, the following three rules for using this procedure should be noted:

1. Never use a consequence-rating scale that includes a value of zero to assess objectives. If a consequence assessment equals zero, the FOM score will automatically be zero. In the previous examples, the scales used to measure synergy, managerial reputation, legality of combination, and team caliber did not contain a zero value. Always use positively valued scales.

2. Scale the objectives so that either the higher values are more preferable than the lower values or the lower values are more preferable than the higher values. Since in the Booker Industries' problem the future sales potential and profit-to-net-worth objectives were naturally scaled so that the higher values were preferable, the remaining three objectives were similarly scaled. Note that this required the legality objective be scaled so that higher numbers indicated a lower potential for a Justice Department challenge. Whatever scaling procedure used, be *consistent* over all objectives.

3. Objectives must be conceptually different from one another. Otherwise, the same objective under two different names will be double-counted. If one objective is to minimize travel time in hours and another objective is to minimize travel time in minutes, these are essentially the same objective; one of them should be eliminated before the choice phase begins. Remember, a rose by any other name is still a rose.

Application to Booker Industries' Problem

When there are many objectives and large consequence values, the FOM scores can become huge. Without distorting the rankings, you might find it useful to rescale the scores by using the following procedure: *Rescaled* FOM_i = FOM_i ÷ *Minimum FOM score.*

Given the FOM scores shown in Exhibit 7-7, the potential acquisition candidates can be ranked in the following descending order of desirability:

Crow Technology
Advance Systems Inc.
Lancaster Inc.
Computer Technics
Continental Numerics Inc.

Exhibit 7-7: Evaluation of five acquisition candidates

Alternative	FOM calculation	FOM	Rescaled FOM
Lancaster Inc.	$(9.45^4) \cdot (.125^{1.8}) \cdot (5^{3.2}) \cdot (6^2) \cdot (2.1^1)$	2,462,572	3.37
Crow Technology	$(7.25^4) \cdot (.139^{1.8}) \cdot (7^{3.2}) \cdot (9^2) \cdot (5.2^1)$	16,888,034	23.11
Advance Systems Inc.	$(6.89^4) \cdot (.107^{1.8}) \cdot (8^{3.2}) \cdot (5^2) \cdot (6.1^1)$	4,774,431	6.53
Continential Numerics Inc.	$(10.24^4) \cdot (.078^{1.8}) \cdot (3^{3.2}) \cdot (5^2) \cdot (7.8^1)$	730,784	1.00
Computer Technics	$(8.76^4) \cdot (.164^{1.8}) \cdot (4^{3.2}) \cdot (8^2) \cdot (1.9^1)$	2,334,853	3.19

Can we say more than this? Because the scales used to measure the objectives ranged from interval to cardinal, the rescaled FOM scores are not meaningful on a ratio scale. For example, we cannot say that, as a candidate, Crow Technology is 23.11 times more attractive than Continental Numerics, nor is Advance Systems Inc. 2.04 times ($6.53 \div 3.19$) more attractive than Computer Technics.

We can, however, be reasonably confident that the rescaled FOM scores are meaningful on an interval scale. Consider Crow Technology, Advance Systems Inc., and Continental Numerics Inc. The increase in candidate attractiveness from Advance Systems to Crow Technology is three times greater than the increase from Continental Numerics to Advance Systems; the ratio of the intervals is: $23.11 - 6.53 \div 6.53 - 1 = 3.0$. Similar statements can be made for the remaining candidates. Simply, this means that Crow Technology is far and away the most attractive acquisition candidate.

On completing what is certainly the most mathematical presentation in this book, and being intoxicated with the power of quantitative procedures, I am reminded of a quotation attributed to Sir Josiah Stamp:

> Public agencies are very keen on amassing statistics—they collect them, raise them to the nth power, take the cube root and prepare wonderful diagrams. What we must never forget is that every one of these figures comes in the first instance from a village watchman, who just puts down what he damn pleases.

Preimplementation Phase, or Anticipating the Unexpected

Solutions to one problem are often the breeding grounds for a new and more serious problem—the cure is worse than the ailment. Thus there is need for a preimplementation phase in which the decision maker assesses the possible adverse consequences of a tentative solution. Among the earliest proponents of this approach were Kepner and Tregoe:

> A manager should take the best alternatives and consider them independently, visualizing each as though it were already in operation. He should question the effect the alternative will have on other things, and the effect that other events will have on it. He is not reconsidering the attainment of objec-

tives, but he is estimating the future possible effects of the actions necessary to attain them. For example, if cost were an objective, he would not consider the cost of attaining each alternative as a consequence, but would weigh the possible effects and trends of these costs over a period of time. He should ask: "If we were to do this, then what would happen as a result? What could go wrong?" At this point, he is looking for trouble, trying to find the potential breakdowns and shortcomings that have escaped his notice so far. These will be hidden and obscure. They will lie primarily along the lines of contact between the proposed course of action and other activities going on in the company.[2]

These recommendations are especially appropriate when several excellent alternative actions (alternatives with similar FOM scores) might be chosen. Kepner and Tregoe suggest that the decision maker should assess the possible adverse consequences in implementing each alternative. An alternative with little adverse consequences might be preferable to one that has a slightly higher FOM score but serious potential adverse consequences.

Adverse-Consequence Worksheet

Even when one alternative is clearly superior—as with Crow Technology—developing an adverse-consequence worksheet will help pinpoint where the solution implementation can go astray. Once these roadblocks are identified, a manager can develop a *contingency plan*. Simply stated, contingency planning is advance preparation to meet a situation that is not expected to occur; but if it occurs, the situation will have a significant detrimental impact on a firm. Since contingency plans are often developed from an assessment of potential adverse consequences, we will consider the assessment first.

We first considered an adverse-consequence (worst case) worksheet in Chapter 2. Its purpose was to help a problem solver overcome an unrealistic fear of failure. An adverse-consequence worksheet was recommended as a means of getting one's fears out in the open where they could be addressed.

Now we will use the adverse-consequence worksheet to preimplement the several highest ranking alternatives. Assuming that Murphy was an eternal optimist, we will now consider what could go wrong as each alternative is implemented. We need to evaluate (1) the seriousness of these consequences and (2) their likelihood of occurrence.

Let's look at an example. Based on the weighted product-of-the-consequences evaluation procedure, suppose that the three highest-rated alternatives have the following FOM scores:

Alternatives	FOM score
A_1	8.75
A_2	8.25
A_3	8.60

Prior to implementing the "best" alternative—A_1—we will preimplement all three alternatives. In implementation a manager should ask: "If we were to implement alternative ___, then what would happen? What could (and would) go wrong? How likely is it to happen?" The answers to these questions are then summarized in the adverse-consequence worksheet. Each consequence must be assigned a degree of seriousness value between zero and one hundred—where a zero rating means that the consequence is trivial and a one hundred rating means that the consequence is a serious barrier to obtaining the decision objectives. The worksheet for our hypothetical example is shown in Exhibit 7-8.

After the adverse-consequence worksheet has been developed, how can we factor it into the decision-making process? First, the FOM scores and adverse-consequence scores (or their reciprocals) *cannot* be added together to arrive at an aggregate index. Since the FOM score measures the degree of goal attainment and the adverse-consequence score measures the potential for disaster during solution implementation, adding the scores would be similar to adding oranges and peaches—beyond mixed fruit cocktail, nothing meaningful is obtained.

So what are the uses of the worksheet? Even though an additive-index value is meaningless, the adverse-consequence scores should be incorporated, if only informally, into your analysis. In this example, the highest FOM alternative has the worst consequence score—this alternative possesses the greatest downside risk. Should alternative A_1 be implemented, or should alternative A_2, with the lowest FOM score but the least Murphy-like potential for foul-ups, be chosen? While there is no universally correct answer, at least you have all the necessary

Exhibit 7-8: Adverse-consequence worksheet

Consequence/ roadblock	Alternative 1			Alternative 2				Alternative 3			
	(1) Seriousness	(2) Probability	(1) x (2)	Consequence	(1) Seriousness	(2) Probability	(1) x (2)	Consequence	(1) Seriousness	(2) Probability	(1) x (2)
Could hurt morale in Division Y.	70	.30	21	Potential coordination problem with Division X.	80	.40	32	Implementation time might be tight.	30	.60	18
								Political factors could kill implementation.	100	.30	30
											48
Critical equipment failure during implementation.	30	.80	24								
Reduce Division Y's ability to react to external changes during implementation.	90	.15	13.5								
			58.5								

information to make an informed decision, and the final decision is yours.

Your decision will depend, in part, on the financial health of your firm, the caliber of the people who will implement the chosen alternative, and your own willingness to tolerate ambiguity or uncertainty. If you cannot cope with uncertainty or ambiguity, you'll want to give the adverse-consequence scores greater weight in the final decision; if you can cope with ambiguity, you'll want to give greater weight to the FOM scores.

In developing the worksheet, the consequences may be transformed into additional objectives that may have been initially overlooked. In that case, you must rank-order the additional objectives, expand the alternative-consequence matrix to incorporate them, assess the consequences for all the alternatives, and finally determine the "best" alternative, using the weighted product-of-the-consequences evaluation procedure.

No matter which alternative is finally chosen, implementation foul-ups are possible. The adverse-consequence worksheet not only helps you assess the downside risks during implementation, but is a starting point for contingency planning.

Contingency Planning

Contingency planning attempts to avoid surprise and its related stress. Individuals, groups, and organizations "go to pieces" when faced with high levels of stress. Under severe stress, the individual may (1) attempt to cope by avoiding the stressful situation, (2) vacillate regarding what action to take, and in the extreme case, (3) exhibit panic-induced irrational behavior.[3] Groups and organizations fare no better. They tend to reach premature consensus as to the appropriate action, their communications channels become garbled, and they are susceptible to "groupthink."[4] That is not all. Under severe stress, problem solvers often take a short-run view of the crisis and institute actions that, in the long run, are detrimental to the firm. Contingency planning can improve a firm's recognition of a problem before it is substantially affected by it (like knowing you're in quicksand before you go under) and can provide a well-developed plan of action. A contingency plan must address three issues:

What can happen?
How will we know it?
What will we do?

The contingency planning process is illustrated in Exhibit 7-9.

The *what can happen* requirements of a contingency plan will already be completed if you have generated an adverse-consequence worksheet. If alternative 1 is ultimately selected (see Exhibit 7-8), contingency plans should be formulated for some or all of the possible consequences. Because developing a complete plan is costly and time consuming, you might consider developing a plan only for the consequence with the highest score—namely, a critical equipment failure.

Next, develop indicators to provide an early-warning system for a critical equipment failure. You might choose (1) amount of downtime per shift or (2) the number of adjustments per shift necessary to keep the equipment within tolerance. Whatever indicators you select, you must establish trigger points, so you will know when to implement your contingency plan. In this hypothetical example, a trigger point might be defined as either when downtime per shift is in excess of 5 percent, or when more than two adjustments per shift are necessary. Whatever trigger you choose, it should be a clear signal that the critical roadblock is about to occur.

Finally, you need to develop a plan of attack. The plan's degree of specificity will depend on the amount of time you can devote to it. However, any plan should be more effective than no prior planning. As the adage goes, "When you're up to your armpits in alligators, it's easy to forget what you're supposed to be doing in the swamp." You will also need to develop a plan to implement your contingency plan. In this case, the plan could be as simple as replacing the present equipment with a spare machine from the machine shop. The plan should specify who

---

Exhibit 7-9: The contingency planning process

Issue	Action
What can happen?	(1) List future events that are potential critical road-blocks to attaining decision objectives.
	(2) Estimate their likelihood.
How will we know it?	(1) Develop indicators and identify trigger points that signal the impending occurrence of the event.
	(2) Select individuals to monitor these indicators.
What will we do?	(1) Develop a plan of attack now.
	(2) Develop a plan to implement your plan of attack.

Source: Adapted from Rochelle O'Connor, *Planning Under Uncertainty* (New York, Conference Board, 1978), p. 18.

will disconnect the old equipment, cart it away, and connect the new machine. One final note of caution—if several departments are involved in implementing the plan, representatives from these departments should be involved in the contingency-planning process to help reduce interdepartmental conflict.

Implementation Phase

Successful decisions are more than good decisions. Once made, decisions must be implemented effectively to obtain the desired goals and solve the problem. Conversely, a good decision may be offset by poor acceptance and ineffective implementation.

The implementation phase can be subdivided into three distinct activities and is based on Edgar Schein's three stages of effecting change in organizations:
1. Preparing for implementation
2. Implementing the decision
3. Monitoring the effectiveness of the solution[5]

Preparing for Implementation

In contrast to operating problems, solutions to strategic problems often alter the *modus operandi* of a firm. The decision to acquire a firm, the dropping of a product line, or the decision to invest in a foreign country can cause profound changes in an organization. Where there is change, there is also likely to be resistance to change. When the need for change is not understood by those who will be affected, resistance to change is not a pathological response. Thus preparation for implementation should focus on overcoming resistance resulting from implementing a solution to a strategic problem. Several strategies for overcoming resistance are presented in the following paragraphs.

Obtain support from top management: This may take the form of implicit support or explicit authorization to implement the decision. Authorization is necessary when the decision maker does not have the final authority to commit the organization to a course of action but can only recommend. Regardless of the form the support takes, the greater the support of senior management, the harder the implementors will work to ensure decision success.[6]

Obtain involvement in the decision process: The greater the degree to which those involved, either as implementors or beneficiaries, understand the basis for the decision, the steps to be taken in carrying it out, and the resulting implications, the greater is the likelihood of successful implementation.[7] If possible, get those that have to implement or live with the decision involved in the decision-making process. This idea was first suggested in Vroom and Yetton's Leadership-Style Flowchart (Chapter 2, Exhibit 2-6). You will recall that one of the eight problem characteristics dictating the choice of leadership style was whether commitment to the solution is necessary to ensure effective implementation. If commitment to the solution is necessary, a manager must involve his or her subordinates in the decision-making process.

Often this is impossible because the implementors or beneficiaries may be physically separated from the decision makers by thousands of miles. If *actual involvement* is impossible, will *perceived involvement* suffice? For instance, Trull noted that several individuals who had not taken part in designing a solution were enthusiastically supporting and promoting its implementation.[8] After the decision had been made, but before it had been implemented, the decision makers and implementors met in small discussion groups to review the problem and its solution. Although the implementors could not affect the solution because the choice had already been made, they felt that they had a stake in the decision and could support it. The basic premise is that people want to do what they have decided to do. The argument is a cogent one and is supported by well-documented studies.[9] In short, make the consumer want to buy into a decision by changing *your* decision into *their* decision.

Understand the political environment: Decisions are made in on-going organizations where the past is as important as the future. Whether we like it or not, the past cannot be erased. Whether a decision is successfully implemented may depend on the sponsor and his or her political and organizational enemies within the firm. Only a naive decision maker thinks that decisions succeed or fail strictly on their own merits.

Implementing the Decision

People either implement or fail to implement decisions. In

the business world there are few decisions so technically precise that they cannot be undermined by a determined employee. Elbing states it this way:

> Man, as the vehicle through which the decisions are implemented, reacts not only to the quality of the decision but to the total socio-technical environment associated with the decision. He cannot be manipulated in the same sense that other resources can be. Therefore, the manager's job is not limited to the exercise of knowledge and skill in choosing desirable solutions; it also includes the knowledge and skill required to transform those solutions into the dynamics of behavior in a particular organizational social system.[10]

Motivating subordinates or peers to implement a decision can be enhanced by properly preparing for implementation. Once the necessary groundwork has been laid, managing the implementation process requires the same human, technical, and leadership skills as managing any business activity.

Implementation is subject to all known foul-ups. In an analysis of over one hundred decisions, Trull noted that decision makers typically underestimate the implementation time.[11] Although no detailed discussion will be attempted, there are a number of analytical techniques available to help a manager schedule the implementation. These include conventional scheduling models, such as GANTT, and milestone charts. Network models, such as the program evaluation and review technique (PERT) or critical path scheduling, can also aid the implementation process. PERT is especially useful when complex activities have to be coordinated to ensure implementation success.

Monitoring the Effectiveness of the Solution

Simply because a solution has been implemented does not guarantee that the original decision objectives will be achieved. First, the original strategic problems may have been improperly diagnosed, and a solution generated from an incorrect diagnosis will not solve the underlying problem. We believe that the decision-science diagnostic method should reduce what some label as Type III error—solving the wrong problem. If the solution fails to solve the problem, rediagnose the problem and cycle through the enriched rational model again.

The world does not stop when solutions are implemented. By the time a solution is put into effect, the business environment may have changed to such a degree that a "best" solution is no longer effective. Just recall the Ford Company's debacle with the Edsel. This means that you must monitor and track the effectiveness of the solution. In turn, you must be prepared to redesign the solution should circumstances warrant. To cling to a "best" solution when the environment is dynamic is to substitute *mechanical* decision making for *effective* decision making. When the environment changes, solutions must be reexamined.

Even if no redesign of the solution is necessary, you should monitor the environment for signs of adverse consequences as you move toward the decision objectives. When trigger points are reached, the predeveloped contingency plans should be instituted.

Remember, the only thing constant in the business world is change.

Application to the Booker Industries' Problem

The selection of the best acquisition candidate is only the beginning of the acquisition decision. At this point, implementation is limited to formal authorization to proceed. Should the board give approval, then Booker Industries can enter into negotiations with Crow Technology. Many decisions still must be made. Ultimately a final go/no go decision will be made. If Crow Technology should be acquired, the full scope of implementation procedures discussed in this chapter should be initiated.

Summary

As this chapter concludes, I am reminded of Neil Diamond's lyrics, "the road is long with many a winding turn." In hopes of reducing your confusion level, the highlights of the enriched rational model for managerial decision making are presented one more time.

Diagnose Problems

Strategic problems should be diagnosed in terms of controllable actions and uncontrollable events, interrelationships between the two, and outcomes—the decision-science diagnostic method. Proper diagnosis reduces the chance of solving the wrong problem.

Define Objectives

There are two classes of objectives. Major objectives screen out unacceptable solutions. Minor objectives must be ranked in order of importance. A simple pairwise procedure for rank-ordering objectives and a graphic-scaling procedure for assigning numerical weights to the minor objectives can be used.

Generate Alternatives

Within the environmental constraints (some of which are self-imposed), generate as many alternatives as possible using specific search and design strategies.

Assess Consequences

Using Ben Franklin's "moral algebra" concept, assess the degree to which each alternative accomplishes the minor objectives. Consider three conditions: assessing consequences under certainty, under uncertainty, and under risk. The latter necessitated a brief excursion into probabilities and expected values. Ultimately, complete an alternative-consequence matrix.

Select "Best" Alternative

Since no alternative is best on all objectives, use a rule to select the "best" alternative. In our example we chose the weighted product-of-the-consequences procedure, because it was dimensionally sound.

Preimplement "Best" Solution

To ensure that the cure isn't worse than the ailment, use an adverse-consequence worksheet to catalog what might go wrong during implementation. If the downside risks associated with a "best" alternative are severe, consider a less attractive alternative, with less adverse consequences. The adverse-consequence worksheet, in turn, becomes an important document in preparing contingency plans.

Implement Solution

Implementation is change, and change is often resisted. Preparing for implementation is essential. Once a solution has been implemented, does it solve the problem? If not, be aware that (1) you may need to redesign your solution due to changing conditions, or (2) you solved the wrong problem.

1. Moshe F. Rubinstein, *Patterns of Problem Solving* (Englewood Cliffs, New Jersey, Prentice-Hall, 1975), pp. 317-322.

2. Charles H. Kepner and Benjamin B. Tregoe, *The Rational Manager* (New York, McGraw-Hill, 1965), pp. 190-191.

3. Irving L. Janis and Leon Mann, *Decision Making* (New York, Free Press, 1977).

4. Carolyne Smart and Ilan Vertinsky, "Designs for Crisis Decision Units," *Administrative Science Quarterly*, December 1977, pp. 640-657.

5. Edgar H. Schein, "Management Development as a Process of Influence," *Industrial Management Review*, May 1961, pp. 59-77.

6. Samuel G. Trull, "Some Factors Involved in Determining Total Decision Success," *Management Science*, February 1966, pp. B270-B280.

7. Ibid.

8. Ibid.

9. Norman R.F. Maier, *Psychology in Industrial Organizations* (Boston, Houghton-Mifflin Co., 1973).

10. Alvar O. Elbing, *Behavioral Decisions in Organizations*, 2nd Ed. (Glenview, Illinois, Scott, Foresman, 1978), p. 322.

11. Trull, "Some Factors Involved," pp. B270-B280.

8
Improving Strategic Problem Solving

In the last two chapters we presented the enriched rational model of decision making. The model is normative in that it recommends how a problem solver ought to make strategic decisions. In the final chapter we will review the individual and organizational idiosyncrasies that must be overcome to implement the normative model.

"Now we're going to tell it the way it really is."
—HOWARD COSELL

"Consistency requires you to be as ignorant today as you were a year ago."
—BERNARD BERENSON

"For man, knowledge is little; habit is everything."
—PESTALOZZI

"Habit is habit and not to be flung out of the window by any man but coaxed downstairs one step at a time."
—MARK TWAIN

"Ask yourself always: How can this be done better?"
—G.C. LICHTENBERG

The enriched rational model depicts how strategic decisions ought to be made in organizations. It is a normative, systematic, and logical approach to decision making. Why, then, is it frequently not used? Although the list is probably not exhaustive, we have identified five areas—problem diagnosis, setting objectives, alternative generation, choice phase, and the total decision process—where theory and practice diverge.

Problem Diagnosis

1. Decision making under risk or decision making under ambiguity?

A decision maker's knowledge of the consequences of alternative actions on objectives may vary from total certainty to total ambiguity. When a decision maker is absolutely sure of the consequences, we refer to this as decision making under certainty. When a decision maker is unsure of the consequences of an action because they depend on uncontrollable events, we refer to this as either decision making under uncertainty (the problem solver is unable to assign probabilities to the uncontrollable events) or decision making under risk (the problem solver is able to make probability assignments). In practice, decision makers often do not even know what the uncontrollable events are, and we refer to this state of bewilderment as decision making under ambiguity.

Ambiguity is the price we pay for an insufficient diagnosis. According to the normative model, a problem solver should diagnose the problem by applying the decision-science diagnostic method. This method forces decision makers to examine critically the controllable actions and uncontrollable events in a messy or ill-defined problem. An effective diagnosis can suggest alternative ways of viewing the problem with each view highlighting certain elements while shading others.

It is difficult to imagine strategic decision making without a diagnostic phase; yet the empirical support is not overwhelming. Mintzberg and his co-workers reported that there was no explicit diagnosis in eleven of twenty-five strategic decisions they investigated. Presumably diagnosis was an implicit and informal activity.[1] More recently, Lyles and Mitroff studied how organizations become aware of and diagnose problems.[2] Of thirty-three strategic decisions studied, only three could be defined as well-structured; the remainder were ill-defined. Interestingly, they reported that in over 88 percent of the cases managers became aware of the problem by informal means (intuition and communication with friends, clients, and vendors) rather than through accounting reports and financial figures. In only two instances was there no explicit diagnosis. However, in nineteen of the remaining thirty-one problems only a single conceptualization and diagnosis was made. While there is no evidence that multiple definitions of a problem are superior to a single diagnosis, it is an interesting hypothesis and certainly ought to be studied in the future.

The Lyles-Mitroff study suggests that although problem solvers are beginning to incorporate a formal diagnosis phase in strategic problem solving, much work remains to be done. Decision making under certainty or risk versus ambiguity—the choice is yours.

Setting Objectives

2. Objectives—rational or rationale?

According to the normative model, objectives evaluate alternative actions. A decision maker must formulate, rank-order, and then assign weights to the objectives that reflect their relative importance to the organization. Most importantly, objectives are formulated *before* we generate alternative actions. Is there support for these propositions?

What little evidence we have is not encouraging. In a study of public administrators, Charles Lindblom, a Yale economist, suggested that formulation of objectives often requires information that is either not available or only available at a prohibitive cost.[3] In his view, objectives do not precede alternative generation; rather, those actions that are feasible define what the objective will be. Instead of using objectives to evaluate alternatives, alternatives generate objectives. Lindblom argues that often objectives are formulated after an alternative has been selected and therefore serve as a rationale to support the selected action, rather than as a means of *rationally evaluating* potential solutions. Studies by Soelberg and Carter support the idea that decision makers often formulate objectives after an alternative has been selected.[4]

3. Rank-ordering of objectives—contaminating influences.

According to the normative model, the minor objectives must be rank-ordered in terms of their importance to the firm. A pairwise comparison rank-ordering technique was proposed. In theory, the rank order of the objectives should *only* be based on their importance in solving the strategic problem. Is this true in practice?

In the middle sixties, the British Air Transportation Board

proposed the city of Stanstead, site of a small existing airport northeast of London, as the location for London's third major airport. Stanstead was a highly controversial choice and failed to win approval. As a result, a Commission of Enquiry was established to develop a set of objectives and evaluate proposed sites. The commission proposed three objectives—surface access, defense, and noise level. In an analysis of the decision, it was noted that the planners considered surface accessibility as the most important objective because it was the most easily *quantified indicator.*[5] Objectives were not ranked on their intrinsic importance but on their ability to be quantified.

Beyond quantification, what other contaminating factors affect the rank-ordering process? Allan Easton believes that objectives that are advanced by powerful, articulate, or troublesome interest groups are often given preference over the objectives of less obtrusive interests.[6] I suppose that was one of the legacies of the decade of the sixties—the squeaky-wheel approach to rank-ordering objectives. Now there is nothing improper with a decision maker asking for inputs from various interest groups concerning the relative importance of objectives; however, when these considerations alone determine the rank-ordering of objectives, effective decision making is the loser.

Finally, there is no evidence that objectives are weighted in advance of making the choice. Rather, the weights appear to be assigned implicitly in the process of making choices.[7]

The chasm between theory and practice is wide.

Alternative Generation

4. Alternatives—one or many?

According to the enriched rational model, you should generate as many alternative actions as possible. We argued that the greater the number, the more likely you are to find a workable solution. Two generation processes were recommended—search and design. How is it done in practice?

The Mintzberg study suggests that organizations prefer to design rather than to search for alternative solutions.[8] Because of time and cost constraints, organizations often design only one fully developed, custom-made alternative. In no case are more than three alternative actions ever developed. Snyder and Paige confirm that decision makers are often presented with a single action rather than multiple alternatives.[9]

Even when multiple alternatives are proposed, they are often minor variations on the same theme. This point is illustrated in Alexander's account of the American review of possible military options following the Vietcong attack on the U.S. airbase at Bienhoa in 1964.[10] According to the Pentagon Papers three options were generated:

A. More of the same and limited pressure on North Vietnam—reject negotiations.

B. Option A plus increasing military pressure on North Vietnam—publicly reject negotiations, privately recognize their inevitability.

C. Option A plus graduated military pressure on North Vietnam—public willingness to negotiate.

The options appear to be clones of one another. Radically different options were either never generated or died in infancy. While documentation of strategic business decisions is difficult to find, myopic alternative generation is probably prevalent in business. After all, before Robert McNamara became Secretary of Defense he was president of Ford Motor Company.

Choice Phase

5. Choice as informal review.

Once all the alternative actions have been generated and their consequences assessed on all the objectives, you should *formally* evaluate the alternatives by using the weighted product-of-the-consequences procedure. However, in actual practice something else happens. Alexander suggests that alternatives are dropped without ever being formally evaluated. He illustrates this phase of informal evaluation with a discussion of three different strategic decisions:

> In some cases, alternatives were eliminated almost intuitively, applying informal selection criteria. Some criteria related to the character and perceptions of the participants, others reflected strongly held organizational paradigms or were a response to intuitively perceived organizational and environmental constraints. For example, in the evolution of Vietnam policy, non-escalation alternatives were dismissed without formal evaluation by a rigid application of the "domino theory," the dominant ideological

paradigm in the U.S. policy establishment. In selecting an airport site, the quantitative properties of the Roskill Commission staff led to an undervaluing of factors requiring judgment rather than purely analytical decisions. And in the case of the University of Wisconsin study committee, perceived system demands—an emphasis on cost saving and the apparent infeasibility of any non-saving options—led to the early elimination of the "creative instrument" options.[11]

According to Alexander, informal evaluation reduces the number of options. However, unlike the systematic choice phase, the informal evaluation process is not based on a review of the merits of an alternative. Rather, the elimination of an alternative is almost subliminal—without considering whether an alternative accomplishes a set of objectives, it is eliminated on almost irrational grounds. Thus, in many instances, alternatives are eliminated by a conspiracy of silence.

6. Choice phase—analytical, judgment, or bargaining?

According to the normative model, the best action is determined analytically by the weighted product-of-the-consequences procedure, which rank-orders the alternative actions. If judgment is used to help make the final choice, it should be applied only after the formal choice phase has been concluded.

In practice, decision makers often use judgment or bargaining, rather than analytical procedures, to select the best alternative. Using judgment, the choice is made by procedures the decision maker does not—perhaps cannot—explain. Many call this intuitive decision making. Using bargaining, the final choice is the result of power struggles between affected individuals or interest groups with conflicting goals and desires.

In their study of twenty-five strategic decisions, Mintzberg, Raisinghani and Théorêt concluded:

Judgment seems to be the favored mode of selection, perhaps because it is the fastest, most convenient, and least stressful in strategic decision making. Bargaining appears in more than half of the decision processes—typically where there was some kind of outside control or extensive participation within the organization and the issues were contentious. . . . Our study reveals very little use of the analytic approach, a surprising finding given the importance of the decisions studied.[1][2]

Judgment can take on several forms. Alternative actions may be evaluated not on their merit but on the basis of imitation of previous decisions, tradition, or sponsorship.[1][3] Alternatives that reflect an organization's culture or way of doing things are often given greater weight. We do not believe these judgmental procedures are irrational, for there is merit in nonanalytical procedures. However, when alternatives are evaluated solely on judgmental factors, it is time to take a more balanced view of the choice phase and incorporate analytical techniques.

The bargaining choice mode reflects the simple truth that political activities are a key element in strategic decision making.[1][4] In a study of British corporations, Grinyer and Norburn concluded that "those involved in the real process of strategic decision making recognized that it is ultimately a political process in which power and influence of individuals change with the nature of the challenges of the company, with changing personal relationships, and with factors like the health of the top managers . . . informal political processes constitute the system by which decisions are really made."[1][5]

The political nature of strategic decisions is clearly depicted in President Truman's attempted takeover of the steel industry. The seizure of the steel mills resulted from a power struggle between two men—Charles Wilson, Director of the Office of Defense Mobilization and his subordinate, Ellis Arnall, Director of the Office of Price Stabilization. Wilson had agreed to permit the steel companies to pass along some of their increased costs in the form of higher prices. Arnall objected, for price determination was his domain, and he refused to allow the companies to set higher prices. Although Wilson was Arnall's superior, Arnall had more political clout with President Truman; in a dramatic showdown, Truman sided with Arnall. Once the price hike was rejected, Truman's decision to seize the mills was inevitable, for without the price increase the steel companies would not or could not give the unions the wage increases they demanded, and this situation would ultimately have resulted in a nationwide strike. In this view of the problem, alternative actions were evaluated on their sponsorship and the sponsor's political clout rather than on their own merits.

Total Decision Process

7. Decision making—explicit or implicit?

Above all else, the normative model is an explicit procedure for solving strategic problems. While some may take exception to its components, there is a definite beginning and end to the decision-making process. Are even these minimal conditions found in practice?

George Steiner noted that although he had helped formulate several major policy decisions in government organizations, he could not reconstruct the detailed processes by which the decisions were made. The forces, events, personalities, and information flows were much too complex. He quoted former White House Press Secretary William Moyers who, in responding to a question about how a particular decision had been made, said: "You begin with the general principle that the process of decision making is inscrutable. No man knows how a decision is ultimately shaped. It's usually impossible even to know at what point a decision is made."[16]

Marion Folsom, a top executive in business, echoes Moyer's thoughts:

> It is often hard to pinpoint the exact stage at which a decision is reached. More often than not the decision comes about naturally during discussions, when the consensus seems to be reached among those whose judgment and opinion the executive seeks.[17]

Faced with a strategic decision, a decision maker not only must eventually solve the problem, but he or she must first plan an approach—the steps to be followed and an estimate of the resources that can be committed. Is even this process explicit?

Like so much else in strategic decision making, planning the problem-solving campaign (deciding how to decide) is informal and flexible, and is modified and clarified as the decision process progresses.[18] In actual practice, following an explicit series of decision-making phases, as recommended in the enriched rational model, is still the exception rather than the rule. We have urged repeatedly that you can make significant improvements in your problem solving by *making the implicit explicit*. Let it be said one more time.

8. Decision making—a linear or circular process?

In the previous chapter you may have formed an impression that strategic decision making is a steady, undisturbed process inexorably moving toward solution. This is probably due more to the sequential presentation of the material rather than to any explicit statement. In fact, if you review the strategic decision-process flowchart in Exhibit 6-1, you will notice a number of feedback loops. Even these do not tell the whole story, for in practice the strategic decision-making process is dynamic, operating in a turbulent system where it is subjected to interferences, feedback loops, dead ends, and other interruptive forces. Strategic decision making has been described as a process of everything chasing after everything else in an attempt to mutually adjust.[19]

Again, the most impressive evidence of the "circular" view of decision making is offered in the Mintzberg, Raisinghani and Théorêt study.[20] They found that dynamic factors intervene in the decision process, causing it to delay, stop, and restart. They classified the dynamic factors into several groups: *interrupts* that are caused by external factors; *scheduling and timing delays, or speedups,* that are affected by the decision maker's work pace; and *comprehension and failure recycles* that are inherent in the decision process itself (only the latter two categories are incorporated in the enriched rational model).

Of the twenty-five strategic decisions studied, a total of thirty-six interrupts occurred that caused either changes in the decision-making pace or recycling to previously concluded decision-making subphases. In seven instances, unexpected constraints emerged late in the consequence evaluation phase, forcing the decision maker to develop additional alternative solutions. In six cases, political impasses caused temporary delays. Typically, they occurred when internal or external forces blocked alternative selection in the choice phase. In one instance, a civic group used legal means to block a new airport runway, while in another, a determined staff group in a hospital blocked adoption of a controversial medical treatment. In the remaining cases, new options emerged after an alternative had been accepted.

The decision makers' responses to the interrupts depended, in part, on the underlying causes. In the face of unexpected constraints, decision makers often incorporated the additional constraints and cycled back to the alternative generation phase. The decision makers' responses to political roadblocks were varied. They included redesigning the solution to overcome the roadblock, engaging in political warfare with the dissident groups, bargaining, or stonewalling and waiting for the resistance to evaporate.

Scheduling and timing delays resulted from the managers' hectic work pace, best characterized by brevity, variety, and fragmentation. Mintzberg studied the work pace of five chief executive officers for one week and concluded:

> The vast majority (of activities) are of brief duration, on the order of seconds for foremen and minutes for chief executives. The variety of activities to be performed are greater, and the lack of pattern among subsequent activities with the trivial interspersed with the consequential, requires that the manager shift moods quickly and frequently. . . . *The manager actually appears to prefer brevity and interruptions in his work. . . . Superficiality is an occupational hazard of the manager.* (Italics added.)[21]

Mintzberg's portrait of a chief executive officer suggests that he or she cannot devote large blocks of uninterrupted time to strategic decision making, as important as it is to the organization.

Proper timing is as important in strategic decision making as it is in the theater. Often managers delay or speed up the decision process to take advantage of opportunities. They seek delays when external political pressures threaten to block a decision, and they speed up when opportunity knocks. The combined impact of the managers' hectic work pace and the orchestrating and timing of the decisions lengthens the decision process. In Mintzberg's study, seventeen of twenty-five decisions had a duration of more than one year.[22]

Strategic decisions are extremely complex. By examining and reexamining a strategic decision, the manager gradually comes to comprehend the problem. Mintzberg and his co-workers found evidence of ninety-five comprehension recycles in which the manager had to recycle in an earlier decision-making phase because he or she still did not understand the problem. Most of the comprehension recycles occurred in the alternative-generation phase, when it became clear to the manager that a naive understanding of the problem had generated unworkable alternatives.

Failure recycles occurred in thirteen instances when no acceptable solution could be found or designed. The decision makers tried several options; among these were (1) remove the constraints and thereby make a solution acceptable, (2) develop a new solution, or (3) accept a previously unacceptable solution.

Given the nature of strategic decisions and a manager's fragmented work pace, decision-making processes are circular, not linear; they resemble the process of fermentation in biochemistry rather than an industrial production line.[2][3]

9. Decision making—moving toward objectives or away from danger?

According to the normative model, we select the action that most closely attains our desired objectives. In this view, strategic decision making is a process of bridging the gap between where we are today and where we want our organization to be tomorrow—our objectives. This seems reasonable, doesn't it?

Not according to Charles Lindblom. Lindblom's manager acts in a remedial fashion, *moving away from problems rather than toward objectives*. The strategic decision-making process is not gap-bridging but rather area-evacuating. Lindblom's manager acts in a serial or stepwise fashion—making incremental changes, reacting to environmental responses, and then remodifying actions to incorporate criticism. Lindblom views decision making as "continual nibbling rather than one big bite."[24] His argument is that normative models fail to recognize man's inability to cope with complexity and the problems of time and cost constraints. While there is little empirical evidence to support Lindblom's position, it certainly offers a different perspective of the manager as problem solver. In the parlance of football, he is not a classic drop-back passer; he is a "scrambler"—moving away from danger today to be able to play tomorrow. He muddles through; he survives.

Divergence Between Theory and Practice: Ills and Cures

What accounts for the nine areas of divergence between the theory and practice of decision making? Lindblom offers three reasons:

1. Problems are complex and overwhelm the cognitive abilities of the manager.

2. The cost of analysis often exceeds the benefits.

3. There is never enough time for systematic problem solving.[2 5]

While it is true that problems are frequently complex, it is not their complexity alone that makes problems difficult. Our own inability to overcome real or self-imposed environmental and individual constraints makes a difficult problem insolvable. As we have often said, we are our own worst enemy. If you believe that you still fall prey to self-imposed constraints, you may want to reread Chapters 2 and 3.

Analysis can cost more than it is worth. In the past, this has been a legitimate criticism of normative models. We believe that the operating and strategic problem-solving models presented in Chapters 4 through 7 are cost efficient. The heavy emphasis on diagnosing a problem before attempting to solve it, on alternative generation techniques, and on preimplementation—all often forgotten elements in normative models—should improve the cost-benefit ratio.

Nevertheless, the gap between problem solving in theory and practice remains wide. We understand that it may be impractical to implement the enriched rational model all at once; thus we offer some suggestions for making incremental improvements in your managerial decision making. They are presented in descending order of importance:

1. Diagnose the problem.

This is perhaps the central lesson of the book. Unlike problems in textbooks, real-world problems are fuzzy messes in need of clarification. You should use the decision-science diagnostic method to help generate two different views of a strategic problem. Once you have mastered the diagnostic method then

2. Formulate objectives explicitly.

Develop an explicit set of objectives. While this may result in conflict between various interest groups, these differences cannot be resolved if they remain hidden. When rank-ordering objectives, try to *minimize* the contaminating influences discussed earlier, such as giving undue weight to the most easily quantified objectives or those proposed by powerful interest groups inside or outside the organization. As your understanding of the problem changes, be willing to modify your objectives. If objectives can be formulated and rank-ordered try to

3. Generate at least two alternatives.

Alternatives are often costly to design, and therefore developing many may be impractical. At an absolute minimum, develop two legitimate alternative solutions and be sure that they are conceptually different. When you have learned to generate multiple alternatives, you should

4. Utilize a formal choice phase.

Your long-term goal should be to use the weighted product-of-the-consequences evaluation procedure for selecting the best alternative. Bargaining and judgment—out in the open—are reasonable intermediate goals that recognize that major changes in decision making are hard to implement. However, implicit formal evaluation where alternatives are preempted without any formal consideration should be strictly verboten.

One step at a time the implicit is made explicit. After you have mastered these four important decision-making skills, you should then incorporate the remaining phases of the enriched rational model into your decision-making process.

A Concluding Thought

Success in business depends largely on the ability to solve problems. Managers must learn to think logically and creatively about the problems they face. This book has been dedicated to these twin goals.

We conclude the book as we began it—with a story. A doctoral candidate wished to do his dissertation under the tutelage of a Nobel prize winner. He approached the professor and inquired if he would serve as his advisor. The professor responded that he would if the student could solve the following problem:

There once was a house with two chimneys in dire need of cleaning, for which two people were hired. When the two sweepers had finished cleaning the chimneys, one emerged clean-faced, the other, dirty.

"Who will wash?" asked the professor.

The student thought about it and answered, "The sweeper with the dirty face."

"Wrong," the professor replied, "the sweeper with the clean face will wash." He explained that the sweeper with the clean face would look at the sweeper with the dirty face and assume his face was also dirty; so he would leave the room to wash himself. Likewise the sweeper with the dirty face would look at the sweeper with the clean face and assume that his face was clean. "So you see, the man with the clean face will wash."

"I understand now," replied the student. "Give me another chance to redeem myself."

The professor again posed the question, "Two sweepers emerge from two dirty chimneys—who will wash?"

The student eagerly replied, "Why that's simple—the man with the clean face."

"Wrong again," replied the professor. "As the clean-faced man leaves the room to wash his face, the other sweeper will ask him why he is leaving the room. When the clean-faced man replies, 'To wash my face,' he will be told that his face is clean. At that point, the dirty-faced man will learn that his face is dirty, and he will go wash up."

"I really understand now," replied the student. "Please give me one more chance."

One more time the professor posed the question, "Who will wash?"

The student was perplexed, for he had given the only two possible answers, and yet both were wrong. After several hours he returned and told the professor that he could not solve the riddle. He then asked the professor for the right answer. The professor smiled and walked out the door.[26]

FOOTNOTES

1. Henry Mintzberg, Duru Raisinghani, and Andre Theórêt, "The Structure of 'Unstructured' Decision Processes," *Administrative Science Quarterly*, June 1976, pp. 246-275.

2. Marjorie A. Lyles and Ian I. Mitroff, "Organizational Problem Formulation: An Empirical Study," *Administrative Science Quarterly*, March 1980, pp. 102-119.

3. Charles E. Lindblom, "The Science of 'Muddling Through,' " *Public Administration Review*, Spring 1959, pp. 79-88.

4. Peer O. Soelberg, "Unprogrammed Decision Making," *IMR*, Spring 1967, pp. 19-30; E. Eugene Carter, "Project Evaluations and Firm Decisions," *Journal of Management Studies*, October 1971, pp. 253-279; E. Eugene Carter, "The Behavioral Theory of the Firm and Top-Level Corporate Decisions," *Administrative Science Quarterly*, December 1971, pp. 413-428.

5. Ernest R. Alexander, "The Design of Alternatives in Organizational Contexts: A Pilot Study," *Administrative Science Quarterly*, September 1979, pp. 382-404.

6. Allan Easton, *Complex Managerial Decisions Involving Multiple Objectives* (New York, John Wiley & Sons, Inc., 1973).

7. Richard M. Cyert, Herbert A. Simon, and Donald B. Trow, "Observation of a Business Decision," *Journal of Business*, October 1956, pp. 237-248; Soelberg, "Unprogrammed Decision Making," pp. 19-30.

8. Mintzberg, Raisinghani, and Théorêt, "The Structure of 'Unstructured' Decision Processes," pp. 246-275.

9. Richard C. Snyder and Glenn D. Paige, "The United States Decision to Resist Aggression in Korea: The Application of an Analytical Scheme," *Administrative Science Quarterly*, 1958, Vol. 3, pp. 341-378.

10. Alexander, "The Design of Alternatives in Organizational Contexts," pp. 382-404.

11. Ibid., p. 398.

12. Mintzberg, Raisinghani, and Théorêt, "The Structure of 'Unstructured' Decision Processes," p. 258.

13. John M. Pfiffner, "Administrative Rationality," *Public Administration Review*, Summer 1960, pp. 125-132.

14. Andrew M. Pettigrew, "Information Control as a Power Resource," *Sociology*, May 1972, pp. 187-204; Joseph L. Bower, *Managing the Resource Allocation Process* (Boston, Division of Research, Graduate School of Business Administration, Harvard University, 1970).

15. Peter H. Grinyer and David Norburn, "Planning for Existing Markets: Perceptions of Executives and Financial Performance," *The Journal of the Royal Statistical Society*, Series A, Part 1, 1975, pp. 70-97.

16. George A. Steiner and John B. Miner, *Management Policy and Strategy* (New York, Macmillan Co., 1977), p. 210.

17. Marion B. Folsom, *Executive Decision Making* (New York, McGraw-Hill, 1962), p. 40.

18. Mintzberg, Raisinghani, and Théorêt, "The Structure of 'Unstructured' Decision Processes," pp. 246-275.

19. Paul Diesing, "Noneconomic Decision-Making," in Marcus Alexis and Charles Z. Wilson, eds., *Organizational Decision Making* (Englewood Cliffs, New Jersey, Prentice-Hall, 1967), p. 186.

20. Mintzberg, Raisinghani, and Théorêt, "The Structure of 'Unstructured' Decision Processes," pp. 246-275.

21. Henry Mintzberg, *The Nature of Managerial Work* (New York, Harper & Row, 1973), p. 51.

22. Mintzberg, Raisinghani, and Théorêt, "The Structure of 'Unstructured' Decision Processes," pp. 246-275.

23. Pfiffner, "Administrative Rationality," p. 129.

24. Charles E. Lindblom, *The Policy-Making Process* (Englewood Cliffs, New Jersey, Prentice-Hall, 1968), p. 25.

25. Lindblom, "The Science of 'Muddling Through,'" pp. 79-88.

26. Question the facts. How is it possible for two men to clean two dirty chimneys and for only one man to become dirty?

Index